Domestic life and domestic tragedy
in early modern England

MANCHESTER
1824
Manchester University Press

Domestic life
and domestic tragedy
in early modern England

THE MATERIAL LIFE OF THE HOUSEHOLD

Catherine Richardson

Manchester University Press
Manchester and New York

distributed exclusively in the USA by Palgrave

Published by Manchester University Press
Oxford Road, Manchester M13 9NR, UK
and Room 400, 175 Fifth Avenue, New York, NY 10010, USA
www.manchesteruniversitypress.co.uk

Distributed exclusively in the USA by
Palgrave, 175 Fifth Avenue, New York, NY 10010, USA

Distributed exclusively in Canada by
UBC Press, University of British Columbia, 2029 West Mall,
Vancouver, BC, Canada V6T 1Z2

British Library Cataloguing-in-Publication Data
A catalogue record for this book is available from the British Library

Library of Congress Cataloging-in-Publication Data applied for

ISBN 0 7190 6544 5 *hardback*
EAN 978 0 7190 6544 6

First published 2006

15 14 13 12 11 10 09 08 07 06   10 9 8 7 6 5 4 3 2 1

Typeset in Minion
by Graphicraft Limited, Hong Kong
Printed in Great Britain
by CPI, Bath

This book is dedicated to my parents,
Jean and David Freeman, with love

Contents

Illustrations

All illustrations are from Herbert Cescinsky and Ernest R. Gribble,
Early English Furniture and Woodwork Vol. I & II, London: Routledge, 1922.

Acknowledgements

Many years ago this book began life as a PhD thesis, and my first debt is therefore to my two supervisors, Marion O'Connor and Andrew Butcher, for their help, support and encouragement at the time and ever since. It was first revised in the light of the generous and perceptive comments of its examiners, Janette Dillon and Ken Fincham, and subsequently took shape in response to the comments of anonymous readers at every stage. I would never have started on the project in the first place without a British Academy Studentship. During those years and afterwards I worked with some wonderful people at the University of Kent, whose willingness to engage in endless conversations about literature and history kept me going as it no doubt drove them slowly insane: Sheila Sweetinburgh, Brian Dillon and Claire Bartram have suffered more than most. The staff at Canterbury Cathedral Archive have been helpful and interested in this project in a way which has made every moment spent there a pleasure.

Working at the University of Birmingham and in particular at the Shakespeare Institute has both delayed and encouraged the final arrival of this book – delayed it because it made me realise just how little I knew about early modern drama, and encouraged it because it is a really inspirational place in so many different ways. Since I have been here, Peter Holland, John Jowett, and more recently Cath Alexander and Kate McLuskie, Rebecca and Juliet have been supportive and generous colleagues with whom it has been a pleasure to work. Martin Wiggins has borne the brunt of my insistent questions about tragedy on the staircase and somehow always responded, not only with the resources of his unfailing memory but also with an enthusiasm which has kept me going. He and Mark Merry have read the whole thing, pointed out glaring errors and offered suggestions which have made it a much better book, and I am enormously grateful to them both, for that huge task and for much more besides. Felicity Dunworth has also read several chapters, and she and Brian have contributed to its eventual completion in many less tangible ways too.

I have benefited from talking about the issues involved here with students in both literature and history departments, and at many seminars across the country and beyond. The Institute's weekly play readings have given me the opportunity to test out all of the plays on a discerning audience, and to think about their relationship to contemporary drama. I've learnt a great deal from discussing things domestic with Lena Orlin over several years, and the influence her work has had on this book is at least partly apparent from the notes. When energy was flagging, approaching the final stages, talking about the plays with Sonia Massai and M. J. Kidnie over pizza gave me new enthusiasm.

The Centre for Reformation and Early Modern Studies at Birmingham has provided a forum for working on material culture in which I've benefited from discussions with Giorgio Riello, Mark Overton, Richard Cust and Graeme Murdock in particular. The AHRC Centre for the Study of the Domestic Interior has also offered many opportunities to think about the topic differently, and I've learnt a great deal from discussion with Jeremy Aynsley, Charlotte Grant and John Styles. Sarah Pearson took time to show me around the extant houses of Kent with an expert eye which really opened mine to the complexity of domestic spaces.

Finally of course, this book about family and household has been influenced by my family – by my parents, to whom it is dedicated, and by our oldest member, my very real uncle John Huskinson. Justin, with whom I share a home most of the time, has had to bear the brunt of the extreme emotions generated by domestic tragedy. This book has been with us for around half of our life together, but he has accepted it with patience and supported me with love. I'm looking forward to the future . . .

Note on the text

Punctuation and capitalisation have been standardised in all quotes from archival sources, but spelling has been left as originally written. Abbreviations have been silently expanded. U/v and i/j have been modernised throughout.

Abbreviations:

CCAL   Canterbury Cathedral Archive and Library
CKS   Centre for Kentish Studies, Maidstone
OED   *Oxford English Dictionary*

Introduction

Man hath no permanent habitacion uppon the earth, for the Lord hath made our dayes as it were a spanne longe, neither doe we knowe the daye of the Lordes visitacion. Whereuppon I call to minde the message of the lord sent to Hezechiah by the prophet Isayah: 'Thus saieth the Lord, put thine howse in order for thow shalt die and not live.' In consideracion whereof I Thomas Stockett of the Citie of Canterbury, gent, in the peace of god the father [&] of our Lord Jesus Christe make and ordeine this my laste will and testamente[1]

Imagine, for a moment, what it might be like to be sitting in the hall of an early modern house. Say it is timber-framed, three storeys high, the upper floors jettied out over the street in front. What are you sitting on? Is it an old 'turned' chair with arms and a back 'by the fyer sid', or one of several stools around the table, or a bench along the wall?[2] Are you sitting on the hard oak or, if you reach down to touch the seat, do you feel a cushion? Perhaps it is one 'of crymson velvett, and ymbrodered with borders of greane sylke round about, saving it lackethe a lytle at one ende'.[3] Can you be so precise because you know it very well indeed, both by sight and touch?

What is this room like? How large is it? Perhaps it has a long refectory table with stools around it. There is a court cupboard 'under the wyndowe', 'an olde carpett and a lynnen cuberd cloth upon yt', 'a bason, ii flower potte, a cupp of tynn and ii stone pottes' on top, and there are 'paynted clothes over the benche'.[4] How many doors are visible? There may well be a little buttery 'opening to the hall', the small cupboard off this room in which the brass and pewter is stored. There might be a 'little place betwene the hall and the shop' with a 'little cupbord' in it,[5] one of those curious spaces which spring up in timber-framed houses when new sections are built on. There might be an entry behind the room, opening on to the back side of the house where the kitchen is.[6] Towards the back of the house the room is darker, and here perhaps is the door to the parlour. It is open and you can see the 'fether bedd wythe stedle standinge in the parlor furnysshed as a bedd ought to be',[7] with its curtains and its tester and valance, with its bolsters and sheets and blankets and coverlets, all 'appropriate' to the status of this house in a way which you can judge intuitively. Then, fading from your vision in the hall, the 'dark room behind the parlour' which has no windows. At the other end of the hall is the window on to the street, and this casts light on the colours of the painted cloths, on the 'olde rownde lokinge glase', and on the 'payre of greate andyrons' in the chimney.[8]

How aware are you of the rest of the house as you sit in the hall? Can you smell cooking from the back side? Can you smell onions and garlic, either in the room with you or upstairs in the chambers; perhaps the four 'bacon hogges that are hanging in the roof'?[9] Is it autumn? Can you smell apples in the loft above, or the oily scent of wool? Can you smell the raw materials and the processes of production going on in the shop; can you hear shears, or hammers? These routine noises must fade away in your consciousness to almost nothing, to a reassuring background which means 'household' to you.

How aware are you of the presence of the rest of the household? The walls are thin and there are holes, cracks, spaces in them, some there by design and others the result of wear.[10] They complicate the division between the hall and the rooms around it. As you listen, you hear 'one coufe [cough] in the howse'. Do you recognise the cough?[11] If it is a stranger, you begin to listen much more carefully, to concentrate and make out sounds above your head. If there are 'no persones in the . . . hall hearing' but you 'alone', the disparity between the exchanges upstairs and your seclusion downstairs will make the hall seem larger and stiller.[12] Those you hear 'in a chamber over the hall' are choosing their words very carefully. They are discussing issues which connect the house to the body and the soul as they 'speake and move' the testator 'to be good unto his wif'.

If you go up, what will happen? You may '[loke] into the chamber and [harken] what was there in doing'; you may see women standing by the bed, and men writing. Is it possible that they may cause 'the doore to be shut fast to them'?[13] How does the testament they are writing affect your perception of this house, its spaces, objects and routines, as the man who is dictating his wishes gives away his household goods? Perhaps, weighing up these possible interventions in events to which you are close but not necessarily privy, your attention is drawn outside the house. It is 'fayre wether but yet a cold wynde' has 'forcyd [you] to shot one of the . . . wyndows',[14] but you can still hear voices because the other noises in the street are low, even in a town like this.[15]

It is specific words which strike your consciousness forcibly, ringing out like a bell: 'Thow art an arrant w[h]ore and an olde bitch and thou maist go lie with thie knaves againe in the chinmney corner upon wooll sackes'.[16] You cannot 'see either of the . . . women' who are speaking. One, Debeney, sounds as though she is 'in an entry of her howse toward the backside', the other, Wyneates, 'in her backside or house very neere one to the other for their houses are next adioyning'. But you know it is 'Wyneates that spake the said woordes' because you know 'well her voice, having heard her talke and bene in her company divers times before'. These are your neighbours, but the words you have just heard are not neighbourly; they demand a different kind of listening from you. If they know you have heard, you will be 'required to beare witnes of them', and in that case you will have 'cause to note and remember the mater'.[17] But they cannot see you here in the hall, so before that happens you will need to decide whether or not to go outside.

Whether you go upstairs, or outside, and how you go, will depend upon who you are. How have you been imagining yourself? Are you the testator's wife, in need of friends to intervene in your husband's testament on your behalf because he cannot equate the final home to which he is going with this one in which you will be left, causing you to sit in the hall in unbearably painful isolation and exclusion, alive to the proximity of sound and the distance formed by his control, even now, over the space of his chamber? Are you his servant, facing the possibility of the fracturing of the household if he dies, called from the hall where you were tending your fire to fetch the necessaries of the deathbed; rushed, troubled, barely pausing to notice these familiar surroundings? Or are you the head of this household, retired for a while from advising your kinsman the testator, pausing to reflect upon the disjunctures of death in a hall filled with the furniture which your grand-parents, parents, godparents and friends have given to you over the years, and to which you have added from the profits of your business in order to demonstrate your status in this comparatively public room? If you are this latter, you may well go straight outside and begin to arbitrate between the women in the street. If you are yourself a woman, you might check your clothing in the mirror, making sure that you are appropriately dressed with headcloth and breastcloth, before taking up a safe position on your doorstep.

This is a consideration of different kinds of representation of the household, an argument which moves from oral tales about its spaces to theatrical performances.[18] And the point of reconstructing contemporary perceptions of the household here is to begin a dialogue about how they might affect the way in which the domestic tragedies of the 1590s and 1600s were watched.

It is possible to reconstruct the early modern house spatially, through the sights, smells, sounds and textures of which it was composed; possible also to consider the way it changes over time, and to locate human rites of passage within its fabric. This can be done using the descriptions which early modern men and women gave, sensitive to differences of construction, colour and fabric, to the qualities of light and the ways in which sound moves between spaces. Such a reconstruction is infinitely richer for an understanding of the social and moral information which those descriptions carry with them. Seeing, hearing, touching – talking about their sensory perceptions of the domestic was always a loaded issue when 'did you hear what happened outside?' means 'are you prepared to become involved in addressing extra-domestic crisis?'; when 'what did you see through the chamber door?' carries the weight of 'how do you balance the importance of your domestic employment against your knowledge of right and wrong?'; when the description and pricing of a bed and its accoutrements draws a creative and yet precise connection between domestic furniture and social status which has the moral weight of being 'appropriate'.[19]

The possibility of recovering these distinctions might be reason enough for such a reconstruction, to engage with how domestic life, so central personally, socially and politically in this period, was lived and understood; to reconstruct, partially as must always be the case, sensory perception and affect as they are inspired by objects, in a period in which domestic space meant very different things – different both diachronically in its meanings for us, and synchronically for early modern individuals of diverse gender and status groups. But in addition, when we see Thomas Arden's murderers shed his blood in his parlour having placed him on a stool, or John Frankford approaching his bedchamber through his darkened house in the night, it becomes clear that we are missing some of the impact of the relationship between action and space upon which such scenes originally depended. It is evident from such a reconstruction that a peculiarly early modern spatial imagination needs to be brought to bear on staged representations if they are to regain the full weight of the implication of action.

This Introduction is intended to open up some of the arguments about the connection between dramaturgy and the imagination, in order to introduce considerations of method. First, however, it seems important to explain the choice of plays on which the following chapters will focus, and how they relate to the various definitions of the genre of domestic tragedy to this project of reconstructing domestic imagination. The genre is infamously hard to define, a difficulty largely based around the various meanings of 'domestic': set in England, set within and dealing with issues proper to the household, and treating the actions of those of less than noble birth. Whilst the first designation offers a more distinctly bounded category than the second, which may include almost any play with a domestic or familial dynamic, many plays which locate their action in England lack the eager interest in the private dealings of their characters which is such an important feature of the contemporary moralised meanings of 'domestic'. Critics of the plays have often, therefore, adopted a definition which focuses on the intersection of the first two meanings of the word, and which takes into account the lower status of the protagonists.

Henry Hitch Adams, for example, in the first full-length treatment of domestic tragedy, defined the central characteristic shared by the plays as a departure from Aristotelian definitions of the tragic as involving the actions of kings and princes.[20] He took domestic to mean both 'any phase of family life' and 'familiar, local', summing up the genre as 'a tragedy of common people, ordinarily set in the domestic scene, dealing with personal and family relationships rather than with large affairs of state, presented in a realistic fashion, and ending in a tragic or otherwise serious manner'.[21] Keith Sturgess, in his edition of three domestic tragedies, describes them as 'attempting to portray the unheroic crimes and passions of ordinary life'.[22] He admits two plays by Heywood (*A Woman Killed With Kindness* and *The English Traveller*) to an otherwise homogenous group of historically based plots which end in a murder because, he says, they share a focus on domestic detail which aims at what he calls a 'journalistic treatment'. Frances Dolan and Peter Lake have also discussed the works in the context of their investigations of murder pamphlets, and this initial motivation for their enquiry leads them to concentrate on those plays which are based on historical events. Dolan, Lake and Sturgess therefore stress the plays' appeal to a sense of the contemporary, the shocking and the local.

Lena Orlin and Viviana Comensoli, in the other principal monographs on domestic plays, have both stressed the novelty of the generic form, and the self-conscious way in which many of the texts set themselves apart from 'classical or aristocratic models'.[23] Comensoli's analysis traces a broad trajectory of representations of family life and interpersonal dynamics from medieval through to modern drama. She invariably defines the tragedies of the late sixteenth and early seventeenth centuries in contradistinction to other types of play: to medieval representations of the domestic unit which do not share the same 'interest in the ideology of private life', and to citizen comedies which adopt the city rather than the household as their 'fulcrum'.[24] Lena Orlin examines the fraught binary between public and private life so crucial to these often voyeuristic plays. In order to do so, she puts broad and flexible limits upon the genre, but ones which highlight the essential materiality of domestic culture in the period: she describes domestic tragedies as plays which concern 'property owners'.[25]

My interests here are very much in sympathy with Orlin's focus upon property. I concentrate on the familiar nature of the local, on the shockingness of the contemporary and on those plays for which the nature of the household is the motivating dynamic for action, and in which the meaning of events is therefore shaped by their location. The texts have long been read in relation to the growing political importance of the household as a unit of governance in the period. It is partly this extra-theatrical significance of domestic and familial behaviour which separates the early modern plays on household subjects from their medieval inheritance. But discussions of the genre have tended to focus on the emotional dynamics between family members, and they have not always taken the centrality of the physical household into account – the significance of the connections between relationships and the confining and defining spaces of the house.[26] I want to consider the type of representation of domestic interiors which the genre offers, and the ways in which this affects the movement of the narrative and the pointedness of its homiletic intention.[27] In what follows I examine the relationship between the spatial containment which is an essential feature of a house, and the dynamics of representation on a comparatively 'bare' stage. This suggests a shift of focus away from both the body of the actor and the authority of the script, not in order to argue that stage and prop are more important, but to think about how they negotiate audience imagination. As my focus is upon the significance of such representations, I concentrate on *A Woman Killed With Kindness*, *Arden of Faversham*, *A Yorkshire Tragedy*, and the English narrative of *Two Lamentable Tragedies*. These plays are unashamedly chosen for the novelty of their presentation of the domestic, in order to expand as far as possible the significances of an approach which considers the intersection of representations of, and attitudes to, house and household.

AUDIENCES AND IMAGINATION

English Renaissance theatrical method has been said to be 'radically synecdochic, endlessly referring the spectators to events, objects, situations, landscapes that cannot be shown them', and has therefore been seen 'deliberately to foster theatre goers' capacity to use partial and limited presentations as a basis for conjecture about what is undisplayed or undisplayable'.[28] Katharine Maus is talking here about the limits of what it is possible to represent within such a theatre, but also of what it is morally acceptable to show. Obviously, audiences understand dramatic action in relation to other plays and within the constraints and expectations of genre. But a theatre which relies upon conjecture suggests a broad and fruitful interaction between narrative suggestion and audience imagination, one which receives less critical attention than the interaction between representations.[29] It raises the question, can we begin to reconstruct how and what the audience might have imagined?

Maus conjures an image of interpretative chaos in which critics are faced with reconstructing meanings as various as the number of audience members: 'Under the gaze of multiple spectators, interpretations proliferate uncontrollably, and in place of consensus one is left with myriad perspectives, each one unique, but none authoritative.'[30] In similar vein, William West describes the concern, which developed when 'theatres' became physical spaces rather than epistemological ones, over the shift from a theory in which theatre was a 'spectacle', to a practice in which 'the theatre is realised as an experience'. The imagined audience, initially envisioned as a group of spectators 'that responded predictably and homogeneously', became something troublingly different – an *active* group who participated through experiential engagement with the drama.[31] Militating against this diversity of reaction is the guiding hand which the form of the representation imposes upon interpretation, steering audiences towards a meaning which makes sense of what they have seen. The Epilogue to *A Woman Killed With Kindness* acknowledges both the expanse and the limits of the range of interpretive responses in three verses about 'An honest crew, disposed to be merry' who call for wine in a tavern. Each has a different opinion about its quality: 'The wine was new, old, flat, sharp, sweet, and sour', because, as the final stanza makes explicit, 'every several mouth hath sundry taste'. The taste, approach, experience and expectations of each audience member will be different, but there must be enough common ground for the drinkers all to agree that they have tasted wine if any performance is to succeed in its fundamental communicative purpose.

This epilogue suggests a fairly obvious, but none the less essential distinction between personal tastes, which might be extended into individual memories and present concerns, and generally understood cultural meanings and probabilities. Seeing a tragedy directly after the death of a loved one will acutely alter an individual's understanding of the play, and the effect of such events can never be fully reconstructed.[32] But the latter category of generally understood meanings, still extremely broad, is the level at which we critically approach the way representations communicate with their spectators. The general significance of the representation lies in its capacity to be sufficiently 'recognisable' to the majority of the audience so that a rough consensus about its meaning can be reached. This does not deny different interpretations, altered by, for instance, gender or social status, rather it recognises that representations negotiate such differences through a particular kind of flexibility.[33]

This flexibility was a feature of what Worthen calls the 'dramatic performativity' of the early modern stage, 'the relationship between the verbal text and the conventions . . . of behaviour that give it meaningful *force* as performed action'.[34] If drama as illusion involves a complex negotiation between the physical and the verbal, between spectacle and poetry, between seeing and hearing, then Alan Dessen has argued that these pairings were differently weighted in the early modern theatre.[35] He discusses how a place 'came into existence when the actor gestured towards something (a pillar, a railing) or some place, thus giving a local habitation and a name to an otherwise neutral area'.[36] If 'Language remained the most sophisticated technology of representation', and 'the illusion often lay not in how something looked but how it was described', then illusion moves in complex ways between the visual and the verbal.[37] And the material qualities of the stage afford what Harris and Korda call 'distracting glimpses' of the 'material, economic' and, one might add, affective histories of the properties and spaces which the audience see, bringing extra-theatrical meanings into play.[38]

Dessen quotes Neil Carson's argument that 'the "scenery" . . . can be said to materialize and then melt away in the imagination of the spectators. The effect is a sort of double consciousness in which the stage, without ever ceasing to be itself, becomes also as needed an open field, a stream, a citadel, and so on.'[39] The physical location of the action – field, stream – is thereby established as an idea, rather than some kind of visual hallucination. '[P]lace' becomes very firmly 'an adjunct of the narrative' in 'a drama of persons, not a drama of places', where 'the absence of a verisimilar prison', for instance, 'yields greater freedom to the imaginative vision of Shakespeare and his audience'.[40] Freed from the constraints of visual particularity, an audience's imagination is able to roam between language, concept and situation, imagining 'imprisonment' rather than 'prison'.

For Dessen, seeing *less* almost always means perceiving *more*, and he makes a crucial case for the centrality of imagination to the creation of early modern theatrical meaning. But there is one place where his argument seems to change tack – to move from its insistence upon the amplification of the physical scene to a closing down of imaginative possibilities – and that is in the staging of rooms. He quotes Lawrence J. Ross's argument that 'Desdemona's bed in the final scene "is not placed in a bedroom" but rather "brings the locale of a bedroom with it"'. Rather than being a furnishing, the bed 'is physically and expressively the center of the action and so placed as to be inseparable from it'. These subtle distinctions, strongly expressed to point up the contrast with a theatre of naturalistic sets, seem to separate Elizabethan props from the rooms which form their extra-theatrical contexts, whilst retaining the effort of the audience's imagination necessary to 'bring the locale of bedroom'. Dessen's own comment on the staging of rooms is a typically subtle attempt to avoid anachronous imaginings: 'Not nurtured by cinema, television, the novel and naturalism, an Elizabethan viewer would not have moved as readily from the signal (bed, throne) to our sense of "room".'[41] It is not entirely clear what 'our sense of room' is, but Dessen's distinction appears to be based upon a sense that enclosed space is fundamentally at odds with Elizabethan staging; that action in a room cannot operate in an equivalent way to action in a field, in a river, under a 'penthouse, bulk or hedge corner'. This is clearly not an issue of imaginative failure. Those capable of imagining a field can obviously imagine a chamber too. It *is* a feature of what Dessen perceives to be a uniquely modern capacity to move from prop to room, rather than the 'general sense of locale' which he considers a more likely mental construction. 'Our sense of "furniture,"' he says, 'can lead to subtle distortions (and diminutions) of Elizabethan effects.'[42] The complexities of these spatialising anachronisms need further investigation.

If asked to 'see' armies converging on the stage, the audience need not picture them. They might rather accept that the logic of that particular situation is to be taken to adhere, that the actors are now to behave *as though* they were part of a large army, as though they were going to battle. And perhaps this is a helpful distinction: just as the dynamics of an army are different to its physical presence, with all the issues of scale and personnel which must be negotiated, so a chamber as a space is different from a chamber as a series of suppositions about likely and appropriate or inappropriate behaviour; the logistics of such a space and its connection to human relationships. This distinction is important because it shifts the focus from the material qualities of representation to the social, moral or political dynamics which pertain to the situations which actors conjure into being. The quality of authority and the rules of engagement which apply within armies as opposed to bedchambers, for instance, will be an important part of the difference which is being signalled rhetorically.

Having said this, though, the chamber is different again. Its interpersonal dynamics are controlled by its spatial design: its size, its position within the house, its furnishings, are what gives it the sense of intimacy on which plays call. Neither marching armies nor streams have the close relationship between the spatial and the interpersonal which characterises domestic space. The opening chapters of this book examine the contemporary facility for spatialising imaginations, for the construction of rooms within oral and written narratives which suggest a sensitivity towards volume, location and sensory perception, as a way of examining just how early modern men and women did imagine spaces, and therefore how they are likely to have responded to the properties and rhetorical identifications of space offered to them by early modern plays.

MIMESIS AND PARTICULARITY

Keith Sturgess's description of domestic tragedies as 'journalistic' in their mode of representation suggests more than just the dependence of several of them on contemporary 'news' stories. It indicates a particular kind of mimesis which developed with the professional theatre.[43] Partly, of course, the change was connected to that theatre's development away from the morality plays, with their presentation of 'preordained patterns of static conflict', to 'the realistic mode of characterisation', which 'was particularly well-suited to represent the movement (the relations and the struggle) between the world and the ego, environment and character', as Robert Weimann has described it.[44] As audience tastes moved away from Moralities, the history play developed as a genre.[45] Histories, as narratives of things which 'really happened', would appear to require a different type of representation to plays about the timeless conflicts of vice and virtue. Describing 'realist' mimesis, Jonathan Dollimore says 'drama was rapidly progressing as a form with empirical, historical and contemporary emphases'.[46] In Madeleine Doran's terms, there was a gradual shift from the 'universal' to the 'probable' and even the 'credible', the latter capable of being verified by comparison to the world outside the artwork.[47]

In this new kind of commercial theatre, grown immeasurably in confidence by the close of the sixteenth century, the portrayal of the domestic environment and the pull of local and contemporary narratives seem particularly intended to invite comparison with experience outside the theatre. Instead of 'falling back on predetermined modes of synthesis', Weimann says, writer and spectator, 'were called upon to analyze the areas of congruity and incongruity between vision and experience for themselves'.[48] The 'relations and the struggle' between 'environment and character' set the didactic projects of the morality play and the domestic tragedy poles apart, despite the continuities which Commensoli traces between their familial preoccupations.

The homiletic intention which Adams saw as motivating domestic plays must therefore operate differently. Halliwell points up the importance of a notion of 'experience' to the Greek tradition of mimesis: 'the whole history of mimeticism manifests a dual concern with the status of artistic works or performances and with the experiences they invite or make available'.

Elsewhere, he describes this as a criterion for judgement of 'effectiveness', imagined as an emotional engagement: 'success in drawing the hearer or viewer into a strong engagement with the possibilities of experience that they depict . . . a world in relation to which the audience imaginatively occupies the position of an absorbed or engrossed witness'. These two types of experience, the one offered as example and the other invited in response, are linked to the nature of the representation. It is, for Aristotle, 'situations of vividly imagined particularity that constitute the primary fabric of mimetic art'.[49] Halliwell also makes the ethical component of mimesis clear. To understand such a representation is to recognise 'and, to a degree which varies according to the work and the recipient, "learn" (though not necessarily anything that can easily be paraphrased) from its representation of human action in a possible world'. In discussing Plato's handling of mimetic art he identifies two lines of approach which correspond to my interests here, 'one fixes on the complex relationship of "likeness" between mimetic images and the features of the world they (purport to) represent, the other on the psychological implications and consequences of mimesis for its audiences'.[50]

The emerging focus on the 'credibility' of representations grew out of Renaissance reconsiderations of such Classical theories of their function. The dynamic between representation and ethical function was hotly debated in early modern England, because it was essential to the legitimising discourses around emerging and developing forms of entertainment. Authors of the pamphlet literature to which many domestic plays are so closely connected were keen to promote their narratives as operating as sermon-like keys to an active process of self-analysis. As Golding said in his *Brief Discourse*, 'the execution of his [God's] judgements should, by the terror of the outward sight of the example, drive us towards the inward consideration of ourselves'. A *process* is suggested here, one which is set in motion by the display of judgement: 'When God bringeth such matters upon the stage', Golding continues, '[the murderers'] faults came into the open theatre and therefore seemed the greater to our eyes and surely they were great indeed[. N]either are ours the less because they lie hidden in the covert of our heart. God, the searcher of all secrets, seeth them and, if he list, he can also discover them':[51] representation has the capacity to provoke the revelatory processes of self-analysis. These dynamics are didactic in motivation and ecclesiastical in form – pamphlet writers borrow the rhetorical structures of the sermon to legitimise their representation of sensational material, to give it moral point, and this affects the meanings of the mimetic representation which they offer.

Eric Carlson's analysis of the quality of parish ministry at the turn of the sixteenth century uncovers an interesting rhetoric connecting intention with the form of representation. It was particularly those who were secure in their own goodness, the 'sleepers', who needed to be addressed, and the urgency of the fight for their souls legitimised an aggressive physicality of approach. As William Jones begs: 'suffer us to meddle with you, to reprehend that which is amisse in you: for we must give an accompt for you. Therefore we cannot let you alone, wee cannot, nay wee must not permit you to sleepe in your sinnes.' The way to awake the sleeping sinner was with a loud noise: 'wee must lift up our voices as trumpets to waken you'. As Stephen Gosson, parson of Great Wigborough but a man with knowledge of the operation of all sorts of different representations, said, anything less was to 'tell you that all is well . . . you shall goe to Heaven sleeping, as men carried in a Coach without any action or motion of your owne'. And that, of course, was a damnable lie.[52]

This argument for the stirring of conscience through loud communication is also central to contemporary pro- and anti-theatrical debates about the theories of audience response. Writers of both persuasions described audiences as '"impressed", "wrought upon," "inflamed," "ravished" by the performance'; Gosson depicts plays as making 'our affections overflow' and as drawing 'the bridle from that parte of the minde, that should ever be curbed'.[53] As William West points out, 'The attraction of the theatre for the humanists was that it promised to teach experientially rather than dogmatically', but in practice this experience was fundamentally uncontrollable.[54] All were agreed that performance evoked strong emotion, but there was sharp disagreement about the way that emotion acted on the audience.

Thomas Heywood, in his *Apology for Actors*, famously suggests the way representation operates upon the conscience, mentioning several cases which demonstrate the revelatory power of drama, ones which he says he chose for 'their familiarness and lateness of memory'. There was the Earl of Sussex's players' performance of the ghost haunting the guilty in *Friar Francis*, which provoked a townswoman 'Till then of good estimation and report' to 'suddenly [screech] and [cry] out Oh my husband, my husband!', and from there to confess that she too was being haunted by her own wronged spouse. In Amsterdam, when a nail was driven into the skull of penitent Renaldo in *The Four Sons of Aymon*, the scene 'strangely amazed' a 'woman of great gravity', who finally confessed to driving a nail into the skull of her husband some twelve years previously.[55] These examples share a focus on the emotional trauma of a revelation effected by dramatic representation, one which is suggestive of a spiritual experience, an unstoppable working of providence within the guilty conscience. The Amsterdam example makes it clear that the particular nature of the murder, the unusual and distinctive nature of the weapon, was what triggered the workings of conscience through the equivalence of representation and historical reality.

Like Hamlet's hopes for his 'Mousetrap', such perfect representations whose effects on the operation of conscience are 'not just similar to, but in fact indistinguishable from, the event itself', appear to belong to the realm of theory rather than commercial reality.[56] In practice, the evocation of audience sympathy, whether in this extreme form of identification or in its more diluted modes of empathy and engagement, is far more complicated than this patterning process of exact correspondences, of course. Equivalences of detail do not threaten the boundary between memory and representation, do not convince that what is seen now is 'real'. Rather it is the inflaming powers of narrative, rhetoric and character construction which provide the context within which the conscience-stabbing energies of the performance can be transferred from actor to audience. And ways of achieving such incendiary effects were debated in all media where a moral project depended upon the audience making a connection between representation and reality. Considerations of sermonising practice elucidate a highly developed and detailed contemporary engagement with the difference between the specific and general properties of the representation of sin as a way of retaining the attention of the faithful. Preachers and divines engaged in a heated debate about the difference between sins such as covetousness and actions such as stealing, between the sinner who suffers from wrath and the individual parishioner who loses his temper. 'Particularising', denouncing specific individuals within the congregation, was considered counterproductive because it spread discord and invited conflict by making parishioners feel unjustly singled out. But the line between general condemnation of sin and particular condemnation of character or action was not as clear as might have been desirable. As Richard Bernard pointed out, preachers were 'said to name men in the Pulpit, and gall some personally: when no man is named'. Simon Hieron explained that 'It cutteth the Sabbath-breaker to hear his profaneness still cryed out upon: it cutteth the adulterer, to hear his viciousness continually found fault with . . .' It was possible 'for a Minister to carry the matter so with that wisdome and power, as that every guiltie person present may find and perceiue himselfe as directly spoken to'.[57] Rhetorical skill made the general *seem* particular, made it possible for it to be *felt as* particular. The perceived power of rhetoric to invoke the strongest of emotions functioned through the dynamic between the general and the particular, by setting the individual's conscience in motion.[58] These arguments make it clear that particularising could be a characteristic of the power and clarity of the representation's effect, as well as a feature of its form. Such an understanding is related to the second of Aristotle's mimetic processes, mentioned above, where the work of identification is done within the conscience of the audience.

Sermon manuals, then, actively discouraged the use of the individual example, and instead advocated the employment of a rhetoric which encouraged conscience-provoking emotional engagement. Unlike Heywood's theatrical example of the driving in of the nail, preachers were to delay the process of specificity until the reception stage of representation. Cheap print, however, gained its examples from the particularised narrative, producing stories of true crime whose didactic efficacy was seen (by those who believed they had any) to lie in their topical currency – applicable because they were a recognisably contemporary product of current moral dilemmas and immoral temptations. Arguably, these stories of true crime fundamentally altered the relationship between the general and the particular in didactic literature by elevating the grubbily topical to a position of active significance. They are a part of the move towards a particularity of *representation*, rather than *reception* in a period in which 'a tendency to draw the general out of the particular' was a fundamental aspect of narrative interpretation, and much else besides.[59] Domestic tragedy appears to be one of the stage's closest flirtations with such contemporary, quotidian tales, and it is therefore an interesting sub-genre for consideration of the extent to and ways in which drama functions as a didactic medium in this period.

So how, in detail, might the process of awakening a conscience through particularity work? The key contemporary word is 'liveliness', used in disgust by William Prynne to describe the nature of staged drama, more pernicious than the written script because of the 'lively representations' of sin to which it gives rise. Seeing events represented in a 'lively' manner induces deep and personal emotional responses in the hearts of sinners, and the meanings of the word 'lively' in the sixteenth and seventeenth centuries reflect this relationship between representation and emotion.[60] The notion of vivid intensity was applied to both images and feelings, and the word carried an additional sense of 'being convincing' which seems to come close to mimesis.[61] Tomson's 1579 translation of Calvin's *Sermons on the Epistles of Timothy* offers an illustration of this relationship between the form of representation and its effect: 'The examples . . . ought to make us feele it liuely, and to the quicke', he says.[62] In drama, however, this 'liveliness' must function differently to the preacher's rhetorical manipulation of emotional engagement with a narrative. It will *always* be more immediate in its offer to the audience of human action for comparison, because it is already in human form. As Prynne's concerns suggest, its supremely 'lively' (in the sense of 'embodied') nature – the characterisation and depiction of scenes, dynamics, objects and situations to which it gives a narrative – invite audiences to connect stage action with their own experience. What is physically presented to the audience's eyes is not essentially particular – the properties, costumes and actors are common to many plays – it rather becomes so in relation to the dramatic situation within which such things are placed.[63]

In domestic tragedies this involves a very distinctive kind of particularity which takes its cue from the familiarity of the local narrative and its clear engagement with audience experience. Peter Lake suggests that the extraordinary nature of these stories works to defamiliarise behaviour. 'These were exceptional cases', he says, 'sent by God precisely to rouse ordinary, secure sinners into a true faith.' He sees their uniqueness as in some way at the heart of their ability to promote introspection. This is the furthest reach of a particularity of representation, one which challenges its audiences with the fact that they will never experience this exact situation, and nevertheless asks them to find it relevant. Lake begins to move towards the way this might work, drawing attention to the narratives' 'startling combination of an almost complete otherness with an all too obvious familiarity'.[64] There is an implicit connection here between the 'ordinariness' of the sinners and the 'familiarity' of the tale which will rouse them. It is by beginning with the 'normal', by staging horrifically aberrant behaviour within an 'everyday' context, that the secure can be made insecure by being shaken out of the complacency of daily routine. True conscience is awakened here and made 'lively' by the relation-ship between familiar location and outrageous action in a mimesis which contrasts the two. The domestic setting is a key aspect of particularity, then, one which harnesses the wild energies and at times absurd discourses of the murder plots to moralising, didactic ends.

Such a process of domestic comparison and identification may well belong to the discourses which legitimise such sensationalism, just as Heywood's nail did. And if this is the theory, then the practice is perhaps more likely to have been that the plays constructed an audience who always knew better, who would have avoided the obvious domestic pitfalls offered to the char-acters, who would have made different choices.[65] But in this very different response, of smug self-satisfaction as opposed to shocked self-examination, the invitation to make comparison between those domestic practices, power dynamics and standards represented on the stage and the ones which take place behind one's own door is conceivably even more strident. Calling upon a sense of appropriate behaviour sharpens the spectator's notion of its con-nection to social status, particularly in a period of growing social mobility.[66] Considering the fatal mistakes of a Thomas Arden or an Anne Frankford demands considerable attention to the details of domestic behaviour repres-ented on the stage.

Towards whichever of these poles of response the audiences for these plays tended, they responded to the invitation to make connections, not only amongst dramatic representations but between personal and staged events. But how did such comparisons work when gender and social status were stratified in such a way as to offer significantly different kinds of domestic experience? In plays whose emotional dynamics are generated by the tensions of gender and status, these differences must become particularly significant. The probable domestic experiences which life as a gentleman or a wage-labourer would offer are radically different, as are male and female attitudes towards household spaces and objects – differences which will be explored in the following chapters of this book. Such variation affects physical standards of living, familiarity with different activities, and consequently attitudes towards particular situations, behaviours and possessions. Responses to the domestic on the stage might fall somewhere between two extremes: that which I as an audience member can comprehend as similar to my own experience, and that which is not just different but totally 'other' to what I know. The latter obviously does not negate engagement, as everyone has an idea of what a study, for instance, might be like, rather it necessitates recourse to imagination as opposed to experience. The point at which experience gives way to imagination defines and reinforces an audience's identity. Status and gender can construct their own sense of exclusion based around the dynamic between knowing and supposing.

In *Playgoing in Shakespeare's London*, Andrew Gurr states that 'the complete social range' of playgoers 'goes all the way from earls and even a queen to penniless rogues . . . and the unemployed' and extends to women as well as men.[67] The chronology of audience patterns is also significant. Gurr concludes that 'citizens were the standard kind of playgoer in the 1590s, but . . . they were a distinctly less normal feature of the later indoor playhouse audiences'.[68] Even after 1599 when the hall playhouses were reopened, he suggests that it was some time before any firm social division became evident between the two types of playing space.[69] The decades surrounding the turn of the sixteenth century, then, appear to have provided the greatest diversity of social status within the early modern audience. By the time domestic tragedy declined, the audiences attending different kinds of playhouse had become divided along hierarchical lines. This suggests that the genre had a broad appeal, and that it had to be particularly flexible in order to give pleasure across such a wide spectrum. One of the principal areas of exploration in what follows is the ways in which particularity can be made to mean broadly. It is a central premise that these broad meanings are a function of the universality of some of the meanings of domesticity.[70]

IMAGINATION AND INTERDISCIPLINARITY

The complex interrelations of the invitation both to recall and to imagine necessitates a detailed interdisciplinary analysis of early modern plays, one which engages with the materiality of stage representations through an understanding of contemporary material culture. Objects focus and pinpoint the relationship between on- and off-stage meanings: 'That which is merely an airy shape, a dream, a passing thought', Hazlitt complained, 'immediately becomes an unmanageable reality' on the stage.[71] It is often the material qualities of production which draw our attention most sharply to the difference between the theatre for which these plays were produced and our own.

Baz Lurhman's ironic inscription of 'Long Sword' on Montague's gun, for instance, gives a small stab of recognition that objects, the way we use them and our attitudes towards them, have changed. We must concentrate on the fruitfulness of this exchange between illusion and reality; between the infinite possibilities of language and the particularity of image with its broad set of meanings if we are to begin to understand how and what audiences perceived in the theatre. The 'alternate social dramas of economic production, exchange and ownership'[72] which objects produce on the stage are harnessed by theatrical performance as the memories, thoughts, attitudes and imaginations of their diverse audiences.

Despite the difficulties of reconstructing audience experience, we have to begin to understand the material conditions under which it was produced if we are to give shape to the attitudes and perceptions to which it gave rise. This will always be a partial process, frustrated by the lack of evidence which would make possible full comparisons between different kinds of individual; hampered by the problems of finding a methodology for imaginative reconstruction which is robust enough to satisfy the different evidentiary demands of literary critics who desire access to the limits of the culturally possible, and historians who demand an analysis of the socially probable.[73] Discussing domestic life means, in many ways, concentrating on ideas common to all. As Heather Dubrow suggests, it is 'common and in many instances quotidian happenings' that offer an essential corrective to the 'outré and extreme events such as witchcraft and murder' which often form the basis of reconstructions of *mentalité*.[74] If we do not investigate the ordinary, the meaning of the extraordinary is infinitely impoverished – partly because we lack a perspective on it, and partly because we cannot appreciate all that might be threatened by aberration.

The approach adopted in the following chapters is an attempt to recover both the elements of a representation which might trigger memory and imagination, and a sense of what might be tapped into – what the audience might bring with them to the theatre.[75] The method is therefore partly that of the historian and partly that of the literary critic. Considering audience perception means examining the productive interrelationships between oral and literate cultures, and it involves understanding how narrative forms move between their differing structures and intentions.[76] Going back to the archive is essential, then, not only in order to reconstruct non-literate perception (with all its gendered implications) but also non-elite perception, the thoughts and feelings of that large middling section of society which Gurr sees as so fundamental to theatre audiences.[77]

Such an approach necessitates attention to a large number of documents, and a rigorous concentration on their interrelationships. If we want to understand how gender and status change response, we have to be able to uncover the internal dynamics of communities, and this means studying coherent bodies of documents.[78] My interest in the coherence of the evidence for this reconstruction, and the possibilities which it offers for a record linkage which traces individuals between documents, is perhaps a historian's interest. But it is an essential method if we are to understand the *relative* meanings of house and household within communities, in a way in which cannot be achieved with randomly chosen examples.[79] Within the limits circumscribed by the survival of evidence, it permits an examination of the meaning of wills and probate inventories in relation to one another – a husbandman's against a gentleman's, a widow's against the mayor's. Seeing a whole community at once means reconstructing the way individuals understand their own limitations and choices, how they perceive their experience in relation to that of their peers.

The arguments presented in Chapters 1 and 2 are, as this Introduction has been, concerned with levels of particularity, and with the point at which knowledge gives way to imagination. This was a society in which the potential to generalise the unseen was at the heart of moral projects; in which the contemporary capacity to infer, to extrapolate information about the likely organisation of individual households from a position outside the doors, organised reputations and made sense of social division. The opening chapters advance a case for widely understood tropes of household life, and for basic similarities of domestic practice which lie behind the variety of urban houses and the diversity of urban experience.[80] Like the meaning which audiences make out of dramatic narrative, the grammar of domestic organisation also operated on what we might describe as a national scale. While the specificities were different for individuals from the county of Kent and those from the county of Essex (as they were for those from the Kentish towns of Canterbury and Sandwich), these were distinctions of degree rather than kind.[81]

Arguing for a national scale does not mean denying regional difference, rather it celebrates it, but it does necessitate an engagement with the relationship between London and the provinces.[82] London's infamously prodigious growth and the national pull it exercised for immigrants helped to breathe economic life into a commercial theatre.[83] The experiences of provincial life which immigrants brought with them, their attitudes towards communal order and personal morality, formed the starting point for negotiation of the capital's social life. The fundamental meanings of the distinctions and inter-relations of the domestic and the communal were what allowed 'Londoners' from different counties to understand one another's practices and expectations, and to appreciate the basic social distinctions which were necessary for society to function peacefully and effectively. The men and women who in all probability formed the audiences for those domestic tragedies played in London had their minds explicitly focused upon ways of defining status within communities by their experience as immigrants outside the theatre. Because they lived in single rooms, in parts of tenements with shared access, outside the structures of patriarchal authority; because so little in their daily life corresponded to the ideals of domestic practice which were so widely promulgated in this period, their attention to the household was sharp and strong.

Chapter 1 takes its evidence from household manuals and from ecclesiastical court depositions, evidence which makes it possible to connect literary didacticism to the written record of oral tales about household spaces and behaviour. It examines the tropes which these discourses share, and the ways in which they employ them – sometimes to similar, sometimes different ends – in order to examine the extent of their currency. My interest is in the relationship between space and behaviour, between the material and the interpersonal aspects of the household. In pursuing the points at which early modern men and women think spatially, and the way they moralise spatial relations, the chapter examines the house from the outside, from the boundary and from the inside. The primary interest of both types of evidence is in the way the marital unit functions within the wider household. Here and throughout the chapters, the interactions and responses of adults to their domestic situation is of primary interest; when children do appear, it is most often as a comment upon their parents' actions.

Chapter 2 investigates the relationship between domestic spaces, household objects and the individuals who owned them in a period in which attitudes to material culture were markedly different to our own.[84] It uses testamentary evidence for the communities from which the witnesses who gave their court testimonies in the previous chapter came, setting the manner in which they furnished their houses and their attitudes towards their possessions against the way they talked about domestic life. Although the method is historical in the disciplinary sense, the chapter is literary in its presentation: in the way it privileges the qualitative over the quantitative in order to find a narrative form which gives the extensive statistical data meaning in terms of contemporary perceptions of status, lifecycle and gender within the household. I am interested in the way objects mediate social relations, but those of affect rather than production and consumption. My primary intention is to reconstruct experience in contemporary terms, which means privileging perceptions which were available at the time, rather than tracing their underlying structures.[85]

Chapters 1 and 2 are intended to make it possible to see differently, however partially this must be attempted; it is hoped that thinking about the plays in the light of the evidence they offer will be a rather different experience, not in terms of sudden and unexpected revelations but in the more modest effects of altered nuances. The remaining chapters treat the four plays under consideration in detail. The main intention of these chapters is to consider how the dynamics of the early modern house were represented on the stage in the broadest terms. The aim is to develop a grammar of specifically domestic representations which stretches from the most subtle of Dessen's spatialisations to the most concrete of stage properties, examining every element of the use of stage space and the linguistic and gestural construction of the household along the way. Investigating the connections between the seen and the unseen, between secret and revelation, between inside and outside, household and community, I consider these plays as offering a uniquely developed domestic mimesis.

It is a central contention in what follows that the household had a striking form and status within the memory. As an example which bridges the theatrical and the personal, not in theoretical terms but in terms of circumstance, Edward Alleyn's letters home while in Bristol on tour with Lord Strange's Men in 1593 usefully crystallise these meanings. On 1 August, he writes to his wife:

> mouse you send me no newes of any things you should send of your domestycall matters such things as happens att home as how your distilled watter proves or this or that or any thing what you will . . . you sente me nott word of my garden but next tym you will but remember this in any case that all that bed which was parsley in the month of september you sowe itt with spinage for then is the tym: I would do it my self but we shall nott com hom till allholand tyd[86]

The homesickness is palpable, and it manifests itself in the way Alleyn mentally follows the domestic routines which form his experience of home while away from it. On 28 September, Henslowe writes to him, including news of his house. John Griggs, a carpenter who had previously been working on the Rose, was now involved in alterations to Alleyn's house: 'your Joyner hath seate up your portolle in the chamber & hath brothe you a corte cobert & sayes he will bringe the Reaste very shortley' (your joiner has set up your portal in the chamber and has brought you a court cupboard [large cabinet for storage on which plate could be displayed] and says he will bring the rest very shortly).[87] He is clearly updating the house, using such profits as his itinerant provincial touring may have produced to pay the playhouse carpenter to improve his most intimate domestic space. As the space alters he must imagine the changes from a distance, and the prospect of seeing them in reality becomes part of an anticipated homecoming, pleasurable as both familiar and different.

If domestic drama necessitates the use of the imagination, and if imagination is built partly on experience and its memories, then mental images of the house are strong. As this small example shows, they involve an intimate relationship between the emotional and the physical, and an awareness of the consolations of material stability within life's cyclical patterns of change.

NOTES

1 CCAL 17.51 f.122v, 1596.
2 CCAL 21.8 f.304, 1587.
3 CCAL 39.9 f.82, 1583.
4 CKS 10.20 f.358, 1592; CCAL 21.4 f.197, 1580; CKS 10.13 f.309v, 1584; CKS 10.5 f.120, 1570.
5 CKS 10.11 f.221, 1580.
6 CKS 10.13 f.116, 1582; CKS 10.20 f.151, 1592; CCAL 28.2 f.29, 1567; CCAL 21.12 f.470, 1596.
7 CCAL 39.10 f.170v, 1583.
8 CKS 10.27 f.143, 1598; CCAL 21.4 f.28v, 1580.
9 William Faunt, tailor of Canterbury, had a standing bed with two featherbeds, needle-work cushions and a bible in the 'great back chamber next the river', plus a bushel of onions, CCAL 21.8 f.304, 1587; Thomas Nethersole of St Peters had onions and garlic in his hall, CKS 10.11 f.214v, 1582; Richard Pordage of St Dunstans had cheese and onions in the chamber over his old parlour, as well as his featherbed, CKS 10.8 f.4, 1575. CKS 10.8 f.4, 1575.
10 Lena Cowen Orlin has uncovered fascinating details of the permeability of early modern partitions, 'Walls and their chinks in early modern England', unpublished paper, 2005.
11 CCAL 39.10 f.123v, 1583.
12 CCAL X.10.6 f.49v, 1551.
13 CCAL X.10.6 f.52, 1551.
14 CCAL 39.1 f.7v, 1555.
15 For a detailed description of noise levels in the early modern town see Bruce Smith, 'The soundscapes of early modern England, city, country, court' in *The Acoustic World of Early Modern England*, Chicago: University of Chicago Press, 1999; see also Jennifer Melville, 'The Use and Organization of Domestic Space in Late Seventeenth-Century London', unpublished PhD thesis, University of Cambridge, 1999, pp. 86–8.
16 CCAL 39.17 f.4, 1593.
17 CCAL X.10.15 f.114, 1566.
18 My interest here is in the way the materiality of the household functioned in men's and women's spoken and written representations of it. There is much work to be done on bringing together archaeological, architectural and historical work on the actual physical nature of house and household in this period. See, for a provocative examples focusing on objects, David A. Hinton, *Gold and Gilt, Pots and Pins: Possessions and People in Medieval Britain*, New York: Oxford University Press, 2005; Lisa Jardine, *Worldly Goods: A New History of the Renaissance*, London: Macmillan, 1996; or, on objects and houses, Matthew Johnson, *An Archaeology of Capitalism*, Oxford: Blackwell, 1996.
19 For a thought-provoking approach to 'feelings, evanescent moods, the unmapped circuitry of intimation and insinuation' in domestic spaces in colonial America see Robert Blair St George, *Conversing by Signs: Poetics of Implication in Colonial New England Culture*, London, Chapel Hill, NC: University of North Carolina Press, 1998.
20 Henry Hitch Adams, *English Domestic or Homiletic Tragedy 1575–1642*, New York: B. Blom, 1965, pp. 1–5.
21 Adams, 1965, pp. 1–2.
22 Frances E. Dolan, *Dangerous Familiars: Representations of Domestic Crime in England 1550–1700*, Ithaca, London: Cornell University Press, 1994; Keith Sturgess, *Three Eliza-bethan Domestic Tragedies*, Harmondsworth: Penguin, 1985, p. 7.
23 Viviana Comensoli, *Household Business: Domestic Plays of Early Modern England*, 1996, Toronto, London: University of Toronto Press, 1996, p. 3; Lena Cowen Orlin, *Private Matters and Public Culture in Post-Reformation England*, Ithaca, London, 1994, p. 12.

24 Comensoli, 1996, pp. 7, 16.

25 Orlin, 1994, p. 9.

26 Diana Henderson's article on *A Woman Killed With Kindness* stresses the fact that 'One element contained in the name [of domestic tragedy] itself remains in the background – *domus*, the home', although she does not then focus her argument on the way the house is represented on the stage, 'Many mansions: reconstructing *A Woman Killed With Kindness*', *Studies in English Literature 1500–1900*, 26.2, 1986, p. 277. In focusing on domestic spaces, this book builds on the enormously productive recent work on domestic processes and economies and their relationship to drama. See especially Wendy Wall, *Staging Domesticity*, Cambridge, Cambridge University Press, 2002; Natasha Korda, *Shakespeare's Domestic Economies*, Philadelphia: University of Pennsylvania Press, 2002.

27 Adams, 1965, passim.

28 Katharine Eisaman Maus, *Inwardness and Theatre in the English Renaissance*, Chicago, London: University of Chicago Press, 1995, p. 32.

29 Jonathan Holmes and Adrian Streete outline Sidney's interest in *imitatio* as something which goes beyond the kind of imitative pedagogical practices found in the grammar school and becomes instead about 'a kind of imitation, but one that imitates the world (broadly conceived) rather than literary forms'. *Refiguring Mimesis: Representation in Early Modern Literature*, Hatfield: University of Hertfordshire Press, 2005, p. 4.

30 Maus, 1995, p. 103, where she discusses 'the displays of the Marlovian theatre'.

31 William West, *Theatres and Encyclopedias in Early Modern Europe*, Cambridge: Cambridge University Press, 2002, p. 10; pp. 116–18.

32 Indeed, this process may not be desirable, as it tells us very little about the communal, as opposed to the personal, meanings of the representation. See Andrew Gurr, *Playgoing in Shakespeare's London*, 3rd edn, Cambridge, New York: Cambridge University Press, 2004, for differences in what he calls 'mental composition' based on experiences as diverse as 'the hat worn by the playgoer in front', and 'the hearer's familiarity with Ovid or Holinshed,' section 4, quotation at p. 98.

33 Anthony Cohen's still valuable explanation of the use of polyvalent symbols of community to produce an illusion of consensus explicates this negotiation: 'What passes as *understanding* is often based on *interpretation*'. He explains the function of cultural products in diagrammatic terms, as filters through which many meanings are distilled and of which many interpretations are made, the two sides of the process meeting at an interface which is their sole point of contact and of seeming concord, Anthony P. Cohen, *The Symbolic Construction of Community*, London: Routledge, 1993 (originally published 1985), p. 73.

34 W. B. Worthen, *Shakespeare and the Force of Modern Performance*, Cambridge: Cambridge University Press, 2003, p. 3. Worthen points out the subservience of the play text: 'Far from governing the shape and meaning of performance, writing is given its significance in performance by the range of its possible uses, by the various social and theatrical conventions that transform it from language into action, behaviour' (p. 12).

35 See Gurr, 2004, pp. 102–15; Alan C. Dessen, *Elizabethan Stage Conventions and Modern Interpreters*, Cambridge: Cambridge University Press, 1984.

36 Dessen, 1984, p. 61.

37 Martin Wiggins, *Shakespeare and the Drama of His Time*, Oxford: Oxford University Press, 2000, p. 98.

38 Jonathan Gil Harris and Natasha Korda eds., *Staged Properties*, Cambridge: Cambridge University Press, 2002, p. 6.

39 Neil Carson, quoted in Dessen, 1984, p. 62.

40 Dessen, 1984, pp. 62, 85 (at the latter he quotes Gerald Eades Bentley on Shakespeare); p. 99.

41 Dessen, 1984, p. 91.

42 Dessen, 1984, pp. 61, 91.

43 Stephen Halliwell describes this kind of realism as 'committed to depicting and illuminating a world that is (partly) accessible and knowable outside art', as a type of which the mirror has often been held up as emblem, *The Aesthetics of Mimesis: Ancient Texts and Modern Problems*, Princeton, Woodstock: Princeton University Press, 2002.

44 Robert Weimann, *Shakespeare and the Popular Tradition in the Theatre: Studies in the Social Dimension of Dramatic Form and Function*, ed. Robert Schwartz, Baltimore, London: Johns Hopkins University Press, 1987 (originally published 1978), p. 200, 'The allegorical mode had provided an altogether different mode of relating the idea (*Wesen*) and the appearance (*Erscheinung*) of reality', p. 202.

45 Wiggins, 2000, p. 23.

46 Dollimore, Jonathan *Radical Tragedy: Religion, Ideology and Power in the Drama of Shakespeare and His Contemporaries*, Brighton: Harvester Press, 1984, p. 71.

47 Madeleine Doran, *Endeavours of Art: A Study of Form in Elizabethan Drama*, Madison: University of Wisconsin Press, 1954, pp. 65–81.

48 Weimann, 1987, p. 202.

49 Halliwell, 2002, pp. 16, 21, 29.

50 Halliwell, 2002, pp. 25, 28.

51 Peter Lake, *The Antichrist's Lewd Hat*, New Haven, London: Princeton University Press, 2002, p. 148.

52 Eric Carlson, 'Good pastors or careless shepherds? Parish ministers and the English reformation', *History*, 88:291, 2003, 432, 430.

53 Katharine Eisaman Maus, 'Horns of dilemma: jealousy, gender and spectatorship in English Renaissance Drama', *ELH*, 54:3, 1987, 566–7.

54 West, 2002, p. 72. See Dawson's comment on the audience's response to the actor's body: 'The blushes, the tears . . . are signs, not symptoms, moments of representation whose point is to establish a set of meanings or, more often, a rush of feeling, that exists aside from the actor's body, in the minds (or "hearts," to use a favorite Elizabethan term) of the spectators' (2001, p. 21).

55 Thomas Heywood, *An Apology for Actors*, 1612, London: Shakespeare Society, 1841, pp. 57–60. Michael McClintock points out the gendered aspect of these examples, suggesting their significance in illustrating 'the theatre's ability to regulate and punish, rather than to promote, social and sexual trespasses'. As he argues, this makes interesting connections to *A Woman Killed With Kindness* and, I would argue, suggests broader congruences between the affective power of theatrical representation and judicial methods of dealing with sexual trespass. McClintock, 'Grief, theater and society in Thomas Heywood's *A Woman Killed With Kindness*', in Margo Swiss and David A. Kent eds, *Speaking Grief in English Literary Culture*, Pittsburgh: Duquesne University Press, 2002, p. 105.

56 West, 2002, p. 124.

57 Carlson, 2003, p. 424.

58 As the unfortunate example of William Storre's sermon on Isaiah's 'very small remnant' makes clear. Francis Cartwright heard the 1602 sermon as a personal attack and, seeing the preacher walking in the town one day, he rushed into a cutler's shop, bought a sword and stabbed him to death for his particularised sermons. Carlson, 2003, p. 425. As an extreme example of a common response, this incident provokes thought in an argument about representativeness.

59 Wiggins, 2000, p. 30. For evidence of the way such practices related to the material culture of the house see Chapter 2.

60 *OED* definitions for its adjectival use include 3b. 'Feelingly; (touched) to the quick', dated 1579, and 4b. 'Of feelings, impressions, sensations, memory: Vivid, intense, strong', dated 1535.

61 4c. 'Of evidence, illustrations, expressions: Vivid or forcible in effect, convincing, striking, telling', dated 1604; adv. 4. 'In a life-like manner; vividly, "to the life"', frequent in the seventeenth century.

62 *Sermons of M. John Calvin, on the Epistles of S. Paule to Timothie and Titus*, translated by L.T., London: Henry Middleton, 1581; *OED* adv. 3b.

63 For a fuller discussion see Richardson in Harris and Korda eds, 2002; for the 'commonness' of contemporary theatrical spectacle and its links to anti-illusionism see Gurr, 2004, pp. 125–6.

64 Lake, 2002, p. 128.

65 I am grateful to Felicity Dunworth for the formulation of this point.

66 For more on the connection between courtesy and good manners and changing social status see Anna Bryson, *From Courtesy to Civility: Changing Codes of Conduct in Early Modern England*, Oxford: Oxford University Press, 1998.

67 Gurr, 2004, p. 58; for women see pp. 65–9 and passim.

68 Gurr, 2004, p. 70. He points out that 'descriptions which suggest that the full range of society was present at plays come from around the 1590s', p. 79.

69 Gurr, 2004, pp. 81, 85–94.

70 This universality is both a part of the ideologies surrounding patriarchal authority, as suggested in Chapter 1, and a material fact, as discussed at length in Chapter 2.

71 Quoted in Harris and Korda, 2002, pp. 10–11.

72 Harris and Korda, 2002, p. 15.

73 For discussion of this issue of the different evidentiary demands of the disciplines see David Scott Kastan, *Shakespeare After Theory*, New York, London: Routledge, 1999: 'different evidentiary standards exist for different projects. If the goal is to discover if something was *thought*, a single reference might well be considered inadequate, too easily explained as idiosyncratic and aberrant; if, however, the goal is to discover if something was *thinkable* at a certain moment, then one example demonstrates the case quite nicely', pp. 49–50.

74 Heather Dubrow, *Shakespeare and Domestic Loss*, Cambridge: Cambridge University Press, 1999, p. 6.

75 Anthony Dawson argues, in relation to theatrical representation and Eucharistic controversy, that 'the habits of thought associated with one arena of culture carry over into the other, finding a different institutional home and corresponding affective register', Anthony Dawson and Paul Yachnin, *The Culture of Playgoing in Shakespeare's England*, Cambridge: Cambridge University Press, 2001, p. 28.

76 For a sophisticated analysis of this relationship see Adam Fox, *Oral and Literate Cultures in England, 1500–1700*, Oxford: Clarendon Press, 2000.

77 Gurr, 2004, p. 58.

78 The testamentary evidence for Kent permits these essential distinctions to be examined inside a coherent model of social relations which, despite some migration, demonstrated a measure of stability not to be found in London. It also offers an example within which the definitions of communities are less fraught with problems: in London parishes were radically different to one another in, for instance, size, population density, wealth, social composition and state of expansion or contraction. See for example, Derek Keene and Vanessa Harding's work on Cheapside in *Historical Gazetteer of*

London Before the Great Fire. Pt 1, Cheapside, Cambridge: Chadwick-Healey, 1987, as opposed to Jeremy Bolton, *Neighbourhood and Society,* Cambridge: Cambridge University Press, 1987.

79 Lena Orlin's ' "The causes and reasons of all artificial things" in the Elizabethan Domestic Environment' suggests a research agenda: the testing of the central issues she raises against the experiences of those of lower social status, in a way which allows the drawing of the kind of parallels which her evidence does not permit; *Medieval and Renaissance Drama in England,* 7, 1995, 19–75.

80 See also the discussion in Chapter 2 below, pp. 86–95.

81 See also the arguments over the question of representativeness, below, pp. 84, 94–5.

82 For an important corrective to the new historicist tendency to emphasise 'London in general and the court in particular', in other words to ignore regionalism and the provincial as well as the non-elite, see Dubrow, 1999, p. 5 and passim.

83 Steve Rappaport quotes John Stow on the image of London as a melting pot 'by birth for the most part a mixture of all counties, by blood gentlemen, yeomen, and of the basest sort without distinction'. Five out of six men enrolled as freemen of the city were recent immigrants in the 1550s, the south-east providing 18.5 per cent of them, Steve Rappaport, *Worlds Within Worlds: Structures of Life in Sixteenth-Century London,* Cambridge: Cambridge University Press, 1989, pp. 77, 86.

84 See for instance Richard Halpern, *The Poetics of Primitive Accumulation,* Ithaca: Cornell University Press, 1991; J. Barish, *The Antitheatrical Prejudice,* Berkeley: University of California Press, 1981; Patricia Fumerton and Simon Hunt, *Renaissance Culture and the Everyday,* Philadelphia: University of Pennsylvania Press, 1999; Margareta de Grazia, Maureen Quilligan and Peter Stallybrass eds, *Subject and Object in Renaissance Culture,* New York, Cambridge: Cambridge University Press, 1996.

85 For a detailed discussion of the challenges to historicist literary criticism presented by 'categorial anachronism' see Glenn Burgess in Holger Klein and Rowland Wymer eds, *Shakespeare and History,* Shakespeare Yearbook 6, Lewiston, Queenston, Lampeter: Edwin Mellen Press, 1996, where the relative merits of a history of phenomena 'visible only in hindsight and with the employment of a way of seeing the world meaningful to us and us alone' are examined, p. 9.

86 Carol Rutter, *Documents of the Rose Playhouse,* Manchester: Manchester University Press, 1984, p. 75.

87 Rutter, 1984, p. 77.

1

'My narrow-prying neighbours blab': moral perceptions of the early modern household

IN LATE SIXTEENTH-CENTURY ENGLAND, domestic life became the subject of scrutiny: just what *was* the household, how might it be made to further God's intentions for the world, what ideals should govern conduct within it?[1] Early modern society responded to these questions eagerly, insistently and at length. Homilies, political tracts, sermons, advice literature, ballads, jests and of course plays sought, and questioned, the answers. The results of such investigations informed the moral standards which under-pinned legal interest in appropriate behaviour, especially the anxieties about moral honesty and personal reputation which structured the concerns of the ecclesiastical courts.[2]

The broad outline of these debates is well known.[3] A sophisticated discourse of the power relations of the household within society was developed, one which saw a metaphorical connection between different kinds of authority and their several spheres of operation. As the king ruled the country, so the husband ruled his household. His authority there was absolute, and those who lived under his roof owed him loyalty and allegiance just as he owed them protection and the wisdom of his government. This system fitted within the larger scheme of patriarchy reasonably neatly.[4] Domestic inequality, like the other discriminations which underpinned society, was seen as fundament-ally productive of order: 'For as in a citie, there is nothing more *unequall*, then that every man should bee like *equall*: so it is not convenient, that in one house every man shuld be like and equall together. There is no equality in that citie, where the private man is equal with the Magistrate, the people with the Senate, or the servants with the master, but rather a confusion of all offices and authoritie.'[5] In order to ensure that an unambiguous sense of hierarchy prevented such confusion, household relations were to be modelled on more complex systems of social organisation. As Richard Brathwaite put it, 'As every man's house is his Castle, so is his family a private Common-wealth, wherein if due government be not observed, nothing but confusion is to be expected'.[6] The idea of commonwealth expresses the seditious potential of family rebellion; the idea of castle articulates the fundamental difference between the household and other social groups: its physical separation and seclusion from the eyes of the community.

Almost as familiar as this structure of domestic authority, however, are the contradictions inherent within it. Although the husband was supreme head of the household, he was also an equal before God with his wife. A wife's place, as Gouge put it, 'is indeed a place of inferiority and subjection, yet the neerest to equality that may be: a place of common equity in many respects, wherein man and wife are, after a sort, even fellowes and partners'.[7] Negotiat-ing the times when equality gave way to subjection was always fraught with social, personal and ideological tensions. Marriage could be discussed meta-phorically as a yoke shared by a pair of oxen who, as a result of their equal stature, might make great headway in the furrow of domestic production.[8] But it could also be envisaged, in the image favoured by St Paul, as a union comparable to that of the head and the body: the married couple incorporated into one form, where the male part of the pair represented the reasonable and reasoning head, served by his female lower members.[9] Although both metaphors aim to express intimacy and common purpose, the difference between the equal oxen and the hierarchised head and body epitomises the problematic connection between the political ideology of household govern-ment and the patriarchal organisation of social power. As Gouge points out, the couple are 'yoak-fellowes in mututal familiarity, not in equall authority'.[10]

The household manuals, from which come the most detailed evidence for the working out of domestic theories, were keen to stress the fact that they dealt primarily with ideals. Writers acknowledged that their advice about subjection was very hard to follow: 'I know this dutie goes against the haire' Whately says to women, 'though it be so plaine, as it cannot be denied, yet it is withall so hard, that it can hardly bee yeelded unto.' But these ideals were nevertheless goals which could be aimed at, and as such domestic subordina-tion was part of the wider responsibilities of Christians to improve the human condition: 'we must remember that this is no more difficult than divers other duties in other cases required of a Christian; and that it is no excuse from our dutie in any case to say it is hard, and who can do it?'[11]

But such ideals *were* intended to be models for, rather than absolutes of, behaviour, and the manuals expounded proscriptions for daily life which were grounded in practice, not theory. Advice is given, for instance, about the appropriate division of tasks between household members; about the way superiors might chastise inferiors to encourage them to change their ways; and about the forms of speech and gesture appropriate to authority and submission. Often, advice is presented in the traditional rhetorical form of a dichotomised pairing which attempts to draw clear distinctions between different roles.[12] The roles of husband and wife, for instance, are described in contradistinction to one another: 'The dutie of the husband is, to get goods: and that of the wife to gather them together, and save them. The dutie of the husband is, to travell abroad to seeke living: and the wives dutie is to keep the house . . . The dutie of the husband is, to deale with many men: and of the wives, to talke with few . . . The dutie of the man is, to bee skilfull in talke: and of the wife, to boast of silence . . . The dutie of the husband is, to dispatch all things without doore: and of the wife, to oversee and give order for all things within the house.'[13]

These dichotomised proscriptions for behaviour turned on three major divisions. There was the distinction between authority and subjection, where 'household' was envisaged as a set of power dynamics between masters and servants, parents and children, husbands and wives. There was the division between the house and the community, by which the duties of the house-holder were circumscribed: for instance Cleaver claims that many tried to 'complaine that their children and servants are disordered, and corrupted *abroad*, when in trueth they were disordered and are still corrupted, and mard at *home*'. The final division was that between the spiritual and the material comforts of the household, where the family 'must seeke to have

Holinesse found in their habitation, whereby God may be glorified, as wel as *riches*, whereby they may be comforted'.[14] Whereas the distinction between authority and subjection involved distinguishing between different types of behaviour, the other two generate their meaning from the firm distinction between inside and outside, and between the material and the non-material. In other words they are intimately concerned with the fabric of the house itself and with the physical qualities of everyday life as boundaries upon and analogies for behaviour.

The texts imagine the household in two different senses; as a physical space which is closed off from the community and therefore controllable, and as a series of interpersonal relationships with their individual dynamics of authority and submission which cohere into a functioning unit of production and consumption. These two aspects are inseparable, and they are defined by one another: people form a household when they are gathered into the same living space, and buildings function as houses when they are inhabited by a family.[15] The two aspects of the household are also used, metaphorically, to explain one another. Rifts within the social fabric of the house produce shocking and irreparable physical results: 'As a kingdome cannot stand, if it be divided: so a house cannot stand, if it be divided: for strife is like fire, which leaves nothing . . . but dust, smoke and ashes behinde it.'[16] Such vivid images of physical threat to the house give form to the crucial importance of the ties which should bind its inhabitants.

Despite the familiarity of this material, two questions crucial to my argument here have yet to be fully explored. The first concerns those relationships between these two meanings of 'household', the physical and the familial: how exactly did understanding of the material qualities of the household impinge upon the relationships between its inhabitants, and vice versa? Although we are by and large studying the textuality of proscription, we do so at least partly in order to reach an understanding of the way it was interpreted in practice. Henri Lefebvre has pointed up the connections and the tensions inherent in different aspects of the spaces within which life is lived: the 'dialectical relationship' between 'the perceived, the conceived, and the lived'.[17] Hanson and Pratt argue that subjectivity is negotiated through 'the traffic between symbolic and concrete spaces'.[18] Understanding the way didactic literature uses the materiality of the house itself to negotiate its human relationships of subjection and authority is suggestive of the connections between mental and physical space.

The second question also grows out of an interest in practice, as it involves the relevance of these textual constructs of behaviour to daily life. This issue has received considerably more attention from historians, who have concerned themselves with the extent to and the circumstances under which these ideals impinged upon domestic practice. It has become clear that, although the literature admonished wives to stay within the household and to speak seldom, the demands of the domestic economy for those of low and even middling status necessitated wives' frequent trips to market to sell their wares aggressively.[19] It is equally plain that, although husbands were to negotiate the complexities of social and financial credit in order to provide for their families, harsh economic conditions, particularly towards the end of the sixteenth century, made this ideal so hard to sustain that for a proportion of the population even the provision of household space itself was under threat.[20]

Alexandra Shepard says that her evidence 'suggests a routine acceptance of a household ideology far less differentiated by gender than that proposed by Dod and Cleaver' in their manual *A godlie forme of householde government*. Instead, issues such as social credit were 'gender-related, rather than gender-specific'; individuals worked creatively with gendered notions of the household, which could be 'selectively applied and invoked'.[21] Laura Gowing quotes a slander case which is richly suggestive of this process of selective invocation of ideals. The incident in question is recorded by 'Agnes Franklin, an armourer's wife of St Andrew Holborn', who testified, 'that with a group of women in an upper chamber of her house she had heard Henry Smith, the minister and preacher of household order, standing by her window in his yard, call Eleanor Hedge, who was standing inside her window about ten yards away looking into the same yard, a whore'. Franklin was presumably aware of what he preached, and enjoyed setting this against what he practised. Gowing sees such a creative reference to the disparity between ideal and practice as a more general feature of her material. 'Street talk', she says, 'reflected and manipulated prescriptions for female behaviour.'[22]

In the context of communal disharmony, recent scholarship has suggested, both men and women were liable to hold up practice for comparison against moral absolutes. Although daily life may not have been lived in self-conscious relation to such fixed ideas, conflict was likely to sharpen perceptions and make individuals hyper-sensitive to moralised readings of everyday situations. My second concern here, then, is to attend to the points at which such ideals were invoked. In practice, this means looking for the familiar and meaningful *tropes* through which they were expressed in different kinds of literature. This will not give direct access to a 'reality' to set against ideals, but it will indicate the contexts and forms in which the latter were brought to bear upon the complexities of daily existence. Such a project makes meaning out of the relationships between different stories about similar subjects, whether those stories were produced as fact or fiction; whether they adopt a tone of high moral seriousness, or the 'throwaway' flippancy of a cheap joke.[23]

In addition to the prescriptive literature studied here, the responses of a socially diverse, although essentially 'middling', range of men and women to the connection between moral lapses and household spaces is investigated through the depositions they gave in the ecclesiastical courts. These courts were extensively used in the period, and they gave a high profile to the disputes they heard and the line they drew between acceptable and unacceptable behaviour.[24] Their disputes were 'centrally concerned with the spatial organization of the household'.[25] Conduct manuals and court depositions have very different moral intentions, approaching as they do the relationship between ideal and practice in different ways, and they operate within distinct sets of 'generic' constraints.[26] The differences between them make it possible to investigate a range of ways of thinking around the central connections between houses and human relationships.

But both sources also share an interest in the relationship between the inside and the outside of the house as a way of defining social order. They both acknowledge the enormous moral and social over determination of the terms 'household' and 'householder'. They also share a *self-consciousness* about ways of making moral meaning through narrative form, and this is crucial to my argument here. Two brief examples of the use of a candle indicate their investment of meaning in image and detail. Gouge's portrayal of the paradoxical inequality, 'similitude, resemblance, and fellowship', between a husband and Christ, offers evidence of his sensitivity to the choice of explicatory metaphor: 'The glorious and bright Sunne in the firmament, and a dimme candle in an house, have a kind of fellowship, and the same office, which is to give light, yet there is no equality betwixt them.' The image moves between heaven and earth just as the comparison does.[27] Similarly, deponents in the court both witness and then retell events with an eye for the effect of the moral implications of narrative details on their audience. They are keenly aware that any detail given within a narrative which answers an interrogatory (or legal question) about whether or not a crime was committed has an inescapable meaning in relation to the guilt or innocence of the parties involved. When several suspicious parishioners of the parish of Reculver gathered outside the church 'about ten of the clock in the night', they looked through the parson's window, and 'did see the said Sir Thomas sitting in his bed naked'. When Margery Lissette 'did bring a cup of drink', the deponent offers the suggestive detail that 'even sodenly the candle was putt oute', and, in case there should be any doubt about the matter, he adds 'very suspiciously': every detail here is added for its moral weight.[28] The descriptions of household spaces and actions are explicitly offered in both types of narrative as carrying moral information. The differences in scale between inside and outside, and the distinctive qualities of household action, make movement between the domestic and the extra-domestic morally instructive.

This chapter is divided into the fundamental spatial categories of the material it treats: inside, outside, and what comes in between.[29] This division makes possible comparison of the broad groups of narrative images of enclosure and its opposites which underlie the significance of household space. Such an investigation suggests how daily life was at times negotiated through the distinctions between them, and the impact this had upon perception of the collaborative relationship between household space and domestic experience for the kind of individuals who formed the audiences for domestic plays.

OUTSIDE THE HOUSE

Any discussion of action outside the house is necessarily gendered, because the ideological connection between women's behaviour and communal spaces was unrelentingly negative: Cleaver, for instance, identifies the woman whom 'wee call the wife Huswife, that is, house-wife, not a street-wife, one that gaddeth up and down, like *Thamer*: nor a field-wife'.[30] Female honour was to be constituted through public invisibility: 'The chiefest way for a woman to preserve and maintain this good fame, is to be resident in her owne house. For an honest woman in soberness keeping well hir house, gayneth thereby great reputation, and if she be evill, it [keeping there] driveth away many evill occasions, and stoppeth the mouthes of the people.'[31] Women's reputation operates on a firm physical boundary between house and community.

On the other hand, as the explicating opposite of good housewifery, the figure of the whore is unsettled, her attention constantly focused outwards: 'And therefore *Salomon* depainting, and describing the qualities of a whore, setteth her at the doore, now sitting upon her stall, now walking in the streetes, now looking out of the window.'[32] Behaviour, as the morality of action and gesture, represented a form of immoral spatialisation seen in this literature as a self-evident analogy between the quality of a woman's movement in space and a lack of control over her body. Such behaviour was, for William Whately, a route to the location of whoredom: 'This impudency and unwomanhood doth track the way to the harlot's house.'[33] In this complex image the moral weight of 'impudence' – action which denies proper power relations – is such that it moves a woman 'outside' and on her way to the antithesis of domestic space. Her behaviour has the power to unmake the physical confines of the domestic, and the choice to perform good or bad actions constructs space as either house or whorehouse. Whateley's 'unhuswifelines' and 'unwifelike behaviour' carry a similar sense of deconstructing identity.[34] 'Inside' is given its spatial meanings in distinction to 'outside', but its nature as a space of intimacy is predicated upon behaviour. In a conception of the production of space analogous to that which took place on the stage, the quality of domesticity is brought into being through appropriate action. Like actors creating a field, but with a razor-sharp moral edge, women produce their households through words and deeds.

For men, of course, the ideal relationship between household and community was totally different. The several spheres in which their daily life operated outside the house were seen to support one another on a pragmatic level. There was a pedagogical aspect to the analogy between household and castle. By ruling the household, men gain the skills to govern on a larger scale: 'it is impossible for a man to understand to governe the common wealth, that doth not know to rule his owne house, or order his owne person, so that he that knoweth not to governe, deserveth not to raigne'.[35] As with everything masculine, this kind of identity works against the separation of domestic and public personas, suggesting a synthesis of ways of being in which differences in authority are those of scale only, and not of kind. If masculine power is in theory identical in its operation within and without the house, then the logic of the process of analogy is that domestic intimacy, for the husband, does not have its own unique dynamics. This point of tension between political theory and companionate marriage produced confusingly contradictory advice.[36]

But correspondence has a temporal order built into it. Masculine credit is *first* forged through the way a man handles the responsibilities of rule within the house, and then broadcast in the community at large: 'the opinion and estimation of another mans goodnesse and wisedome, the which reverence is not onely honoured within the doores, but also shineth and extendeth it selfe into the cittie, so that he is taken for an honest man'.[37] The light of good household relationships pours out of the house, allowing neighbours to judge a man's public capacities by analogy: 'he is reputed for a wise man, considering that he can so moderately handle so difficult and hard matters . . . and that he may easilie conserve and keepe his Citizens in peace and concord, that hath so wel established the fame in his owne house and familie'.[38] If the household offered a testing ground for masculine identity and was the place where honour began, where it was shaped, then it was only outside its boundaries that it could be promulgated.

Philip Julius, travelling around the country in 1602, famously remarked that 'In England every citizen is bound by oath to keep a sharp eye at his neighbor's house, as to whether the married people live in harmony'.[39] His comment underlines what the wealth of court material suggests so strongly: Protestant notions of the right ordering of communities would succeed only if those communities regulated themselves internally, a goal which necessitated careful observation of neighbours' comings and goings. Amussen states that 'The scale of local society made it possible to know and judge the behaviour of neighbours, even new arrivals',[40] and the evidence for towns of all sizes shows that individuals could be hypersensitive to the goings on around them. Even in the unwieldy and ever-developing metropolis, early modern men and women were conscious of belonging to a social unit which was small enough to ensure that such surveillance was possible: perhaps as large as a parish, perhaps as small as a street or tenement.[41] Spatial proximity produced intimate knowledge, and the rhetoric of 'neighbourhood', meaning everyone's charge to ensure the moral uprightness of their local community, turned that knowledge into a currency with which to purchase local honesty.[42]

The intimacy of communal knowledge had implications for the processes of arriving at the truth in the ecclesiastical courts. What was brought to court was a web of small suggestions and clues, embedded within social and personal dynamics of huge complexity. Out of this information the courts strove to establish innocence or guilt in relation to countrywide definitions of moral probity and their related systems of acceptable (i.e. externally verifiable) proof. It was within these negotiations, between the local and the national and the partial and the impartial, that deponents told their stories of domestic and non-domestic behaviour.

Because the courts could bring wrongdoers to justice only if they could gain access to the closed, privileged world of mutual knowledge and responsibility which the neighbourhood fosters, the tales deponents tell necessarily begin from a high level of familiarity with the habitual actions of those who live in close spatial proximity. Deponents structure their narratives in relation to a sense of the regular and the routine, where any departure from custom offers potential evidence of wrongdoing, and they are sensitive to the timing and direction of movement in relation to moralised connections between the house and the community.[43] The courts encourage a complex grammar of the legitimacy of actions, which can be assessed by their positioning within the common patterns of social intercourse. Presence and absence in the street at key moments are used by deponents to suggest moral worth. Leaving the house can be assumed to suggest certain activities by the time and direction of the journey, and hence its relationship with legitimate social movements. Visual clues, such as a basket or a milk pail, are useful additional details in narratives of the actions of others because they help to explain and legitimise the assumptions of the deponent.[44] These narrative forms indicate the significance of household practices in establishing an impartial testimony.

Richard Grange is accused of keeping his sister Margaret, suspected of being a whore who 'everie daie lyveth suspiciouslie in running about at hir will and pleasure and commeth not unto the church'.[45] Her movements are out of control: she leaves the house too often, but she does not leave it when she should, for expected and credible purposes. The whore whom Agnes Butterwick is accused of housing has also been a common sight to her neighbours, who have 'many tymes seen [her] before, that in the said Agnes Butterwick's house and also going and commyng to and from the same'.[46] Her going and her coming are used to identify, visually and spatially, her relationship to the house in which she is living, which forms the beginning and the end of every journey she makes. Her reputation is constructed by the nature of those journeys within the town and 'brought back' to the house, which becomes a repository for it. Such narrative expressions of the proscriptive advice for women position the building centrally in terms of its importance. They directly echo the moralists' focus on extra domestic journey and movement as the mark of the whore, and demonstrate the general currency of the notion that 'houses' have a moral identity, defined in part by their inhabitants' movement in the street.[47] Agnes Butterwick, herself a contentious figure, was beaten by her husband 'because she wold not geve attendaunce with hym, as he said, but rather be abrode . . . saying . . . that he had rather his wyfe remayned at home spyning and carding woll'.[48] The report calls the woman's honesty into question by putting the familiar gendered patterning of 'home' and 'abroad' into the mouth of her husband, and implicitly contrasting what she might be doing outside the house (she was a midwife) with the honest domestic activity of the spinster.

The notion of honest employment such as spinning has a wide significance in these narratives. It enables deponents to structure their narratives of significant events as a rupture in the decent routines of the community. It also permits them to stress the fact that they and their associates were going about their daily business (and were therefore involved only as impartial witnesses) by stating that events took place as they were, for instance, taking chickens to be carved.[49] This 'baseline' of normality is an important way of characterising immoral behaviour, particularly noisy public disturbances, as an aberration which breaks out of the smoothness of communal routine. As John Buck is 'syttynge at his dore of his house', for instance, he 'fortuned to heare the said Agnes Graves and Agnes Ungley chide to getheres very muche. And at lenght stryved to gethers, so that the said Agnes Graves caught the said Agnes Ungley by the thrott, and where apon the said Agnes Ungley cryed out and said that the whore had her by the thrott.' He has to part them, and all present are then called to bear witness. The dynamic between the peaceful street and the slander gives shape to the prominence of outside sins and their disruptively performative quality.[50]

But this narrative trope logically offers its own moral antitype to such laudably productive ways of spending time. Deponents also tell stories of 'routine sins', ones whose long history presents particularly damning evidence of wrongdoing. The churchwardens of Headcorn parish recorded an accusation of adultery between William Welles's wife and Robert Humphrey 'and the matter so evident that it is knowen where and howe his hawnte is used'.[51] The word 'haunt' seems to encapsulate a sense of behaviours which, unlike the one-off lapse, have become habitual, and which are therefore located in a physical 'other' to the household. Stephen Osborne of Eastchurch on the Isle

35

of Sheppey met George Segar, accused of having sexual relations with the parson's wife, on Beacon Hill, where he talked to him about the time he was spending with the woman. Segar promised not to see her again, but in fact he apparently did so more than ever 'in places and tymes unconvenyent and mete'.[52] Transgression becomes a routine; an immoral behaviour ingrained. Sins prominent enough to be known in this way threaten the moral identity of the whole community, and the case therefore moves from informal arbitration into the court.

Deponents are sensitive to the 'unconvenyent places' in which such activities take place as potentially peripheral to the social control of communal scrutiny. In their descriptions of the locations for illicit sexual activity, they are able to express both their vigilance in spotting it and their attitudes towards the free rein given to lust. The lengths to which couples are seen to go to secure privacy from the gaze of their neighbours strongly suggests that no right and proper place is available for their actions, as sexuality outside marriage is forbidden. Magdalene Lewis of St Paul's parish in Canterbury deposes that 'about mydd of the harvest tyme and that apon a workynday . . . this deponent was sitting and spynyng at her dore situate in Ivy Lane with other her poore neighbours sitting by and spynnyng'.[53] Into this honest and hardworking scene bursts Margaret Richardson who says she has come from the fields, 'and told this deponent and other there present how that the mornyng of the foresaid workday betwene 6 and 7 she toke Margaret Raven in a hedge comyng owt with a knave . . . and that she and the said man had plaide the whore and knave togither'.[54] Helen Joyseman of the same parish says she met Richardson in the market that morning where she told her that while battering a sheaf of corn which she had taken from the field she saw the couple, 'the man creping away after and whipping over the hedge, and she going a long the hedge till she cam to the foresaid stile wher she whipped over'.[55] The association between exigency and an ill rule over the bodily appetites is strong, and the field as a setting makes it possible to ally the sin with animal imagery. The couple run along the hedge and then jump over it. Isabel Valyor's testimony records the jubilant cry of Margaret Richardson as she passed Raven's house: 'here be privye whores com they leaping in the f[i]eld on this fasshion'.

In a case that uses similar imagery James Mortimer, seeing a woman rise from a dyke by a hedge outside the city walls of Canterbury, said to the man who was walking with him that 'theye had started the heare oute of the bushe'. This euphemism, making explicit reference to the chase which ends in possession of the quarry of sexual fulfilment, is linked to their description of the place where the couple had been. Here 'the gras was as flat crusshed downe as was possible and yn the place rounde aboute the gras and nettles verrye highe and rancke'. The couple had created an animal's den by flattening the vegetation, leaving a screen to hide them from the road. In Mortimer's description the grass and nettles which remained standing were 'as high as a man so as a man, going ynto the same mighte have hidden himself'. As he tells it, the prodigious growth of the wild vegetation has colluded with the baser animal instincts of those who make their 'home' within it by shielding them from the eyes of all but the most morally vigilant.[56]

Activities which are the opposite of domestic are characterised by their attempts to set up what amounts to an 'anti-house' – a haunt or den complete with its own recognisable anti-type to domestic productivity, the sexually motivated and regulated routine. Deponents suggest the especially pernicious nature of wrongdoings, and simultaneously insist upon the objectivity of their evidence of sin, by characterising it in relation to domestic practice. Intimate actions necessarily, inevitably, create a kind of domesticity, but it is one which is relocated outside, under the hedge or in the ditch, in between legitimate areas of jurisdiction, needing to be unmade at every liaison.

BORDERS AND BOUNDARIES

Whilst the moral integrity of the household was unambiguously undermined by the discovery of illicit sexual activity, it could also be affected by the circulation of domestic information as rumour or tittle-tattle. Writers of advice literature, of course, focused on the inevitability of garrulousness in women. Jacques du Bosc entreats 'those women who have not the inclination to speak little, to consider that if there be a time to speak something and also to say nothing, there is never any to speak all'. But the feminine tendency to be 'full of words, powring out al in her mind', is particularly disturbing to him because it involves 'babling of her household matters, that were more fitter to be concealed'.[57] Whilst the way in which men exercised their domestic authority within the house would naturally shine out into the community as a whole, female household matters should be 'concealed' within – either not important enough or inappropriate to discuss outside.

Coming at the topic from the perspective of 'street literature', Joy Wiltenburg discusses the relationship between boundaries for behaviour and concepts of shame. She quotes a ballad written from the perspective of an English husband who has allowed his wife to control him:

> But let not my neighbours of this understand;
> For that if thou dost, I know it will be
> A shame to thy selfe, [and] disgrace unto me.

The boundaries of the household, she says, 'become important in managing shame' in literature which does not only advocate concealment but also entertains the notion of deliberate and effective revelation. Wives in the street literature she discusses 'regularly appear as speakers in their own songs on conjugal ills . . . perhaps encouraging women to view their grievances as matters to be spoken of rather than merely endured'.[58] These complicated relationships between the interior physical space which is woman's proper domain, the honour which she must maintain by staying within it, and the speed with which the spoken word can leave the front door to undermine household stability, are linked in interesting ways to notions of performance within the community. When it goes *wrong*, the domestic becomes shared; it is performed as complaint, impersonated as gossip and occasionally staged as Skimmington.[59] In each case, its status as a common problem should lead to a solution. Laura Gowing's comment on the confusion often made between 'public or private *issues* and *events* and public and private *spaces*' is very pertinent here, an essential aspect of the peculiarly early modern tensions around the management of domestic information for the greatest communal good.[60]

The extent to which communal intervention is linked to the movement of knowledge out of the household through the discourse of gossip is demonstrated by the case of Beatrice Garman. She asks the advice of Richard Quilter of Kingsdown about the behaviour of her husband William, who 'did haunt Goodman Gauntes wif from place to place, who could not goo to Canterbury, Sandwich or Dover but [he] would follow her'. Beatrice uses a telling analogy, saying her husband pursues the woman 'as it wer an Anthony pygg'. His routine has become merely a shadowing of Mistress Gaunt's, his moves dictated by her own like the faithful pig of the saint. Beatrice feels that something must be done at the point where the story of her husband's behaviour is becoming as popular a legend as the image which she uses to illustrate it: a kind of fable, an often-told tale. She also gives evidence for the public status of the tale, 'saying moreover that she was ashamed to heare of it, and that the chiefe yomen of the countrey talked of it in Master Hamondes house'.[61] The domestic has here become the public property of gossip, broadcast abroad as a form of leisured amusement, but eventually brought to the court for resolution.

In addition to the attention paid to individuals' physical movements in and out of the house then, deponents are also sensitive to the way in which actions travel as complaint and as gossip. The notion of 'common fame' which is so regularly invoked in the courts, referring to things so familiar that they barely need to be proved, expresses both the sense of broadcast and the idea of knowledge held *in common*: the sharing of the domestic outside the household.[62]

But boundaries were also important in a much more physical sense. Work on the London archives has stressed the connection between the crowded nature of urban space and the peculiarly material qualities of the disputes which take place within communities. John Schofield's work has demonstrated the incredibly complex and fragmented spaces in which daily life was lived as London expanded, and Lena Orlin's investigation of the viewers' certificates for the town outlines the physical complexities of living conditions.[63] Gowing describes the pressures on ideals of female behaviour which were caused by 'disputes over building rights, access to water or light, or shop space' in an environment in which 'houses were frequently being subdivided, extensions or windows added to walls, and penthouses built on to the street'.[64] In towns experiencing these pressures towards the end of the sixteenth century, levels of tension about the material boundaries of household life ran high.[65] Lena Orlin describes seemingly impossible situations in which the spaces of different householders were troublingly interwoven with one another: 'Mercer Richard Smythe was told he had to live with the drains running through his bedchamber, but Thomas Blunte was advised, somewhat ominously, not to "annoy" Smythe "with no manner of corrupt water or any other thing going through it".'[66] The firm delineation between different spheres of life in which authority was to be exercised was severely problematised when the physical boundaries between domestic units overlapped, and shared spaces and complicated boundaries must have made the ideal of the domestic castle incredibly hard to apply to daily practice. While the house was to form a coherent moral unit seamlessly divided from the outside world, within which mutual responsibilities could be established, it was rarely so regular as a physical entity and frustration worked into the cracks between the physical and the ideological boundaries of the household like frost. The ideals of 'household' must have undermined those individual masculine identities which could not be constructed in relation to the honest stability of the term 'householder'.

The borders of the early modern house were problematic because the jurisdiction of its inhabitants technically ended there, despite a perceived area of 'personal space' around them which should prevent others from coming too close. The 'thickness' of borders – their status as more than an edge – was legislated for in the provision for eavesdropping: a necessary space between buildings for the runoff of excess rainwater.[67] In the fierce focus which crowded urban space forced upon the boundaries between the personal and the communal, such sites became a focus for dispute because they stood at the point where outside became inside.

Within the ongoing variance between the Clintons and their next neighbours in St Paul's parish in Canterbury, the Nowres, one point of tension in particular was generated by the nature of their shared space. Mrs Nowre's servant John Naylor was woken in the night when Roger Clinton, 'standing in his yarde and loking in at a windowe into the parlor of the house of the said Nowre' ominously tells him to get up and fetch his dame out of the shop, where she is allegedly having illicit sexual relations with a tapster.[68] It is this connection, between the Clintons' yard and the Nowres' parlour window, which permits a particularly prominent kind of contact. A week after the previous incident, 'Joane Clinton . . . stode in her yarde and loked into the house of the sayd Joane Nowre at a windowe'. The latter was at the time at supper with some guests in the parlour, but nevertheless carried on a conversation with her neighbour through the window: 'Joane Nowre said unto the sayd Joane Clinton "what meane yow to eaves drope my house", and Joane Clinton sayd she woulde stande in her owne grounde and loke into the house of the sayd Nowre.' Both are legitimately standing on their own property, but it is the direction of Clinton's gaze which irritates Nowre. Rather than turning her attention inwards towards her own domestic space, she is looking outwards, penetrating the walls of her neighbour's house. Her posture is presented as a metaphor for the attention which she pays to Nowre's business, her intention not to regard but to intervene, with a gaze which does not look on, but through. The incident comes to a climax when 'Joane Nowre called for a dishe of water and flownge into the face of the said Joane Clinton'. Playing on that original meaning of eavesdropping as an antisocial intrusion of water, Nowre physically drives Clinton away from their common boundary and material and social nuisances are punningly connected.

The other crucial spatial issue which this case raises is the relationship between domestic privacy, or 'enclosedness' and the honesty of those who lived within the house: when *is* it morally acceptable to say you have looked into another's domestic space? When a wrongdoing has been identified, neighbours are legitimately allowed to look *in*, to use windows and doors intended for egress as a point of access, in order to make the domestic public. In the course of the normal routine, however, such unbidden proximity is an unwanted intimacy, and is read as an invasion akin to the twin sexual and spatial meanings of the verb 'to occupy'. These tropes of the penetration of household boundaries are at the heart of the creation of a moral distance between deponent and accused: a hierarchised detachment in which the former takes the high ground on the latter because of their suspicious behaviour. It is this moral dynamic which keeps the household private, and prevents the penetration of its boundaries.

The legitimisation which moral suspicion gives to others to make the private public is explored in interesting ways in the case of Goodwife Ford. When an old woman reports that the sexton of Ash has entered the house of Robert Ford 'about 8 of clock at night at Bekettes tyme, her husband being then away from thence, and his wife being in the house', a group of men meet together to investigate the allegation.[69] Two of them 'kept the doore of the said Robert Fordes house on theone strete and William Solley and Robert Jervys kept the dore on tother side of the said house on the garden side'. When both exits were secure, 'Mr Henry Seth knocked at the dore on the streate side, whome the goodwife Forde, being within, asked who was there. "Mary", said he, "I your land lord am heir". And she asked what he wold have . . . [to whom he replied] that he wold com in and see what good rule she kept there.' He invokes the morally weighty concept of the 'good rule' to be kept by wives in their husbands' absence, and his own anomalous position as owner of the physical house, but not head of the family who inhabit it. Seth's overall ownership of the property, however, carries little weight with Mistress Ford, 'she replying said agayn she knew hym for no officer and therefore shuld not com yn ther'. As he is neither constable nor borsholder (a parish officer whose role was comparable to that of a petty constable), officials who are legally entitled to have doors opened to them, she is unwilling to allow him access to her house and its contents (at this moment allegedly including Thomas Stonard the sexton). It is only the threat of violent destruction which removes the obstacle from Seth's path: ' "Then", quod he the said Seeth, "I wille offer my self at this tyme or els break up the doore".' As barrier, the door becomes focus for their competition over jurisdiction and control of domestic space, opened only after several different types of power (of possession, legal and physical, of moral superiority and of patriarchal authority) have been measured against one another. Unexpected and unexplained movements generate suspicion, and communal action which makes the domestic public by opening the house up to scrutiny is thereby legitimized.

All these cases which focus on the boundary, the border between the house and the community, work within two fundamental organising paradigms of narratives about the household. They bring into play the complex injunctions of a range of prescriptive advice which counsels that women should stay within the house, and that any kind of argument conducted in public is unseemly and damaging to personal reputation and communal harmony, but that the dictates of good neighbourhood should ensure that individuals are sensitive to the needs of others within their communities.[70] Although both offer moralised images of the relationship between the inside and the outside, the tropes are in many ways directly opposed to one another in their interpretation of the permeability of the household.

In the first trope, the house is constructed as 'other' in relation to the street, and the illusion of a strict division between public and private behaviour is fabricated as a dichotomy, with the façade of the house as its dividing line. On either side of this barrier cluster the exclusive pairings inside and outside, invisible and visible, as the house becomes the perfectly sealed container of virtue imagined in the proscriptive literature. An example is provided by a Master Beale and his wife, who were arguing in the street with a Master Ringer and his wife outside the latter's shop. The deponent heard 'both Beale and his wife brawling . . . with the said Ringer's wife, which [who] then did stand knetting or sewing in the street. And in their chiding the said Beale and his wife did call the said Ringer's wife hore and naughty hore.' They add that 'if he [Ringer] were a man as he is a cuckhold knave, he would then fetch in the said hore his wife'.[71] There is the double meaning of stopping her running out of control and removing her from the street, from the gaze of those who might be offended by such a sight. When John Pensaxe and Roger Greenham were 'settyng downe togither at the doore of one Edmunde Deale', they 'hard sodenlye a greate crye and noyse of one crynge, "thow arraunte whore bytche foxe whoore, chartham whoore", and hearyg so soddeyne and great noyse this dept looked abowte and espyed the sayd Margarett Baker in an upper chamber of hyr owne howse lokyng out of the wyndowe towardes them'. Her head poking out from a window 'right over agaynst the place where this deponent the said Roger Greneham and Elizabeth Deale then satte', she repeats the insults, adding 'and I will cut of thye whoores nose'. John then suggests that Elizabeth 'goin to hyr howse that therbye the said Margaret Baker myght leate of hyr raylynge'.[72]

The stage-like quality of the street prioritises it as one perfectly created to ensure maximum visibility, and visibility demands action, it insists upon a reply, upon a progressive dialogue either of verbal insult or social meaning and interpretation. The façade of the house, rather than allowing deponents to see without being seen, is constructed as a totally separate, non-interactive area. In this scheme, community exists solely in communal spaces, and such spaces are unsuitable for the honest as they present dangers to the reputation. Within the house, relationships can be controlled, but in the street, one might encounter people with whom one would not normally associate. The employment of this trope draws attention to the implications of such a metaphorical clarity of spatial division, by offering to divide the morally (and perhaps also socially) inferior from their superiors.

The second trope is one of a mutual responsibility and community which transcends physical barriers. Sound is used here as a mediator which insists upon a dependence between the personal and the communal by invading the established space of the former with the concerns and preoccupations of the latter.[73] Individuals are related to 'the community' as an abstract notion of alterity outside, but the nature of the town as a collection of individuals well known to one another is also insisted upon. Thomasine Bellinger of St Peter's parish in Canterbury provides an example in her deposition. Thomasine, 'hearynge say before that the said John Graves now deceased was very sicke, and this dept beyng in hyr bedde and hearyng the bell of the same parishe knowllyng in the night, supposyng that yt was for the sayd Graves, arose out of hyr bedd and went to the said Graves his howse situate in St Peters aforesayd to vysitt and to comforte him if she were able'. Using her detailed knowledge of the well-being of her fellow parishioners, Thomasina alters her habitual routine and makes her way to the place where she is needed. The alderman James Nethersole, 'lying in his bedde' at ten or eleven o'clock, 'herd the said Joane Graves go up and downe in the streate pitiously lamentyng and monynge', and 'ther upon' he did 'aryse and went to the sayd Graves his howse, slyppyng on his night gowne, and for that the moone dyd then shyne very bright, he went without candle'.[74] Both deponents stress that it is their position within the local community which allows them to interpret the meaning of the sounds they hear in the first place, and their reiteration of the tolling of the bell in the silence of the night translates such shared knowledge into a narrative of moral imperative. Rupture in the social routine, represented by extraordinary journeys, is here constructed positively. The movement of individuals out of their rightful places demonstrates their unselfish prioritisation of the needs of those outside over their own personal comfort. By presenting the noise of the bell as penetrating the houses of the parish, the spatial interconnection is made clear, and any dichotomous relationship between inside and outside, between personal and communal, is denied.[75]

The examination of these two tropes of the significance of the house as boundary demonstrates above all the flexibility of the connection between physical spaces and moral ideals. Women who come and go during the night are, of course, whores. But Thomasine uses exactly the same spatial dynamic to present herself as an honest neighbour – a good citizen who ministers to the needy whenever such an act of mercy is necessary. Through narrative, boundaries are used as a way of exploring the extent of responsibility and intervention in morally sound affairs. Meaning is contingent upon the identification and reiteration of permeating sounds – the slander, the bell – as a way of indicating the appropriateness of the action undertaken.[76]

The project of the ecclesiastical courts was to ensure that domestic activities were equally subject to moral justice as their more physically open counterparts, and to insist that the same precepts of Christian morality and charity governed behaviour in every space under the watchful eye of God's providence. In reality, of course, crossing boundaries involved changing behaviour, changing clothes, gestures, words, and reconsidering the way in which situations should be approached. But a rhetoric of the needs of others which takes precedence over such concerns was available, and available to women as well as men. Open or closed, honest or privy, the permeability of the boundaries between the house and the community was always morally suggestive, because spatial opposites invited comparison with moral absolutes – if goodness was within, then iniquity must be outside, or vice versa.

INSIDE

Inside the household, domestic manuals concern themselves with routines and their associated objects. Deponents are also interested in the productive tasks of daily life, but their concerns are with the visceral closeness of intimate living too, and the troubled spatial relationships to which it gives rise.

In addition to the often-negative divisions of behaviour which the writers of household manuals used to describe the relations of domestic authority and subjection, they also employed similes and metaphors, which tended to encourage a more positive process of comparison.[77] In order to explicate the endlessly frustrating, subjective nature of human relationships, about which it is very hard to generalise, their similes tended to make recourse to the physical. The similes are often biblical in origin and conventional in use, but nevertheless, in the context of describing household behaviour they take on a literal referent which is almost comic. Taking his text from I Peter 3, Cleaver argues: 'Like as a vessell the weaker it is, the more it is to bee favoured and spared, if we will have it to continue: even so a wife.' Later in the text, he expands the analogy: 'A christall Glasse, is a precious and profitable vessell, yet brittle: so is the married woman . . . As therefore a man doth more care-fully take heed of breaking such a glasse, then some earthen or tinne vessell, the one being more base, and the other more strong: so likewise should the husband have such regard of the frailetie of his wife'.[78] Gouge suggests that the joining of the couple in matrimony be thought of as a process of 'gluing': 'Things well glued together are as fast, firme, and close as if they were one intire peece. Yea we obserue by experience that a table will oft times cleaue in the whole wood, before it will part asunder where it is glued: so as an husband ought to be as firme to his wife as to himselfe: and she to him.' Here it is the very material stuff of the household which bears the weight of anchoring and concretising the nature of husbandly behaviour in a commonly understood domestic practice.[79] Before marriage care must be taken to choose wisely, as a woman would select a vessel, 'there is no woman almost so unwise or unwarie, that will buy *an earthen pitcher* . . . but she will view it well first, ring it, and trie it whether it be found whole or no.'[80] Individuals must do their duty willingly, as 'A good work may be marred (you know) by an ill manner of doing it; as good stuffe maybe spilled by the bungerly making'.[81]

Because of the structure of these manuals, reaching out as they do between heaven and earth in an attempt to produce an integrated concept of Protes-tant domestic life, the writers move with speed between a notion of the house as a physical entity and as a body of individuals interlinked through a variety of intricate bonds of obligation. In Cleaver's complex pairing, love of spouses and love of houses are intimately related: '[A] modest and chaste woman that loveth her husband', says Cleaver, 'must also love her house, as remem-bering, that the husband that loveth his wife, cannot so well like of the sight of any tapestrie, as to see his wife in his house.'[82] The conventional point about confining wifely activity is imaged as a merging of the woman into the decorations on the walls – prioritised as *more* desirable than the sight of expensive furnishings, but nevertheless allied to them in her constant presence and function as an ornament. Although the material is at all times inferior and posterior to the spiritual, it is even so the very stuff through which human understanding has to function – that which is closest to its nature and to which its limited comprehension can extend; subordinate in importance, it nevertheless forms the starting point of knowledge. In making this comparative move, writers conflate the neat distinctions between the human and the material, between a love patterned on Christ's own for his people and the responsible handling of crockery.

The recourse to material comparisons in order to describe human relationships is particularly prevalent in images of the house itself. William Whately describes the consequences when men fail to take up their natural position of domestic authority: 'That house is a misshapen house, and (if wee may use that terme) a crump-shouldered, or hutch-backt house'.[83] There is an implicit acknowledgement within his parentheses that the metaphorical slippage which seeks to clarify concepts risks merging the categories of 'body' and 'house' in peculiar ways. The pairing is gendered male here, playing on the meaning of house as familial lineage, but it is often gendered female too, because of a woman's inferior strength. The wife's moral imperfections are imagined as a physical fault: 'she knoweth her selfe to be feble, and nedfull of many thinges, & busye about many trifles, & lyke unto a ruinous house, that muste be underset and upholden wyth manye smal proppes'.[84] Trying to explain why it is wrong for a wife 'secretly to purloyne and powle from [her husband], for to pranke up her children, or her selfe, her house and chambers in braverie', Cleaver presents an image which is a curious mixture of the pragmatic and the metaphorical: 'it is a close undermining of her house'.

This is not only a metaphorical concern; the connections between spouses and houses also offer a set of practical comparisons. Writers use the link between physical environments and emotional bonds to check a reader's precipitate haste towards the institution of marriage: 'If thou wert to take *an house*, or hire but *a servent*', Gattaker admonishes the reader, 'how carefull wouldest thou be to make diligent enquirie of the commodities and discommodities, conveniences and inconveniences, easements and annoiances.'[85] House and wife are to be investigated as physical environments. One's wife 'must bee continually conversant with thee, at thy table, in thy chamber, in bed, in thy secrets, and finally, in thy heart and breast', the intimacy moving between house and body in an increasingly visceral closeness.[86] The wife's ministrations round out the husband's activities: 'shee is the last that leaveth thee at thy departing, and the first that receiveth thee at thy returning: thou departest from her with sweete imbracements and kisses, and with sweete kisses and imbracements she receiveth thee at thy returne home'. The qualities of the marriage partner *become* the nature of the household: 'Who so now chooseth him a wife, or shee a husband, that is infected and tangled with such noysome vices, hee seeketh not a spouse . . . but an hell, a painfulnesse, and destruction of all expedient, quiet, and vertuous living'.[87] A wicked spouse, as a 'hell', is a whole environment within whose moral compass the qualities of one's life are defined. As Gataker's reworking of the passage from Proverbs puts it, 'an evill wife is *as the raine dropping* in thorow the tiles, that maketh him weary of the house, that vexeth him so that it driveth him out of doores'. She is 'a continual evill companion with him at bed & boord, such as he cannot shift off or shun'.[88] In these images the writers try to come to terms with the two meanings of the household, as a space and as a conjunction of human relationships of relative authority and subjection. Although it is a woman's moral honesty which creates domesticity, both spouses have the ability to make the bounded area of the house itself into a heaven or a hell. Although the extent of male authority must stretch past the edges of the house to the limits of human relationships, where the two meanings of household are concentrated together in domestic space they become uniquely powerful.

Men, of course, are to rule the day-to-day business of the household in a devolved way. They are to pass control of the physical stuff of the house and its daily routines of production and consumption to their wives, and this gives women a power which resides in particular kinds of skill. It is a 'charge laid upon wives to *guide the house* . . . so as therein husbands ought to referre matters to their ordering, and not restraine them in every particular matter from doing any thing without a speciall licence and direction', Gouge says.[89] The housewife must order her domestic domain with expert precision, as her success in its organization has direct implications for her family's prospects: 'good husbandrie and good huswifery, consisteth not so much in having much or little, as in the wise, carefull, discreet, & good forecasting of that, which God in mercie hath inabled and inriched them with, to see every thing well ordered, and imployed to a good end and use'. The wife patterns and controls the rhythms of production and consumption: 'She must have a good forecast to contrive and dispatch things in due time, and good order, that necessaries bee not wanting when they should be used, and confusion doe not make more labour then is needfull.'[90] If the natural result of insubordination within the house was anarchy within communities, then a lack of order amongst its physical goods would lead to financial ruin.

She must have an intimate knowledge of every inch of her domain: 'She must lay a diligent eye to her household stuffe in every Roome, that nothing be embezeled away, nothing spoyled or lost for want of looking to, nothing mard by ill usage, nor nothing worne out by more using then is needefull, nothing out of place, for things cast aside, are deemed to be stolen.' The active nature of this supervisory role is striking.[91] The household, in these examples, is imagined as a castle constantly under threat from both within and without, where objects spontaneously disintegrate or creep away into obscure corners. The sheer level of energy which female work within the house should involve is made clear by Cleaver: 'She borroweth of the morning and the evening, for to dispatch her businesse. When she is up, doth she sit downe and cap a stoole? NO, shee looketh that her servants have their necessaries, that they may goe soone to their worke . . . She must not thinke to sit and commande, but she must be a stirrer in every place.'[92]

Household goods were often the products of female labour, and they were sustained, maintained and kept in good order by women's further work. In other words it was in the material qualities of the house that a wife exercised her authority. Reading between the different evidence for moral absolutes and qualities which are desirable in practice, it becomes obvious that the kind of domestic power available to women was that of order – a physical and spatial issue of controlling the domestic environment of things.[93] To put things in good order was, through the connections between objects, their associated routines, and prescriptive behaviour, to be an 'honest' woman.

But there is a potential tension between the husband's overall domestic authority and that part which he devolves to his wife. Gouge makes the important distinction that she must 'so rule others as she be subject to her husband, and not command any thing against his command'; she must act as her husband's representative only, over whom 'if she take any authority, she usurpeth it'.[94] Ownership becomes important here, central to the notion of the overlapping spheres of matrimonial authority: 'For as in mixture of wine and water, though the greater quantitie be water, yet we call the whole wine, so in the common goods of the family, though the wife should bring the greater part, we call all the husbands.'[95] His ultimate control over domestic space rendered the woman's power there potentially subversive, unless it was a metonym of his own. Within the troubling relationship between theory and practice, for instance, a wife actually had a much greater operative power over her children, her servants and her household stuff than her husband did.[96] Where these different kinds of authority overlapped, the consolations of ultimate control might not have been so great on a day-to-day basis because men did not fully understand what went on in the complexities of the routines of production and consumption. Different kinds of agency, operating in different physical spaces at different times of the day, were in occasional competition with one another, and moral stories often exploit those tensions.

The routines of food production and consumption, for instance, central to the household tasks assigned to women, were used by deponents as a way of identifying the particularly insidious nature of moral lapses within the household. A Mistress Robinson, in Sturry church on the Tuesday before Wye fair, said that she had asked her man William 'why he came not home to breakfaste'. The answer she received initially offered a rejection of the communally binding ties of breaking the fast within the household: 'and the saide William saide he coulde have a better breakfaste at his cosyn Bigges than she his dame coulde make hym'. But William went on to set this against a notion of appropriate domestic practice at his cousin's house too: 'For whan the churle her husbande sitteth churlyng by the fyre in a chaire she the saide Bigges wyf will wyncke uppon hym . . . to come in to the buttrie.'[97] Master Biggs's position in his chair by the fire is that due to him as household ruler. His wife moves about the house carrying on its day-to-day running while he enjoys the more sedentary pursuit here parodied and hence dismissed as 'churling' (as opposed to 'lording'). The business of female ministration, however, far from supporting his position of authority, radically undermines it.

Other depositions employ the domestic routine more explicitly to characterise the wrongdoing they describe. Richard Alcock of Tenterden is accused of having 'carnall copulacion wyth the [said] Bennet's wyf in the meane tyme while he was eatyng hys porege, before she dyd bryng in the meate'.[98] Similarly, an unnamed man is accused of having 'carnally to do with [Joan Colson] whilest an oven full of cakes were a bakyng'.[99] It is also suggested, by a group of women who move out of a hall in Luddenham and into a parlour to discuss the matter more privately, that 'he dyd eate parte of them with her when he had don'.[100]

It is their position within the daily routine which characterises these events as immoral: 'anti-domestic' and therefore 'antisocial'. The focus of the cases upon the production and consumption of food is partly pragmatic, in the sense that it stresses the small temporal gaps between chores into which women must fit their crimes, during which their position in the service areas of the house (rather than its more public rooms) gives them a spatial advantage. As high-status men of the house sit around tables involved in the rituals of dining and the consequent cementing of friendships, women gain control over other areas of the house for the duration of the meal. This is pragmatic rather than absolute spatial control: a by-product of the social obligations of the status of those around the table, and the etiquette of the meal itself.[101]

It is also possible to analyse the comic potential of the descriptions of 'sins within routine', especially here perhaps the detail of the eating of the cakes. Although this fact undoubtedly works to compound the crime, it also seems intentionally readable in terms of appetite, patterning as it does several different types of hunger. The juxtaposition of work and sex, of the domestic and the antisocial, of the control of routine and the license of licentiousness, of smooth running and of rupture, and of the appearance of normality and its perversion – all of these are comic pairings, and they make the tales seductive to repetition. They situate bizarre aberration right at the centre of the domestic. But within the representation is an anxiety: such humour threatens the overall hierarchical control of the household by suggesting that what is seen from the perspective of the hall table may be an illusion; that as dishes come and go with faultless ease, the pauses between them may not represent the duration of production, but the illicit consumption of the economic and moral worth of the household.

Such tropes treat the destructive potential of female domestic control, but the binding ties of hospitality also function in more positive ways.[102] Deponents use them to signal mutual obligation, and presence in the house is associated with a unique series of responsibilities and appropriate behaviours. Being inside, behind the walls of the house, involves becoming a part of the household itself. William Clerk, examined about his relationship with John Wright, who is accused of trading beer on a Sunday, says that 'many tymes now adaies he hath seen . . . the said John Wright carryng beeir to and froe in Canterbury . . . and at such meting of hym this deponent hath saluted hym'. Having defined their public relationship, the way in which their daily routines caused their paths to cross, he considers their personal friendship: 'And divers and many tymes within the tyme that he hath before deposed he this deponent hath been in the company of the said Wright in divers honest places in Canterbury and hath droncke with hym together in honest company, and somtymes he hath been at this deponent's house.'[103] The description of their relationship moves from the chance encounter, to the choice of each other's company in the public interior space of the ale house, to the invitation to spend time together in one another's own houses. As the spaces involved become more reserved, so the element of chance in their meeting consequently diminishes, and the time and place of their encounters can therefore be used to define their mutual familiarity. The narrative moves neatly through different masculine interactions and their related spaces.

This notion that presence within the house is morally binding takes on a particularly sharp resonance when relationships have broken down. In a case over a disputed contract of marriage between Mary Richards of Canterbury and the young King's School scholar Thomas Cocks, Joanna Pilkington deposes about her invitation to breakfast at the house of Richard Richards, the girl's father. The meal is presented as a habitual affair amongst friends, distinguished only by Joanna asking Thomas Cocks 'whye he dallied so with Marye Rychardes'. Thomas answers that they have previously made promises of marriage to one another, and these are then formally repeated in front of Mary's friends and family. The public iteration of the contract is sealed by breaking the morning fast together, a meal translated from social occasion to semi-ritual status. Cocks is placed at the table within the family which he should shortly have entered, and food is shared between them.

In his own deposition, the girl's father explains the significance of the house itself in their courtship:

about a seven weekes before christemas laste paste the saide Cockes came to this deponent's house with Daniell Welkinson, the which was the firste tyme that the said Cockes ever frequented this deponent's house when as yn the presence of this deponent's doughter he did as yt were aske this deponent leave to frequente his house saying that he would have cum thether a hole yere before that tyme, and that because so longe tyme he fansied and loved his doughter[104]

The formal request to 'frequent the house' is used as an indication of the closeness of the relationship, forming as it does a significant step in the courtship process. The deponents who support the existence of a contract between the couple focus their narrative upon these two events which involve Cocks's entry into the house, as a way of demonstrating his position within the family. In asking to frequent it, Cocks allies the license of physical entry with the wooing, and hence 'knowing' of the girl: to form a relationship with her must involve locating himself physically within her family.

This spatial intimacy, reserving actions from the sight of the whole community and thereby clarifying and intensifying their meaning, is at the heart of deponents' interests in the household. Whilst these depositions present its positive potential for developing closeness between individuals, cases concerning sexual immorality implicate domestic space in the troubled early modern conception of privacy. Margaret Raven's triumphant proclamation, in the case quoted above, 'here be privye whores com[e] they leaping in the f[i]eld on this fasshion', exuberantly sets the intended priviness of the act of whoredom against the openness of the fields, the energy of the couple's activities and the public broadcast of her slander. Privacy here is a matter of moving away from the prying eyes of neighbours. Within the house, however, the ability to hide actions takes two different forms. One aspect of the anxiety generated by the succinct tales of illicit sex and cookery mentioned above is that their position within the domestic routines of food production circumvents a need for spatial privacy. Rather than being hidden physically within the house, these women and their lovers are concealed temporally inside the complexities of household business. Their activities might be overlooked because they seek invisibility in a non-spatial way. But the secrecy afforded by physical concealment within the house is the most problematic aspect of the evidence, because it invariably exploits the authority which individuals feel they have over the household itself.

When events come to court, physically restricting access to spaces is presented as diminishing moral control over them. As a suspicious action, locking a door justifies further investigation.[105] Anna Jones sleeps with Thomas Holt in her chamber on the ground floor 'the doore being shut to them', but this does not stop her maid opening the window. The maid, careful to include the detail of the closed door in her deposition, had to weigh the control of domestic space in her mind. As she knew what was taking place in the chamber, she suggests, her moral imperative to discover the truth and exhibit it legitimises her extraordinary practice. Weighing against this authority, which only really functions retrospectively (if she is right and if she can prove it) is her mistress's command over the rooms of her husband's house. Her eventual invasion, at which she 'did open the wyndow of the chamber and saw her and hym to gither apon the bedd, saying, "what Holt, are ye heare?", and so went a way', underlines these competing authorities by its partial and temporary nature, figuring the potential of domestic space for secrecy as a set of rules governed entirely by moral precepts.[106] The description of the relative moral authority of a wife engaged in adulterous activities, and a servant of blameless reputation, feelingly demonstrates the chaos which ensues when household heads behave inappropriately. It hints at a 'world turned upside down' image of a servant becoming mistress in her control of household space.

This case considers a wife's control over the household in her husband's absence. The household manuals admitted the possibility of this scenario, indeed it was in some ways one of the less confusing areas of the unequal rule of husband and wife. 'Yet the Scripture alloweth', says Dudley Fenner, 'uppon necessarie occasion of warfar, service to the common wealth, church, or necessarie affaires of their own, somtimes a long absence.' It is in such circumstances that the wife must be at her most alert, 'And in her husbands absence, to see good orders observed, as he hath appointed: to whatch over the manners and behaviour of such as bee in her house, and to helpe her husband in spying out evils that are breeding, that by his wisedome, they be prevented or cured'. While he is gone, the wife must physically stand in her husband's stead, being 'his eies, foot and mouth, when hee is away'.[107]

Standing in their husbands' stead, representing his authority in order to ensure the continued smooth running of the domestic routine, the less-than-perfect doubles of male authority which the depositions describe seem to assume that their crimes will go unnoticed. This is clearly an important point of contention, as the cases brought suggest that these women felt a security in their ability to control their domestic environment which extended to committing adultery within it. The subversive expectation is that a wife's status as domestic ruler will provide privacy from the gaze, if not the knowledge, of others by dissuading them from entering spaces even though they are aware of what is taking place there. A three-layered seclusion prevents those of lower status, if not from comprehending actions then from actually seeing them, and if not from seeing them then from broadcasting the information. The distinction between others knowing roughly what happens in one's intimate domestic spaces and being morally justified in intruding (and so actually seeing one perform those actions) perhaps provides a working definition of privacy within a society. The depositions demonstrate the fact that this is not an issue of the construction of spaces but rather of the control which individuals can exercise over them, and they test, and of course dismiss, the idea that spatial control extends to the performance of sin.

If the legitimacy of intervention is always a contest of moral and social authority between the performers of sin and their various audiences, then it is often gender which acts as the feather which tips the scales one way or another: a woman's authority as domestic head in her husband's absence is set against the power of a man from outside the household. The case of Henry Seth the house owner and Mistress Ford the tenant, quoted above, is perhaps the clearest example of this weighing of gender and power: 'Mr Henry Seth knocked at the dore on the streate side, whome the goodwife Forde, being within, asked who was there. "Mary", said he, "I your land lord am heir". And she asked what he wold have.'[108] Is this property to be considered his to enter, as a male landlord, or hers to defend, as the castle of the wife of a tenant?

These dynamics are played out at length in the deposition of Robert Marleton, a 'sojourner' in the house of Mr and Mrs Osborn.[109] Marleton gleans his evidence for his hostess's adultery from a position 'standing . . . apon a stayeres out unto the yard' of their house, watching the woman's movements with a Mr Wallop. The latter was walking 'up and downe in the ketchin about half an hower' while the former 'brought her husband of bedd', after which time she 'cam downe owt of her chamber into the ketchin unto Wallop'. After sending the maid out for apples, Mrs Osborn set her candle aside and followed the man into the bakehouse where they stayed for a quarter of an hour. She then 'cam out of the backehouse to the ketchin and tourned her about the candle which she had set by and brusshed her clothes behinde her with her handes', turning herself around and smoothing her skirts behind her. On Wallop's return 'she went into the hall and he out of the ketchin door, out of the house, and sat a while at the gate'.[110]

This description offers no proof of a sexual encounter, but it is neverthe-less richly suggestive in its presentation of movement between spaces and the gestures which accompany such transitions. The narrative is constructed around the relationship between hall, kitchen and bakehouse, the last seem-ingly a detached building in the yard of the house. The tale sets up the outer limits of the house as areas less susceptible to scrutiny, and as spaces which are opposed to the constraints and obligations of family life. The couple use the kitchen as a kind of middle ground where they meet before either leaving together for a more private space or departing in opposite directions. It is here that the light, simultaneous discoverer of spaces and delineator of the path taken through them, is left behind, and this detail is, of course, highly moralised.

Marleton's organisation of the spatial elements of his tale situates him at an elevation from which he can observe her journey not as a series of consecutive spaces viewed independently, but as a complete itinerary: his moralised relationship to the events in question is one of omniscience.[111] The unbroken vision which the deposition elucidates is suggestive of wrong-doing because it presents a series of actions which are coterminous but not coherent. They suggest her employment of different personas within differ-ent spaces – performing as wife, then lover, then wife again. As she reclaims the light to illuminate her way back to her husband's bed, so Mistress Osborn readjusts her clothing. Neatening the back of her skirt seems an eminently liminal gesture of reintegration into the space of the house proper, a perfect-ing of the self-image and a reorientation towards a different role and new set of expectations.

But Marleton's deposition goes on to focus on another event which took place 'apon a certayn night whan the go[o]dwife Osborn's husband was out of the way'.[112] On this occasion Mistress Osborn goes to Wallopp's chamber in the house, where she again stays a quarter of an hour. Marleton does not see the couple at all, although he 'hard them speake or swisper togither'. It is only when her husband is present that she must move to the peripheries of the house; when he is not at home, then, his wife is said to use the house as her own, showing her as confident that her temporary role as householder will afford her privacy from intervention. She is not unaware of the sinful nature of her actions, Marleton suggests, as she came 'without any light', but the scales of domestic control have tipped sufficiently for her to use domestic space differently.

Marelton is not standing alone on the stairs while he watches his hostess with Wallopp, he is accompanied by his 'bedfellow' Spycer. The corroboration offered by a second witness is significant, not only because the memory of the event can be confirmed, but also because it begins to address the almost impenetrable web of loyalties and affections, the relationships of authority and deference which are unique to depositions about events 'inside'. A stand-ard interrogatory asks the deponent how well they know the parties litigant. It is often answered by stating the duration of acquaintance and the type of occasions on which they meet, as demonstrated by William Clerk's deposi-tion above, and it aims at assessment of the likely partiality of the witness. When both witness and accused are a part of the same household, however, even in the more distant relationship of sojourner and hostess, bias becomes an essential aspect of the narrative. The evidence given by such close associates is that of intimate observation of glances, gestures, half-heard sounds over a long period of time; it is different in nature to the signs of occurrences outside. It also offers a strikingly different set of spatial dynamics between the watcher and the watched.

William Alcock of Canterbury and his friend Thomas Boys, both gentlemen, were walking together 'in the body of Chrystchurche' Cathedral when Crench, one of Boys's servants, passed them.[113] Boys called him over in order to ascertain the truth of certain rumours which Crench had been spreading about two of his fellows. Crench, having asked leave to 'tell him the whole truthe', retells his tale officially (Boys says it was in the hall of his house), now as a proof of sexual incontinence which has to convince the gentry, rather than what had no doubt been a comic slander to amuse his peers. He says that

> the said Colbrand and Elizabeth Purfry articulate had bene ... walking together and being come home to the said Mr Boys his house the sayd Colbrand and Purfry stayd together in the entry and he the sayd Crench went in and lighted a candle and went up into his chamber and there pulled of[f] his shoes

Crench, who has to return to lock the doors, implicitly provides a temporal and physical space for the couple to begin something that he could later observe. Able to move quietly now, he 'came downe in his hose and heard the said Colbrand and Purfry rumbling againste the walls and blowinge in the entry and heard the said Colbrand say (Oh sweete Besse sweete Besse)'. Because this is a relationship between two household servants, the closeness of their intimate liaison and the almost claustrophobic lack of privacy within the house seem connected to the bonds of domestic responsibility which should remind them of the significance their immorality has for their master's house.

Crench is able to 'catch them in the act' because he can exploit the spaces within his usual domestic routine in order to produce the spectacle to which he is a willing audience. Alerted by the deviations from the usual practice of others, hiding behind the cover of his own habitual movements, he is able to negotiate the house in the dark through his familiarity with its layout. Such tropes of interior detection are credible because of the intimate knowledge shared by those of the same household, of its routines and of the building itself – its potential to provide cover for those they follow and for their own clandestine movements of 'discovery'. The physicality of familiarity is striking at several levels in Crench's deposition.

This duplicity of routine, which seditiously folds abnormal behaviour into the illusion of normality in a similar way to the 'baking of cakes', is a part of the uniqueness of domestic observation. But it is a dangerous narrative strategy for deponents to adopt because the relative weight of the honesty of observer and observed is delicate. Such actions can only be legitimated by their end result: Crench controls the 'space of revelation' but not, it must be assumed, the nature of the event which takes place, because he cannot be seen to have coerced their actions, only to have found an ingenious way to give evidence of them. But there is a suggestion, in the pressure to which Crench's tale is subjected, that the act of witnessing is in some ways also seen as one of *participation*. A slight shift in the moral standing of the parties might make this an exclusive performance of sexuality engineered to gratify its voyeuristic audience. These cases are problematic because the deponent must acknowledge that, in order to obtain his information, both he *and* the accused are involved in secrecy and the deception which hiding necessitates.

The crucial aspect here is the physical position from which Crench observes the couple. Returning to the contention between the Clintons and the Nowres provides an instructive parallel. Joan claims to have 'harde William Harris the tapster at the Quenes Armes and goodwife Nowre' together in Nowre's house, 'and ther they were blowing'. The barrier between inside and outside leads, inevitably, to an exercise of the imagination, aroused by the noises which travel from one space to another. Her husband Roger adds, 'that he had put his heade in at a hole into the shoppe' and heard them together. The detail of the hole is used as a metaphor for clarity and shared sensory experience, as part of his attempt to present a narrative of perceptions in which understanding is undeniable, and signs cannot be construed differently.[114] The almost-sharing of domestic space through the permeable barrier of the wall appears calculated to do two things. First, it offers a more credible kind of evidence, without the exposure of either witness or performers to the moral threats of total revelation which would accompany the opening up of the house to the street. Second, it attempts to substitute knowledge for imagination. But it does so by stressing 'hearing better', without being able to see, as seeing would make the act of discovery into one of 'audiencing', of the duration and intention of enjoyment of an inappropriate spectacle. This case points up the curious dialectic between fantasies of what *might be* seen and interpretations of what *is* seen in narratives where proof is hard to gain, and where sexual acts could not in any case be described in the court.

Whilst the Clintons stand outside the house, listening in from behind the wall, Crench and his fellow servants are all inside. The sharing of domestic space, with its perceived intimacies produced by its separation from outside, makes it much harder for him to claim the same kind of physical separation from the event he watches. And without that clear distinction between a public space of watching and a private space of performance, this tale begins to look much more like one of involvement.

The tale which Crench has told thus far is a cleverly crafted narrative of domestic discovery, comic in its use of aptly descriptive verbs (rumbling, blowing), and in its repetition of the alleged speech of passion. But Crench, presumably thinking that he had reached a meaningful conclusion, is further questioned: 'then sayd Mr Boys aforesaid "what of all this?"' Crench applies an explicit meaning to his narrative in response: 'the said Colbrand did there occupye the said Elizabeth Purfrye'. But he is still met with the paucity of his proof: 'quoth Mr Boys "howe canste thou tell?"'. At this point the narrator realises that the story has become one about his own honesty, hinging on the plausibility of his tale, in the face of the threat to the reputation of Boys's household which such crimes offer. He begins to back down a little: 'then sayde Crenche "I hope you will not seeke advantage of me, I did not say he occupied her but I *thinke* he did" '.[115] The substantiation he is forced to provide now is unique in detail within the evidence, but common in the way it stretches out towards the irrefutability of material proof: 'for sayd he, when they were goon owt of the entry I fetch[ed] a candle to locke the dore and there I sawe his nature [sperm] ly uppon the ground'.

The circumstantial details of these sins – their locations and the evidence which remains after the event – help to tie the actions in question to a material world outside the narrative, one which will enable deponents to present evidence whose physicality suggests objectivity. Many different types of narrative circulated about such sexual crimes, even this single case hints at several different types of story – a slander full of comic potential, a formal reiteration of a story about unruly servants told to their master in a tone of moral seriousness, an official narrative deposition given in the court and written down by a scribe. In each case, however, it is the dynamics between watching and acting, suspicion and knowing, hearing and not seeing which are key to interpretation of events. They generate, we can imagine, the humour of Crench's slander and the moral meaning of his more serious tale. But they are also shaped by the teller's status, in this instance as a domestic servant. Although the moral project of social scrutiny extends to all types of human behaviour, in all possible kinds of space, it is within the household that the dynamics of watching and acting are the most overdetermined and potentially damaging to the reputations of all involved.

Space functions in complex and flexible ways, then, in the representation of events. The depositions studied here demonstrate the currency of the images of inside and outside, discovery and display, which the plays use: tropes at the heart of the definition of immoral behaviour. The clarity of spatial dynamics, particularly the distinctions between inside and outside, attract to themselves the less clear-cut divisions between right and wrong, proof and conjecture, as a narrative move by which deponents can insist upon clarity through analogy. Type and anti-type reflect and clarify one another, and distinctions can therefore be used to define behaviour as aberrant.[116]

Also striking in this evidence is the unique set of problems thrown up by domestic space, particularly with regards to its connections to a level of partiality which problematises the distinction between audience and spectacle. Household spaces tie individuals together in ways which are both stabilising and troubling, implicating them in endless permutations of interconnection. Those connections, for all their visceral closenesses, are always conditioned by the shaping effects of gender and status upon the power dynamics of spatial control.

NOTES

1 From the late sixteenth century onwards, manuals advising on matters of conduct within the family and between the genders were published in large numbers. For their relationship to changing ideas about marriage see Anthony Fletcher, 'The Protestant idea of marriage in early modern England', in Fletcher and Peter Roberts eds, *Religion, Culture and Society in Early Modern Britain*, Cambridge: Cambridge University Press, 1994. For the audience for conduct books see Bernard Capp, *When Gossips Meet*, Oxford: Oxford University Press, 2003, pp. 11–12.

2 These courts were central to the definition of moral boundaries in early modern England. They saw an unprecedented increase in business between the mid sixteenth and the mid seventeenth centuries. For more on their significance see J. A. Sharpe, '"Such disagreement betwyx neighbours": litigation and human relations in early modern England', in John Bossy ed., *Disputes and Settlements, Law and Human Relations in the West*, Cambridge: Cambridge University Press, 1983, p. 168; Martin Ingram, *Church Courts, Sex and Marriage in England 1570–1640*, Cambridge: Cambridge University Press, 1987, pp. 13–15, who sees their rise in significance as beginning after 1570; Laura Gowing, *Domestic Dangers: Women, Words, and Sex in Early Modern London*, Oxford: Clarendon Press, 1996, passim.

3 For extracted examples of the texts see Kate Aughterson *The English Renaissance: An Anthology of Sources and Documents*, London: Routledge, 1998, and Lloyd Davis ed., *Sexuality and Gender in the English Renaissance: An Annotated Edition of Contemporary Documents*, New York and London: Garland Publishing, 1998; for readings of their views on marriage and gender see for instance, S. D. Amussen, *An Ordered Society: Gender and Class in Early Modern England*, Oxford, New York: Basil Blackwell, 1988, E. A. Foyster, *Manhood in Early Modern England: Honour, Sex and Marriage*, London: Longman, 1999, S. Mendelson and P. Crawford, *Women in Early Modern England, 1550–1720*, Oxford: Clarendon Press, 1998, Alexandra Shepard, *Meanings of Manhood in Early Modern England*, Oxford: Oxford University Press, 2003.

4 See Shepard on the relationship with patriarchy, although she does also stress that the patriarchal meaning of manhood was not the only one available, and that it was in any case increasingly irrelevant to the growing number of men without a household to govern, 2003, esp. chapter 3.

5 Robert Cleaver, *A godlie forme of householde government*, London: Thomas Creede, for Thomas Man, 1598, p. 175, my italics.

6 Richard Brathwaite, *The English Gentleman*, London: John Haviland, 1630, p. 155; Gouge says 'a familie is a little Church, and a little commonwealth, at least a lively representation thereof', p. 18, William Gouge, *Of domesticall duties*, London: John Haviland for William Bladen, 1622.

7 Gouge, 1622, p. 356.

8 See for instance Cleaver on the importance of a good match in age and estate: 'For as two horses, or two oxen, of unequall stature, cannot be coupled under one selfe same yoake', 1598, p. 148; Gouge refers to 'all those places where a wives yoke may seeme most to pinch' in his Dedication, 1622.

9 Paul to the Ephesians 5:23, 'For the husband is the head of the wife, even as Christ is the head of the church'. See, for instance, John Calvin, *A commentarie upon S. Paules epistles to the Corinthians*, translated by Thomas Timme, London: Thomas Dawson, 1577, 'Thus the man consisteth not wythout the woman, bycause otherwyse he should be a head cut of from the body: neither dooth the woman stande wythout the man, bycause then shee would be a deade body', f.130.

10 Gouge, 1622, p. 303.

11 William Whately, *A Bride-Bush: Or, a Direction for Married Persons*, London: Felix Kyngston, 1619, pp. 192, 202, 213.

12 See Dudley Fenner, whose particular turn of phrase, 'Contrary to this is ...' seems to epitomise the technique of opposition; *The Order of Houshold, in Certain godly and learned treatises*, Edinburgh: Robert Waldegrave, 1592. Davis, quoting Newman, describes 'Fenner's dialectical method' which 'aims to limit the meanings of these qualities, and effectively introduces a "sexual division of behaviour and labour" in its "representations of ordered family life"', 1998, p. 167.

13 Cleaver, 1598, p. 170.

14 Cleaver, 1598, dedication; p. 17, my italics.

15 Capp quotes William Austen, 'He that hath no wife, hath no house', 2003, p. 16.

16 Cleaver, 1598, p. 215.

17 Henri Lefebvre, *The Production of Space*, translated by Donald Nicholson Smith, Oxford: Blackwell, 1991, p. 39.

18 Quoted in Laura Gowing, '"The freedom of the streets": women and social space, 1560–1640', in Mark Jenner and Paul Griffiths eds, *Londinopolis*, Manchester: Manchester University Press, 2000, p. 131.

19 Mendelson and Crawford, 1998, passim, esp. chapter 5.

20 Alexandra Shepard has stressed the fact that, in reality, 'Men ... as well as women, undermined, resisted, or simply ignored patriarchal imperatives', 2003, pp. 248–9. She also draws attention to the work of A. Hassell Smith on the Norfolk village of Stiffkey in the 1590s, 'where more than 50 per cent of the families lived in some sort of shared or divided property', p. 203. For contemporary concerns about vagrants who had no home at all see A. L. Beier, *Masterless Men: The Vagrancy Problem in England 1560–1640*, London: Methuen, 1985; see Raffaella Sarti, *Europe at Home: Family and Material Culture 1500–1800*, London: Yale University Press, 2002, chapter 1, for the frequent disparities between 'house' and 'family'.

21 Shepard, 2003, p. 202; p. 247.

22 Gowing, 2000, p. 136; p. 139

23 Dubrow outlines the significance of reading these cultural relationships outside a model of 'simple equivalence' which posits the centrality of one aspect of the metaphors of rule, the political or the familial. Metaphor, she says, 'not only expresses responses to cultural and social patterns but also can, as it were, represent the relationship between these levels of meaning', 1999, p. 7.

24 Sharpe, 1983, p. 168; Ingram, 1987, pp. 13–15; Gowing, 1996, pp. 264–5. Although responses from different individuals and in different dioceses obviously showed some local distinctions, the images of house and household are remarkably uniform. The examples presented here are therefore representative ones only, and are where possible compared to evidence from other courts. They are taken from the complete run of cases in both the Archdeaconry and Consistory courts of Canterbury from the 1540s to 1600.

25 Gowing, 1996, p. 269.

26 The manuals are prophylactic and admonitory whereas the courts deal with crisis, often after long periods of unofficial mediation; the courts wage war against the secrecy of vice whereas the manuals allude to domestic problems indirectly, and only over the question of marital violence do they enter an arena more serious for the soul than incompetence. Manuals were produced by the literate for the developing market for printed matter, within the constraints of a genre of advice literature with a distinct sermonising tone and a wealth of biblical references, whereas depositions offer

narratives constructed in relation to the demands of evidentiary proof, heavily formulaic and yet peppered with verbatim phrases and oral forms.

27 Gouge, 1622, p. 344.

28 CCAL X.10.2 f.90, 1543. Recent work on deposition narratives, from Natalie Zemon Davis's work on pardon tales, through Carlo Ginzberg's investigations of witchcraft trials, to Gowing's work on ecclesiastical court cases, has stressed the importance of formal tropes to an understanding of the way in which the texts are shaped. N. Z. Davis, *Fiction in the Archives*, Cambridge: Polity Press, 1987; Carlo Ginzburg, *Ecstasies: Deciphering the Witches' Sabbath*, Harmondsworth: Penguin, 1990; Gowing, 1996. Adam Fox's work (2000) has demonstrated the complexities of the relationship between oral and literate cultures, showing how sensitive early modern men and women were to the effect upon their audience of the form of the narratives they told, in terms of the shape which their tales took, the details they chose to include and the language in which they chose to tell them.

29 The extensive literature on 'separate spheres', mainly focused on a later period, is only tangentially related to my argument here as it by and large fails to distinguish between 'private' and 'domestic', and to engage with the relationship between activities and physical spaces. The literature is usefully summarised by Amanda Vickery, 'Golden age of separate spheres? A review of the categories and chronology of English women's history', *The Historical Journal*, 36, 1993. See also Roger Chartier ed., *Passions of the Renaissance*, Cambridge, MA, London: Harvard University Press, 1989.

30 Cleaver, 1598, p. 223.

31 His meaning, he says, is 'not to have the married wyfe continually lockt up . . . but to consider hereby, what respect she must have in going abroade', Edmund Tilney, *A briefe and pleasant discourse of duties in mariage, called the flower of friendship*, London: Henrie Denha[m], 1568, E2v–E3v.

32 Cleaver, 1598, p. 223.

33 Whately, 1619, pp. 194–5.

34 Whately, 1619, pp. 178, 211.

35 Cleaver, 1598, p. 16.

36 Fenner suggests diversity: 'government must bee performed with all comelinesse fit for the houshold, which is, that agreable fitnesse or conveniencie, which woorthily becommeth the diversitie of persons in the familie . . . For all these have not one and the same Rule of decencie . . . Nowe as there is comelinesse peculiar to the subjection of Children, so of servauntes', 1592, p. 4. Other writers draw a distinction between actions with and without audience, advocating avoidance of public familiarity because it undermines the couple's authority. William Whately suggests that wives 'Leave *Tom* and *Dicke* to call thy boy by, and call thine husband, husband or some other name of equall dignitie to that', 1619, p. 200.

37 Dudley Fenner, *The Order of Houshold: Described Methodically out of the Word of God with the Contrary Abuses Found in the World*, 1584, in Davis ed., 1998, p. 176.

38 Cleaver, 1598, p. 178.

39 Quoted in Orlin, 1994, p. 7.

40 Amussen, 1988, p. 86.

41 For the communities of early modern London see Ian Archer, *The Pursuit of Stability*, Cambridge: Cambridge University Press, 1991, chapter 3; Gowing, 1996, passim, esp. pp. 22–4.

42 Pamela Allen Brown describes neighbourhoods as 'schools for manners and behaviour, unofficial courts of local judgement, and stages on which neighbors created the performances that built reputation and identity', *Better a Shrew Than a Sheep: Women,*

Drama, and the Culture of Jest in Early Modern England, Ithaca: Cornell University Press, 2002, p. 14.

43 Alexandra Shepard stresses the significance of hard work in witnesses' tests of credit, 'Honesty, Worth and Gender in Early Modern England, 1560–1640', in H. R. French and Jonathan Barry eds, *Identity and Agency in English Society, 1500–1800*, Basingstoke: Palgrane, 2004, esp. pp. 93–4.

44 See for instance CCAL X.10.7 f.332v, 1568, and CCAL X.10.7 f.130, 1560, where women can be shown to have been going to or coming from market because they hold baskets; CCAL X.10.12 f.15v, 1564, where a woman is taken to be going milking because she has a pail on her arm.

45 CCAL X.1.6 f.48v, 1564.

46 CCAL X.10.8 f.54v, 1561.

47 Gowing quotes the accusation of Margaret Smith to Anne Fanne, her lodger, 'thou art a whore thou hast dishonested my house', 2000, p. 136, a phrase which encapsulates the active contribution she has made to domestic reputation in typically contra-distinctive terms. See also Melville, 1999, chapter 2, for an analysis of how London deponents 'related to' their houses based on the terms they used to describe them.

48 CCAL X.10.8 f.87, 1561.

49 The accused 'went to the house of Mr Fookes . . . with chekins to have them carved', CCAL X.10.7 f.111, 1560. See, for the importance of this kind of routine setting, Davis, 1987, p. 47, and passim.

50 CCAL 39.6 f.27v, 1568. For London examples see Gowing, 1996, passim; for Cambridge see Capp, 2003, p. 95.

51 CCAL X.1.7 f.21v, 1565.

52 CCAL 39.8 f.140, 1577.

53 CCAL X.10.7 f.110v, 1560.

54 CCAL X.10.7 f.111, 1560.

55 CCAL X.10.7 f.111v, 1560.

56 CCAL X.10.11 f.202v, 1570, see also, for example CCAL X.10.6 f.36v, 1551, where the same metaphor is used.

57 Jacques du Bosc, *The Complete Woman*, trans. 1639, quoted in Aughterson, 1998, p. 470; Cleaver, 1598, p. 96.

58 Joy Wiltenburg, *Disorderly Women and Female Power in the Street Literature of Early Modern England and Germany*, London: University Press of Virginia, 1992, pp. 102, 95.

59 On the Skimmington Ride as a form of communal punishment see Natialie Zemon Davis, 'Women on Top' *Society and Culture in Early Modern France*, Stanford: Stanford University Press, 1975, ch. 5; David Underdown, 'The taming of the scold: the enforce-ment of patriarchal authority in early modern England', in A. Fletcher and J. Stevenson eds, *Order and Disorder in Early Modern England* Cambridge: Cambridge University Press, 1985.

60 Gowing, 2000, p. 133.

61 CCAL X.10.12 f.16, 1564.

62 The dynamic between private issues and their public discussion is also important in the London evidence; see Gowing, 1996, p. 120. For thought-provoking evidence of the function of publicity in cases of marital violence see Capp, 2003, pp. 103–14.

63 John Schofield, *Medieval London Houses*, New Haven, London: Yale University Press, 1994; Lena Orlin, 'Boundary disputes in early modern London', in Orlin ed., *Material London*, Philadelphia: University of Pennsylvania Press, 2000; Janet Senderowitz Loengard, *London Viewers and Their Certificates, 1508–1558: Certificates of the Sworn Viewers of the City of London*, [London]: London Record Society, 26, 1989. These

'certificates' were the reports of the masons, carpenters and tilers appointed by the City of London to examine the site of a reported 'nuisance' dispute.

64 Gowing 2000, p. 137.

65 For the effects of urban expansion see for example Peter Clark ed., *The Early Modern Town*, London: Longman, 1976; Peter Clark ed., *Small Towns in Early Modern Europe*, Cambridge: Cambridge University Press, 1995; 'Introduction' in Jonathan Barry ed., *The Tudor and Stuart Town*, London: Longman, 1990; Nigel Goose's article on 'Household size and structure in early-Stuart Cambridge', in the same volume, on problems of definition of 'household' and the complexities of reality; and the influential article by Miranda Chaytor, 'Household and kinship: Ryton in the late sixteenth and early seventeenth centuries', *History Workshop Journal*, 10, Autumn 1980, 25–60.

66 Orlin 2000, p. 365.

67 'To stand within the "eavesdrop" of a house in order to listen to secrets', the latter being 'the space of ground which is liable to receive the rainwater thrown off by the eaves of a building', *OED*.

68 CCAL 39.23 f.159, 1599.

69 CCAL X.10.15 f.92, 1566.

70 The street is, for instance, seen as an inappropriate place for fighting by Richard Birwell of Canterbury who was struck while sitting at his master's stall by William Twyne. The former 'willed hym to avoide, for that it was not a place to quarel or fight in, nevertheles offering to fight with hym in the feld', CCAL X.10.8 f.5v, 1562. Fighting in the street would cause a public disturbance, multiplying rather than terminating conflict.

71 CCAL X.10.2 f.36v, 1541.

72 CCAL 39.4 f.50, 1563.

73 See Bruce Smith's rich descriptions of soundscapes, 1999. The deposition evidence demonstrates the additional significance of the moral aspects of listening.

74 CCAL 39.7 f.51v, 1574.

75 On ideals of good neighbourliness see Capp, 2003, pp. 27–8.

76 For London examples see Gowing, 1996, pp. 98–9.

77 For the use of simile in the sermons to which these manuals are often related in style see J. W. Blench, *Preaching in England*, Oxford: Basil Blackwell, 1964, chapter III part 4.

78 Cleaver, 1598, pp. 162, 204.

79 Cleaver, 1998, p. 162; Gouge, 1622, p. 112; I Peter 3:7, 'Likewise, you husbands, dwell with them according to knowledge, giving honour unto the wife, as unto the weaker vessel, and as being heirs together of the grace of life; that your prayers be not hindered'.

80 Thomas Gataker, *A good wife Gods gift and, a wife indeed. Two mariage sermons*, London: John Haviland, 1623, p. 63.

81 Cleaver, 1998, p. 191; Whately, 1619, p. 208.

82 Cleaver, 1598, p. 229.

83 Whately, 1619, p. 98.

84 Cleaver, 1598, p. 89, and Juan Luis Vives, *The Office and Duty of an Husband*, London: John Cawood, 1555, E1v.

85 Gataker, 1623, pp. 62–3.

86 The final closeness is of course the 'one body' which the couple make. Gouge offers the following analogy for wife-beaters: 'furious, franticke, mad, desperate persons will cut their armes, legs, and other parts, mangle their flesh, hang, drowne, smother, choake, and stab themselves', 1622, p. 78.

87 Cleaver, 1598, pp. 142, 151.

88 Gataker, 1623, pp. 5–6.

89 Gouge, 1622, p. 367.

90 Cleaver, 1598, p. 68, p. 91.

91 Cleaver, 1598, pp. 92–3; for a full discussion of the wife's active supervision see Natasha Korda, *Shakespeare's Domestic Economies: Gender and Property in Early Modern England*, Philadelphia: University of Pennsylvania Press, 2002, chapter 3.

92 Cleaver, 1598, p. 92.

93 As Mendelson and Crawford put it, 'Women of every social and matrimonial status assumed a kind of "psychological" or "moral" proprietorship of goods and possessions through their knowledge, labour, and customary use', 1998, p. 219.

94 Gouge, 1622, pp. 258–9.

95 Gouge, 1622, p. 301. He continues: 'the use of the body is a proper act of the matrimonial bond, wherein the difference betwixt superiority and subjection appeareth not: the wife hath as great a power over the husbands body as the husband over the wives, which is not so in the goods, no one thing can be named wherein the power and authority of the husband more consisteth, then in the goods.'

96 Amussen, 1988, p. 63.

97 CCAL X.10.3 f.43v, 1548.

98 CCAL X.10.2 f.16, 1541.

99 CCAL 39.9 f.126, 1580.

100 CCAL X.10.6 f.126v, 1556. For similar tropes in the London evidence see Gowing, 1996, pp. 197, 206.

101 De Certeau's descriptions of the creative use of a culture 'disseminated and imposed by the "elites" producing the language' can helpfully be applied to this resourceful kind of activity. He points out how proverbs, for instance, are '*marked by* uses; they offer to analysis the *imprints of acts* or of processes of enunciation', *The Practice of Everyday Life*, Berkeley, London: University of California Press, 1984, pp. 21, xiii. His distinction between 'place' as something stable and 'space' as '*a practiced place*' – for instance, 'the street geometrically defined by urban planning is transformed into a space by walkers' – is relevant here and throughout, p. 117.

102 For a detailed analysis of the operation and changing meanings of formal hospitality amongst the elite in the period see Felicity Heal, *Hospitality in Early Modern England*, Oxford: Oxford University Press, 1990.

103 CCAL X.10.8 f.82v, 1561.

104 CCAL X.10.11 f.210v, 1570.

105 In Gowing's London evidence too, 'The word "private" was frequently associated with illicit sex; locking a door was good ground for suspicion', 2000, p. 36. See also her thought-provoking discussions of early modern privacy in 1996, passim, esp. pp. 70–2, 269–70. For the euphemistic use of this trope see CCAL X.10.13 f.156v, 1571, where a woman claims the moral high ground by stating, 'I have never been locked in a chamber from my husband', as the man to whom she addresses herself had with another's wife. For a stimulating discussion of public and private in seventeenth- and eighteenth-century London see Melville, 1999, chapter 3.

106 CCAL X.10.8 f.203, 1562.

107 Fenner, 1592, p. 37; however, Gouge reprimands those men who 'living themselves in one place (suppose at London) send their wives unto some countrey house, and there even mew them up, as Hawkes, never caring to come at them, but are then most merrie, when their wives are farthest off', Gouge, 1622, p. 234; Cleaver, 1598, p. 60; Fenner, 1592, p. 43. The acutely paradoxical nature of the advice on this issue

can be seen in Fenner's concern that men 'keepe not the authority and chiefdome in all matters: that women usurp any part of it', p. 35.

108 CCAL X.10.15 f.92, 1566. This case offers a reminder that Coke's famous assertion that 'the house of everyman is to him as his Castle' was a prelude to a discussion of the moments when public officers could legitimately enter its doors, Sir Edward Coke, *An Exact Abridgement in English*, London: M. Simmons for Matthew Walbancke, and H. Twyford, 1651, book 5, pp. 221–3. See Ingram's pertinent insistence that 'these spying cases did not represent normal, spontaneous, neighbourly behaviour but carefully planned, *legally purposeful* activity', 1987, p. 245.

109 For detailed analysis of the position of lodgers within the early modern London house see Melville, 1999, passim.

110 CCAL X.10.12 f.79v, 1564.

111 Similar tropes of a wife's use of household space and the positions taken up by the deponent are common to the London evidence, Gowing, 1996, pp. 188–206.

112 CCAL X.10.12 f.80, 1564.

113 CCAL X.11.3 f.74ff, 1598.

114 Lena Orlin's work on the physical realities of such gaps and openings should be borne in mind here, 2005. I am not arguing that such a hole did not exist, rather about the reasons for *saying* one existed. For the wide significance of this trope see Gowing, 1996, p. 190.

115 My italics.

116 Heather Dubrow connects domestic transgressions to the distinction between *heimlich* and *unheimlich* because of the way they 'parody the familiar in general and the familial in particular', 1999, p. 13, and, as Terence Hawkes points out, the one defines the other through their contradistinction. Hawkes, *Shakespeare in the Present*, London, New York: Routledge, 2002, p. 11: 'the *heimlich* is defined by the fact that the *unheimlich* appears'.

2

'Choose thee a bed and hangings for a chamber; Take with thee everything that hath thy mark': objects and spaces in the early modern house

RECONSTRUCTING THE MORAL dynamics of household spaces leaves half the story of domestic life untold, of course. Every room that was crossed and every door that was shut enclosed the objects which made spaces into houses. Early modern men and women had a great deal invested in the possessions they used in their daily lives. The things with which their households were furnished were caught up in what Keith Wrightson has called the 'recasting of the economic world', a reorientation towards a market economy.[1] Wealth was often invested in objects, but it was also *displayed* through objects. They articulated social status and the familial, affective and gendered relationships between individuals.

William Harrison, faced with the considerable task of describing his country, followed his opening disquisitions on the church, the universities and the counties of the land with an explication 'Of Degrees of People in the Commonwealth of England'. These divisions came early on in his description because they were central to contemporary political projects. They were also crucial for the sumptuary legislation which set materiality at the heart of the troubled connections between different ways of achieving status.[2] Harrison's subsequent structural divisions of the nation involve such categories as towns, land, commerce, religion, animals and of course food and diet, apparel and attire, and 'the manner of building and furniture of our houses'. Many of his categories are materially orientated and this allows him to refer back to his initial status divisions, playing them out from their ideological centre into the dizzying detail of the gradations of hunting dogs and the distinctions in doublets. Describing England partly entailed recounting the way in which its visual appearance reflected and advertised its social structures and their moral connotations.

Within the category of domestic objects, Harrison identifies substantial recent change. He notes that 'The furniture of our houses ... is grown in manner even to passing delicacy'. Beginning at the top of society, he homes in on items particularly suggestive of this new 'delicacy': 'Certes in noblemen's houses it is not rare to see abundance of arras, rich hangings of tapestry, silver vessels, and so much other plate as may furnish sundry cupboards to the sum oftentimes of a thousand or two thousand pounds at the least, whereby the value of this and the rest of their stuff doth grow to be almost inestimable.' The way the domestic articulates the wealth and status of the nobility almost reaches the limits of expression in its profusion of provision. Moving down to the next of his four large social groups, he notes that, 'Likewise in the houses of knights, gentlemen, merchantmen, and some other wealthy citizens', it is possible to 'behold generally their great provision of tapestry, Turkey work, pewter, brass, fine linen, and thereto costly cupboards of plate, worth five or six hundred or a thousand pounds to be deemed by estimation.' According to the old men of Harrison's village, who provide evidence of social change from their long memories, the 'abundance' of the nobility and the 'great provision' of the gentility are now, for the first time, echoed even further down the social scale. Whereas 'in times past the costly furniture stayed there', now 'it is descended yet lower even unto the inferior artificers and many farmers'. Those who labour for their living with their hands have, 'learned also to garnish their cupboards with plate, their joined beds with tapestry and silk hangings, and their tables with carpets and fine napery'.[3]

At each stage in the social hierarchy Harrison picks out the same categories of goods – fabrics for decoration and vessels for dining. He does identify subtle but resonant differences – the nobleman's arras, tapestry and silver; the citizen's turkeywork,[4] pewter and brass; the farmer's bedhangings, table carpets and linens – but the overall thrust implicit in his argument about the wonderful change in furnishing is that society is becoming more coherent in its domestic practice. Across the social scale people were beginning to *share* a common sense of more refined ('delicate') and therefore superior domestic interiors, and to enjoy notably more luxurious and comfortable living accommodation than their forebears. This is not the consumer revolution of the later seventeenth and eighteenth centuries, where new types of furniture, china and utensils for hot drinks were acquired, often from Far Eastern markets, for their novelty and their association with novel domestic practices.[5] It is, perhaps, its precursor: an interest in directing funds towards domestic goods, albeit larger numbers of 'traditional' items like linens and pewter, amongst those below the status of the gentry.

Harrison's lists demonstrate the various ways in which objects carried information about status: through the material from which they were constructed (arras and pewter), through the function they served (bedhangings and napery) and through the way they were displayed (silver plate exhibited on the cupboard). It is the consonance of particular objects and specific forms of behaviour which characterise 'delicate' living in *The Description*, a lifestyle which the labourer has had to 'learn' as a whole new set of practices from his betters.

In the broadest terms, recent investigations of material life have borne out Harrison's assertions. The material culture of domestic life was expanding at the end of the sixteenth century. In basic terms, households were filled with more goods in 1600 than they had been in the 1560s and a shift in attitudes towards domestic possessions, clearly marked but hard to quantify, accompanied their proliferation.[6] People owned larger numbers of featherbeds, many more stools and chairs. They owned different types of tables of different shapes and sizes, and an enormous number of tablecloths which they kept in more chests and cupboards. Beds, seating and storage facilities were increasingly likely to be found in larger numbers in households across the social scale, whereas increases in ownership of curtains, cushions and carpets, cupboard cloths and pieces of silverware seem to have been confined to more prosperous households.[7] These were not, by and large, *new* items, they were varieties of the old which permitted diversity in day-to-day practice.

This was a crucial period of change in the material household: shifting economic patterns were leading to consumerist tendencies, increasing the numbers of domestic objects very considerably over a short period of time; and yet there were still few enough items around the house for each to have a very personal and intimate significance. Later, when a much wider *variety* of objects were owned, things would be very different. In one way, domestic items became less significant as their numbers increased because they became more common. But in another way, the expanding ownership of domestic items seems to have been causing a kind of nostalgia about the uniqueness of objects. England was poised between two extremes: the conservative domestic culture of its medieval heritage, less socially 'visible' because it was not linked to social change, and a new one in which objects were necessarily divorced from their connections to familial transformation and ancestral mnemonics because they were too diverse, too novel, and too ephemeral in their charms.

For a society balanced between domestic plenty and relative paucity, still mid-way in Harrison's process of the downwards diffusion of abundance, household items were usefully capable of fusing economic with other meanings. The information about status which Harrison identified in the furnishings of the household was just one aspect of the complex language spoken by early modern domestic objects. They also had the potential to carry information about human relationships, to maintain a close connection with the spaces in which they were kept, and to offer mnemonic access to the occasions on which they became a part of the household. Whilst these meanings were commonly understood, their particular manifestation was profoundly affected by status and by gender. In what follows, individuals' descriptions of their household are examined as evidence of broader cultural patterns of thought about domestic materiality.

Such information is important for an understanding of domestic tragedy in several ways. Primarily, it demonstrates just how much was invested, culturally, ideologically and personally, in the household. Beyond this it continues the process of reconstruction of those ideas about the house which audiences might have brought with them to the theatre. I am arguing here for a notion of the domestic which was inherently metonymic – one in which individual objects repeatedly stood for, made reference to and negotiated between whole environments. These meanings were available to be exploited through the use of props and other indications of domestic space, and responses to the drama were conditioned by the extent of their common currency amongst the audience.

DOMESTIC GOODS AS BEQUESTS

Domestic goods, discounting the extraordinary fortunes of discovery or pilfery, were most likely to be made within the home, bought from a manufacturer or a previous owner, or given either as gift or post-mortem bequest. As recent work has established, the balance between these different ways of acquiring goods was changing in this period, as households moved from domestic production to the purchase of a wider range of items in the marketplace.[8] But this very shift was focusing attention on the method by which objects were acquired, giving their provenance an added significance.

The evidence explored here demonstrates the primary importance of the interaction between objects and the lifecycle of the family. The meanings of individual items were constructed around marriage and death, tying these fundamental familial disjunctures to the objects which symbolised changing circumstances and relationships. Marriage and death constituted the two events at which material property was likely to change hands in the most obvious, physical, sense of changing location. And because both events involved changes to the personnel of the household, they offered the greatest challenge to the continuity of family-determined patterns of domestic life: to the coherence of the social and cultural meanings which Harrison identified in the use of particular kinds of object.

The evidence analysed here comes from last wills and testaments, because such documents offered their writers an important context in which to display their understanding of the significance of their goods.[9] Following the complex processes surrounding the production of the document, those objects given in wills were spoken by the deceased, written into the manuscript, read back to the witnesses, reread in the church or other public place, and finally discussed within the community as they were distributed by the executors. Even those making an inventory of the deceased's goods were often made aware of the intended destination of the willed items, lending a considerable and officially documented cultural visibility to such a way of transferring ownership. Writing objects into wills makes them a part of the ritualised, as opposed to the informal, transfer of ownership. It gives *personal* meanings and relationships an interestingly *communal* status which was symbolised by the physical movement of the object itself across the boundary between houses in those cases where altered ownership meant changed location.

Each individual object gains a meaning from its position in relation to all the others which the testator might leave – both those with which it shares a discursive space in the document, and those which were not given. To understand fully the value of a bequest the recipient must be aware, either directly through experience or indirectly through cultural probability, of all the objects they might have been given. This is part of a more general contemporary tendency to understand objects metonymically. In pre-mortem transfers, all of a person's goods were given through a deed of gift, but the written record of the legal transaction was symbolically represented by the accompanying gesture of handing over a single item to stand for the whole.

So when Stephen Ruck, erstwhile mayor of the port of Sandwich in Kent, transferred his estate to his young son Matt who was himself sick of the 'yellow jaundice', he 'delivered him a goblet or cup as part therof in the name of the whole'.[10] There was a clear contemporary facility and willingness to consider the one as a metonym for the many, where discrete collections of material objects were closely interrelated in the imagination.

THE LANGUAGE OF BEQUEST

The descriptions which testators give of their possessions offer vital evidence for the particular aspects of the objects which they considered most striking.[11] Their descriptions distinguish between items of course, but in doing so they simultaneously identify objects and mark them out as special – worthy of the extra time and paper consumed in recording them in detail. These descriptions extend beyond the need to discriminate between different beds or chests into a pride in their status-defining qualities and a sensitivity to their histories.[12]

Testators drew attention to the family provenance of the goods which they left by stressing the history of the object's ownership. For instance, Stephen Hollinden of Canterbury gives his son Lawrence 'a brasse pott that was my father's', and Richard Allen, also of Canterbury, gives his young son John the ring 'my mother gave me'. These men see the value of the objects they give their sons as lying partly in their connection to a previous generation. For women, the implications of such a practice are rather different. Katherine Kingwood of Tenterden gives her son Thomas 'the stayne clothe[13] that was my father's'. The cloth suggests the importance of household possessions in maintaining a sense of dynastic identity in the face of the loss of family name which comes with marriage. The language she uses to pass the object on to her son suggests that Katherine's ancestry had meaning through these objects, and it draws attention to his position in relation to his matrilineal family.[14]

The gift both defines and reflects upon individual identity, foregrounding the individual's position across three generations of a family. Such time-depth is of course comparatively rare, and much more common are bequests which draw attention to provenance across two generations. Several testators mark an object's connection to a predeceased spouse. In addition to his grandmother's ring, Richard Allen also gives his son the great cauldron 'that was his mother's', and Martin Brooke gives his wife's daughter a 'blacke se[a]med sheete which was her mother's'. Christopher Courthop, a gentleman of St Dunstan's parish in Canterbury gives his son John two blankets 'of his mother's spynnynge', and Henry Larke of Faversham gives his daughter Elizabeth a silver ring 'which was hir mother's weddynge rynge'.[15]

The significant number of bequests from men of their late wives' goods suggests that these gifts form a kind of unofficial testament on behalf of the mother, or at least a recognition by her husband that the fact that she made or once used these items will give them greater worth as a gift to her children.[16] However, it is not only women's wishes which are respected in this way, Elizabeth Bespytch divides between her son and daughter the six silver spoons her husband gave her in his will.[17]

These descriptions are part of an official, technical discourse which ensured that wishes were respected by enshrining them in legally meaningful phrases; in doing so it drew attention to memories of ownership: Alice Pinnock of Sandwich, for instance, gives her married daughter Margery Brown a bedstead and bedding 'in a full satisfaction of her father's bequeth' which she is already using. This stresses the idea of a kind of guardianship of goods, through which a testator can entrust the control of objects within his generation for the use of the next. John Wilde of Woodnesborough gives back 'so much pewter' as was in his sister's inventory to his nieces when he makes his own will, along with their mother's great chest. Presumably keeping careful note of what was due to his nieces throughout the time between his sister's death and his own, his will suggests that members of the wider family were also used as protectors of children's rights to property.[18]

But in many cases it seems that formal guardianship of the objects from will to will is less the intention than a desire to record previous ownership for the added affective value which it gives to the bequest. John Elner gives his son Bartholomew two rings, including the 'greatest set with a stone' from his brother-in-law, and James Pettyt gives his sister a chest that 'was my brother's'. Within wider kinship networks the same system operates: Alice Wilde gives her godson a chest 'which was his mothers standing at my beddes feet', for instance.[19] Thomas Crispe elucidates the material continuity implicit in these bequests, willing his son Samuel two spoons, one of which 'shalbe *the selfe same* spone which his godmother gave unto him'.[20] These gifts clearly do not merely represent attempts to ensure adequate financial recompense for past legacies.

At the other end of this process of looking far into the future to safeguard the provenance of household items, testators can be seen considering the future of their possessions beyond the death of the initial recipients. Isabel Glover gives her sister a great kettle and a harness girdle which are to go to the sister's daughter after her death. Nicholas Upton, a jurat of Faversham, gives his son a bedstead and cupboard in the chamber over the hall, after the death of the testator's wife, and Lewes Jones gives his son a great brass pot, a chafer, and a great stupnet,[21] but with the stipulation that his wife should have use of them during her life.[22]

Wishes, and with them memories, extend across time. They are preserved over several generations; taken on by women as the intentions of their sisters, and then by daughters as the desires of their mothers. These brief narratives of non-elite thinking about objects suggest that testamentary structures encouraged individuals to consider their household possessions as a focus for memory and a structure for understanding familial relationships in the widest sense. Some individuals are of course especially sensitive to the familial provenance of goods. Henry Aldey, for instance, gives to his cousin Thomas Wydehope 'my silver and gilt standing cup with a cover which was his aunt's', to another cousin a silver spoon 'which was his aunt's with the ymage of christ uppon the topp of the same' and to his sister 'my playne rynge of goulde which was my wive's'.[23] As a gentleman living in Canterbury high street and preparing to be buried in the south aisle of the Cathedral, Aldey's sense of family identity might be expected to be strong. But there is, nevertheless, no rigid connection between material *sensibility* and social status – individuals with only a few items to leave also attach such significance to them.

In contrast to the homogeneity of rights over domestic objects which the household manuals valorised, these narratives show a particular sensitivity to different types of possession. At any one time, the objects which served daily routines might have combined the extended wishes of several individuals, memories of their eventual owners essential to preserve, and their relationship to past and future held in mind. Using household goods on a daily basis clearly meant, on some level, using-in-relation-to-provenance, seeing individual objects as related to a history which might indicate an emotional response, but also a set of domestic practices peculiar to the way in which they were used by their original owners. These meanings must have come into focus at moments of life crisis, and perception of the unique qualities of domestic life sharpened as the family grew or diminished.

This focus on objects is suggestive. Money is interchangeable – its worth is not inherent in its form; livestock die and are born between the making and the execution of testaments; property and land are divided between individuals in less material ways than spoons. Necessarily, smaller items which are in daily use bear the weight of the transmission of familial identity and emotional connections to the dead. But the use of domestic objects differs from that of, for instance, clothing. Doublets and kirtles, cloaks and petticoats have had exclusive use in the lifetime of the testator, and their closeness to the body forms a clear bond between object and identity.[24] Domestic goods are used by all, in the sense that they may be handled by many within the household. But their use is also common because the fruits of the labours in which they are employed are shared by all, in cooking, eating and sleeping, and this defines a notion of belonging and of community.

Some wills, however, stress the opposite of this connective quality of the material, foregrounding instead the disjunctures of change as the significant element of the objects which are given. Again in response to legal distinctions, many contain reference to both the items which women brought with them to marriage and the event of marriage itself as a temporal marker by which goods can be distinguished. George Stransham of Faversham, for instance, gives his wife Joan two silver goblets which he had bought 'since the . . . mariage' and 'one paier of braclettes which I redeemed for her since the marriage'. Robert Marden of Tenterden gives to Margaret his wife 'all such howseolde and howseolde stuff as she browghte unto me at our marriage or which I had with her at the tyme of mariage', John Crothall of Tenterden gives to his daughter Winifred a chest 'which my wife brought me', and James Benchkin of Canterbury gives back to his wife Katherine an English Bible, a testament and two English Psalters which were hers before he married her.[25] The 'marks', to which the quotation from Heywood's play which heads this chapter refers, existed to define visually just such ways of grouping objects.

These descriptions are partly generated by the legally binding terms of jointures or dowries, and such terms therefore inculcate a pattern of thought in which objects come to stand for the temporal progression through life. Although part of the joined household of husband and wife, these items are still recognised as having distinct provenances. Particularly in a time of high instances of remarriage, the significance of the temporal and familial specificity of objects was clearly important to maintain, and to direct towards appropriate kin. John Harris, for example, gives his young daughter all his 'last wiffe's' linen, and Richard Watters gives his wife Faith all she brought with her to their marriage, plus his other wife's best gown.[26] The detail suggests the nature of this type of emotive significance: not a mawkish sentimentality, but a record of past relationships and their material remains. Marriage, at least in 'ideal' principle, formed an independent domestic environment, in a house of a couple's own, and in the same way that it linked two people, so it linked their goods: two parts (not necessarily equal) of the same whole, rather than an integration which destroys individuality. Individuals and objects correspond very closely in their formation of household.

Domestic objects' perceived ability to carry and transfer identity is perhaps most clearly represented by the ubiquitous chest. This is most prominent in the evidence for dowry chests, where young girls' marital identity is kept safe for them until they come of age. John Neale's daughter Margaret, for example, is given a whole range of domestic objects which are to be 'put in a cheste and there safely to be kepte . . . until the day of her mariage'.[27] But chests are significant for men too: John Allen, for instance, receives a joined chest from his father Richard 'which I browght to Canterbury and all the evydence and wrytinges therein' concerning his father's lands and tenements.[28] As Richard changed his geographical location so this chest, which contained and protected his most important documents, provided a link between one part of his life and the next. There is a strong sense of the need to perpetuate for the next generation physical continuities which had provided comfort and coherence in the past, and the portable space of the chest neatly encapsulates the important items of identity which are needed in a world where service or migration into towns was a reality for many.

The domestic object as bequest both marks difference and provides continuity: it offers the opportunity to explore a series of rites of passage or radical changes in the life of the testator, but it can also bridge disjunctures, and its very physicality can have a cohesive power in times of change. There is a stability inherent in this conception of household objects which offers a powerful image of the domestic as rooted in time, and in the community of human connections with both the living and the dead.

Some individuals, however, also draw attention to objects which have a provenance outside of the family, referring to the places where the items were purchased, or the person from whom they were bought. Edward Knight of Woodnesborough, for instance, gives his wife Cicely a brewing kettle which was bought at Word and a broad pan which was bought at Sandwich, a few miles from where they lived.[29] William Gayny of Sandwich wills that a joyned 'court cubberd which I lately bought at London and intend to place in the parlour' should remain in his house for his heirs for ever.[30] Such descriptions place objects relative to the event of purchase, and set them against the household as it stood at that moment. But there is evidence to suggest that a stronger sense of individual agency was ascribed to such bequests. Knight additionally mentions the people from whom he has purchased his cart and his bed, but he identifies no bequests from members of his family. He was not an insubstantial man but he seems to have showed a pride in his own achievements rather than evincing an interest in family heritage.

The preamble to the will of Jose de Toor of Sandwich elucidates this relationship between patrimony and personal agency particularly self-consciously. Jose, a Flemish woolman living in Sandwich at his death, begins his testament quite conventionally by referring to the disposition of the goods God has given and lent him. However, he also declares his intention to dispose of those goods which he has 'conquered' himself.[31] The choice of vocabulary indicates the perceived possibilities for advancement in this period, and the significance of material possessions as a way of articulating the successful exploitation of those opportunities. The relationship between goods conquered and goods passed on points to a multiplicity of meanings for the domestic object in relation to the identity of both giver and receiver, one closely tied to the connections between individual and familial identity in a period of social change.

The 'national' social information about the use of domestic items which Harrison gives is in this manner particularised and personalised: the way Henry Aldey used his 'silver and gilt standing cup with a cover', for instance, combines with the general cultural meanings of such vessels. Harrison clearly saw domestic possessions and practices as specific to different status groups, and individuals appear to have been acutely aware of their connections to status, but also to have viewed them as carrying the personal qualities of their owners' individual identity. The particular and the general come together in the physicality of the object.

OBJECTS AND SPACES

Objects were not only woven into networks of kinship and community through testamentary discourses, they were also carefully located within the household by testators who were sensitive to the significance of their physical position. Writing the object's location into the will, for instance the great new featherbed 'as it standeth in the grene parlour', stresses its connections to the room in which it was kept and used, and literally brings its context to mind.[32] These types of description are connected to the specific function of the object. By drawing attention to, for example, a chest as being in the parlour, the appropriateness of that particular chest to the domestic routines carried on in the room is stressed: it might suggest a specific size or style of chest especially associated with one type of item. By describing the bequest in such a way, the testator is drawing attention to his own organisation of the domestic interior, that which he considers fitting and appropriate. When the beneficiary receives the chest, an explicit spatial context comes with it: placing it within their own parlour invites comparisons (physical, economic, hierarchical, aesthetic and mnemonic) between the two spaces.

These connections take on a rich additional significance in the case of the bed of the testator, frequently described as 'that which I now lie upon'.[33] If, as is borne out by the dates of the testaments and their probates, the majority of these wills are being written upon the deathbed, then the bed 'which I now lie upon' might be more than a phrase which refers to habitual use, it might also be an indication of the context of the production of the will itself.[34] The deathbed scene offers a conventional image, familiar across many different media from woodcuts to plays. Large numbers of testamentary court cases offer narratives of such events: when William Knell writes Thomas Wood's will, for instance, he is 'sitting apon a stole nere to a trikkill bed wher the testator did lye sicke in his bed'. He describes an event at which the testator is the subject of everyone's attention, centrally positioned in his bed as he describes the bequests he wishes to leave. Knell's particular image is of the intimacy of close concentration in the night: 'he saiethe that the curat did sitte apon the side of the bed, and hold the candell'.[35] Lying upon his bed, surrounded by friends, relatives and spiritual advisers, the will-maker has a particular perspective on the goods he devolves. The household which is organised around him can be subtly shifted – its ownership transferred even if its physical constitution stays the same. Items are described in concentric circles of proximity: the featherbed 'that lieth under the bed that I lie on', the chair 'by my bedsyde', or my chest 'now standinge at my bedes feete'.[36] If we consider the will as the product of an event, then the testator's chamber is its ground: the room encloses the process and gives it context. To give your own bed to your son as he stands next to it situates it in relation to the process of will making, and focuses the emotions involved in such an event into the object.

The spatial connection which testators make between objects is a part of their wider interest in the 'wholeness' of domestic space, the way objects and furnishings come together in rooms. They are concerned, for instance, to preserve the unity of their furnishings by bequeathing them to a single individual. Edward Knight wills to his son John the bed, the bedstead, the table, the cupboard, the form, and the painted cloths from his parlour, almost every object in the room.[37] But he gives these goods on the understanding that none of them will be removed from its position. And he is not alone in underlining the importance of the relationship between specific pieces of furniture and particular rooms. Robert Fayle of Faversham leaves instructions that the table, form and wainscot[38] in his hall should not be moved, neither should the walnut tree ceiling in the little new parlour, or the cupboard, table, form, bedstead, new featherbed or new boughton work[39] coverlet lying on it.[40]

There are also examples of explicit concern for the form of a room: Elizabeth Bassock in 1583 says 'the hall I will not have stirred as longe as my leace last'.[41] Other testators are anxious about the fate of particular types of furniture: William Gervise of Tenterden is concerned that the beds, tables, forms, shelves, cupboards, pans and brass pots should remain to the use of his son William in his house, and others still leave particular instructions about the fate of their fixtures and fittings: William Gayny of Sandwich wishes all his glass and wainscot to remain in his dwelling house for his heirs for ever.[42]

Such instructions are obviously linked in many cases to a wish to provide suitable furnishings for the house when it comes into the hands of the testator's children, and to avoid the risk of spouses selling off the most valuable of the household goods before this time.[43] John Iden indicates the possible consequences of such a denuding of the house when he gives his lease of the White Hart to his wife Richardine, 'provided allwayes that it shall not be lawfull for my sayde wife nor her executors or assignes to take and carry away any the longe settles nor glasse wydowes fastned in the white harte and leave that howse destitute'.[44] Like clothing to the body, domestic objects, and especially the fixtures and fittings which are directly applied to the fabric of the house, cover it in an appropriate and becoming manner. These testamentary discourses deal explicitly with threats to the household, imagining the disjunctions of death as involving the possibility of differing attitudes and priorities with regards to the domestic interior; the importance of the personal over the familial, the pragmatic over the long term.

Many of these additions to properties are also obvious signifiers of status; they are examples of the objects which Harrison pinpoints as being especially effective transmitters of such information, and they must be preserved in order to ensure that the future generations are able to maintain the social position attained by their parents. When whole rooms are left intact, there is clearly an attempt to prescribe a spatial organisation, to impose a way of ordering the household on the next generation, by insisting on the right relationship between object and room. For instance, Edmund Deale, whose wife Elizabeth was called 'bytche foxe whoore' as she sat outside his house in Canterbury, is quite explicit in his bequest to her of the best featherbed in the chamber over the buttery with its tester,[45] valance[46] and curtains of white and green silk, which was 'occupied in the same chamber'.[47] These examples suggest that even the relatively low-status individuals discussed here saw their domestic environment as a representation of personal taste and social status, and that the coherence of these meanings was significant enough to them for them to go to some lengths to preserve it. Despite the tendency of this type of evidence to compartmentalise individual things and people into the discrete units of bequests, testators spend a considerable amount of time attending to the coherence of the rooms themselves. In this period of increasing social mobility, the dynamic between stability and change, the familial and the personal, is under a scrutiny which is expressed in domestic terms.

BIOGRAPHIES OF DOMESTIC POSSESSION

The goods which testators bequeathed clearly held the weight of the transfer of a notion of 'household' between friends and relatives and from one generation to the next. Understanding which objects were particularly significant in such transmissions suggests the range of meanings which cohere around them in other types of representation, not least as the stage properties used in plays. The limits of the conceivable stretch from the ubiquitous chest to items which are much more rarely given.[48] Into the latter category fall seating, books, fireplace equipment, embellishments such as curtains and wall hangings, and fixtures and fittings such as window glass and wainscot.[49] Windows may be rarely given because they were infrequently owned, particularly at the start of the period, and because they fall into the curious category of 'just about moveables' – connected to the fabric of the house but capable of being removed. Stools are different, however, as they were an essential household item, but clearly not thought especially suitable as a bequest. Some rarely owned specialist items such as looms, and objects apparently considered inappropriate as gifts such as spinning wheels and close stools, seem to represent a different kind of gift – a rare exception at the farthest reaches of testators' strategies. Also in this category are shelves, benches, valances, testers and fringes for beds, desks, ladders, lutes, combs and looking glasses.[50]

Pragmatic considerations are clearly tempered by a conception of appropriateness which singles out those substantial pieces of furniture which formed the focus of the rooms in which they were kept: beds, cupboards and tables are all popular, as are chests and the important items of dining equipment which fill them. It may well be that stools, for instance, were routinely given outside the context of the will, but ownership of them did not carry this particularly heightened kind of significance. There is no direct relationship between objects owned in large numbers and popular bequests (silverware is more frequently bequeathed than tables, for instance). Similarly, the probable over representation of wealthier testators does not appear to make the passing on of high-status items such as looking glasses and lutes any more likely. Although some frequently given items were financially valuable, for the gifts as a whole domestic function seems the most important criterion affecting bequeathal.

Looking around an early modern house in the light of this list of common bequests it is clear that the ownership of certain items was significant enough to alter their meaning – to raise the issue of their provenance in the minds of the viewer. And there is a temporal aspect to the development of such significance: particular types of object were more appropriately given to specific individuals at certain points in their life. Understanding these complex notions of appropriateness helps us to reconstruct the links between different types of domestic object, such as hall tables or bedsteads for instance, and the gender and maturity of their owners. If we are to understand the changing significance of such goods and their effect on an individual across their life, it is necessary to reorder the information from individual testaments into a narrative which traces the most probable pattern of receiving and giving for a 'typical' subject.[51]

If one were to follow a representative girl of middling wealth through the matrix of her relationships to different testators, then one would see her household possessions added to in different ways at different stages in her life. As a grandchild she might receive pewter, cooking utensils, and a share of silver spoons, such as the two 'called maiden heads' which John Snothe gives to his granddaughters, and these may, with other goods, be stored in her own chest within her parents' house.[52] The spoons in particular are likely to be part of a larger set, carefully divided between siblings, and her possession of a share of this larger collection would define her as part of that close group within the family. They may well be given with a specific age or status in mind, once she is of twelve years of age, or, more usually, 'at her marriage'.[53] On the death of her godparents, and perhaps in addition to objects they had given her at her christening, she might receive more items towards her dowry: household goods such as 'twelve plain napkins' of linen, the best pewter dish and a brass pan, and sometimes even a chest with a lock and key, explicitly provided for storing these household objects.[54]

When her father died she could add to these items larger stocks of similar things, and perhaps extend her personal stores to another chest, perhaps one 'that was her mother's'.[55] She might also be given a bed and bedding at this point, usually an everyday one, but just occasionally and if her family was of sufficient status the joined bedstead 'standinge in the greate parlor of my mansyon howse'.[56] If any of her brothers or sisters died before she did she might receive additional, possibly more expensive bedding, and maybe another chest with a considerable amount of her sibling's clothing within it, from neckerchers to a black cloth kirtle 'welted[57] with two weltt of velvett'.[58] This, along with a piece of their jewellery, she might then add to her own garments, allowing her a greater variety of apparel, and the possibility of a set of clothes which could be reserved for special occasions.[59] If there was such a crisis within her own generation, its physical consequences would be symbolised by the redistribution of the sets of goods which had initially been divided between siblings.

As a woman of marriageable age, her accumulated goods would become part of the negotiations of her status in the marriage market, representative of her family's prosperity. Her 'worth' within a new household would be partly expressed in the complex relationship between the financial dowry they could provide for her, her material contribution to a new household, her domestic skills, and her personal and physical presence. The way in which men regarded her would be shaped by this intricate image. The objects she added to her store in the process of courtship negotiation might be less valuable but of considerable significance: the household gifts such as knives and candlesticks given to her as markers of the progression of love by her suitors.[60]

On her marriage, her accumulated possessions, at present stored in various rooms within the house where she was living, would join those of her husband. All would be used together, but their provenance would be remembered, and the goods would become symbolic of the unity of marriage in their physical amalgamation, in the way they served the daily needs of the household as a group, but also in the recognisable distinctness of their origin, perhaps as a part of her dowry.[61] They may indeed have had 'her mark' upon them, like 'the spone that hathe the letters of her name graven on the topp' which John Neale gives his daughter Margaret.[62] The items put away in chests she might place in the chamber she shared with her husband. The amount of goods she brought with her, particularly perhaps those in excess of her clothing and cooking utensils, would define the relative status of the couple's families, and provide a sense of continuity with these wider groups of kin. Conversely, however, individual but socially important objects, such as a single silver spoon, might invite esteem of a different type.

After a married life during which their household goods were used in common, ownership of the majority of the bedding and the household stuff in its chests and cupboards might pass into her hands shortly after the death of her husband. This might be limited to 'all such moveables and goodes which were hers before I married with her and none other', or it might include 'all my moveables, plate and juells'; the disparity between the two might reflect previous divisions, strategies and choices made between husband and wife as a part of the legal framework surrounding their marriage, or it might indicate the affective qualities of their union.[63] What she did not own herself would belong to her children, either put away for the future in other chests, or in use, but with the clear knowledge of its final destination. As a widow with children too young to find work, life would be financially testing, but this period would also mark the pinnacle of her control over the goods of the household. When her son came of age and inherited the house, she might move her own lodgings within it to make way for him, perhaps occupying a chamber and having the right to cook and use the communal rooms of the house, 'with free and lawfull entrye ingress egresse and regresse', provisions set up in her husband's will and therefore anticipated throughout the minority of her son.[64] Within her new household, scaled down in terms of domestic activity, its focus now primarily upon herself, the smaller number of objects she used daily may well be close to the dowry goods with which she left her father's home to begin married life. These goods might offer a healing context to the disjunctures of grieving and the physical consequences of her changed position within the hierarchy of the household.

Now that she was no longer running the house, she might also be aware of a reorientation of the friendships and social interactions of which her days consisted. She might begin to spend more time with other widows, drawing comfort from their support and companionship.[65] As these women died she might receive small gifts in their wills, not of the central domestic items necessary to set up new households, but perhaps a petticoat, an old gown or a pair of shoes.[66]

As an older woman, she would then be faced with choices when making her own will. But she would come to this complex process of sensitive division having experienced what it was like to be a beneficiary in a series of different relationships, with a variety of personal and social expectations attached to them. The objects which were hers to bequeath might well include those from her grandparents, her mother and father, her brothers and sisters and her husband, not to mention godparents and friends. As well as acting as an aid to the memory of her relations with those to whom she had been close, these objects would remind her of different stages in her own life, and of the relative experiences of dependence and independence, of levels of control over the domestic routines of the households in which she had lived. Her knowledge of the rooms in which her objects had been used and the routines in which they had been employed would allow her to draw comparisons between the way these households had functioned. Memories of relationships and her position within their relative balances of power in the patriarchal society into which she was born might then be linked to her place within the domestic environment of the giver.[67]

Following a man of appropriate status to be this woman's husband offers a very different narrative of possession and use. As a boy he would perhaps be given his grandfather's best brass pot,[68] or his grandmother's best featherbed,[69] and perhaps some of her silver spoons.[70] As he grew up he would be aware that his ownership of these objects indicated the nature of the household of which he would one day be head, its prosperity and even its aesthetic principles. His ownership of them would begin to dictate his attitude towards domestic items. On his father's death he might, particularly if he was the eldest son, inherit the hall table and forms, the hall cupboard and its embellishments – those items whose ownership symbolised control over the central communal room of the house.[71]

If he was still a child, very little would change physically, apart from the financial hardship caused by his father's death. His ownership of significant items, including the best featherbed with appurtenances, would very rarely have involved actual use.[72] Instead, he would reach his majority in the knowledge of eventual possession, perhaps only after the death or remarriage of his mother.[73] The objects which he inherited and his attitude towards their use would mark his relation to the house as qualitatively different from that of his sisters, even at this early age.

If he was of age, he would take command of the family home, presiding over its communal spaces and responsible for the physical and moral welfare of all those living under its roof. His own successes and failures in the career he chose to follow would be measured by his ability to add to, or the necessity subtracting from, this initial domestic store. After his mother's death he might sleep in his father's bed. If he had brothers, they might leave to set up their own houses, taking some of the contents of his rooms with them, some furniture and some cooking utensils given by father and grandfather.

His father and mother between them would have planned as carefully as they could to balance the needs of the generations against one another, providing first for one another and then for the marriage of their children.[74]

This planning, the purchase of sets of divisible goods such as silver spoons and pewter and additional furniture to provide, for instance, a chest for each child, would enable him and his brothers to form households of their own. He might now begin to purchase goods with his wife if he found success, discussing what was needed and perhaps travelling to the most appropriate place to buy it, or responding to the change of fortune of other families by purchasing the goods they offered for sale.[75]

On his mother's death, he might inherit more household stores, and be able to exercise his control more freely over all the rooms of the house. He might choose to alter it now, by extending it, or by refitting it with panelled walls and decorated ceilings perhaps, as he began to establish himself within the town. As a prosperous craftsman or merchant he might be asked to use his knowledge in the valuation of inventories, moving around the houses of his neighbours, assessing the worth of their household items.[76] This would no doubt sharpen his sense of his own social position in relation to his peers.

The goods which his wife brought with her would express the parity of the status of their families, even as his fundamental legal ownership of them from this point on underlined the disparity of their genders. But there might also be other items within the house, given in trust for friends, for nieces and nephews who may live with him if they are orphaned, or given to his own children by relatives and godparents.[77] These may be used, daily or occasionally, by the women of the household and then returned to the chests in which they are kept. At this point in his life his control over domestic space would be at its height, and the complexity of the groups of domestic goods which he is responsible for, although he may not use them on a daily basis, at its most sophisticated. He can appreciate success and family status through the number, type and quality of these objects, but he must also be aware that such material achievement is dependent upon the honesty of his whole household, especially that of his wife.

As the children of the house leave to set up their own homes, if he lives long enough, he might retire into a section of the property, leaving the majority of it under the control of his eldest son.[78] As an elderly man with time to spare, he might be asked to witness, perhaps to oversee, the wills of his friends and peers.[79] The gifts which they give him in recompense would make a growing collection of personal items, garments such as a 'sleeveless jacket of changeable silk', jewels such as a 'best turkeyse [turquoise]'. They would come with more or less explicit anticipations of reciprocity; the ring 'desyringe hym to be good to my wyef as my whole trust ys in hym'.[80] These bequests would increase his status amongst those who saw him wear them, and they would extend the ties of his professional and personal life within the community beyond the graves of his peers, reminding him perhaps of his own mortality.

Making his own will, perhaps in his father's bed, perhaps in one he had purchased more recently,[81] he must account for all the property which he has been given in trust, ensuring that his own life closes with all 're-placed'. He is perhaps in a position to consider leaving furniture to his grandchildren, imagining their needs in their own domestic spaces as he lies at the centre of his own, his past and their future symbolised in the objects which he can see before him. The domestic goods which he had begun to understand as his own from boyhood, to consider a part of the capital for which he was responsible even though he may never have used the more prosaic of them, would be given away in a final articulation of his domestic role of overall authority.[82] They will be much older now, some perhaps decayed and of much less worth, some long ago relegated to the processes of reuse and recycling which translated the value of their raw materials into other forms, the ones which do remain having a notable durability.

The objects with which this couple's house is filled, organised explicitly into their wills at the time of their death, provide a kind of narrative of the rites of passage which they have experienced, the relatives and friends which they have lost, and the successes and failures of which their life has been constituted. There were many objects which did not fulfil a role in articulating such a narrative, of course: ephemeral items such as the ballads and woodcuts pasted to the chimney breast, the wooden utensils used for everyday meals, the working tools long ago sold off or given to apprentices or sons, and the objects used day in and day out for the production of beer, or puddings or pies.[83] But testamentary discourses intimately link the items which Harrison identified as markers of social status to personal and familial identity: affective and economic, private and public significances merge in the domestic object. Abstracted from their daily use, these things are temporarily 'taken out' of the almost-invisibly familiar routines of the household, and held up to particular scrutiny for their role in these different types of identity.[84] The trajectories described here are underpinned by affective relationships and guaranteed by respect for the wishes of friends and family. In other words, although objects play a central role in negotiating the disjunctures of lifecycle, the comforts and consolations of their material stability are threatened by crimes which jeopardize human relationships: by adulteries and by murders.

Household rooms

The old men in William Harrison's village linked their astonishment at the great 'exchange of vessel' which had taken place within their lifetime to an amazement at the changes which had taken place in the structure of the houses themselves. They noted 'the multitude of chimneys lately erected', a striking contrast with 'their young days', in which 'there were not above two or three, if so many, in most uplandish towns of the realm (the religious houses and manor places of their lords always excepted, and peradventure some great personages)'.[85] Harrison records this change in the roofscape of his parish as indicative of a blurring of the visual clarity with which one could traditionally tell the dwellings of the elite from those of their inferiors. But the increase of chimneys was of course an outward manifestation of more fundamental changes which were taking place inside the late sixteenth-century house: the ceiling over of the open hall which necessitated the transfer of its central fire to a stack at one side.[86]

This process of change saw a decisive move away from the traditional spatial organisation of the house, with its large central hall stretching the full height of the building, with service rooms at one end of it and living quarters at the other. 'Ceiling' the hall sometimes provided one 'Great Chamber' over its whole length, more often several smaller rooms. As the main sleeping accommodation moved upstairs, the parlour began to develop as a new living space on the ground floor. Within the increased number of individual rooms it was possible to differentiate much more clearly between different spaces, both for different activities and for distinct groups of individuals. Between 1560 and 1600, for instance, fewer individuals were sleeping in their halls, a change which indicates a contracting number of functions for each room.[87] Work on London houses has also stressed the expanding provision of separate chambers and privies for male and female servants, changes made possible by a greater number of upstairs chambers.[88] When Crench goes upstairs to 'slip off his shoes' in his master's house, he goes to one of these servants' chambers, shared no doubt with Colbrand.[89]

By the turn of the century, the way in which individuals thought about daily life in relation to their houses was greatly altered. Considering sleep now meant thinking about going upstairs, rather than about rearranging the furniture. Thinking about a meal, the householder might well consider retiring to the parlour rather than eating in the hall. It has also been argued that the division of 'the context of production of material goods and services from the physical and social context of household relations' accelerated in this period, giving much clearer spatial expression to the change between work and leisure and production and consumption.[90] Dividing actions physically is suggestive of a need to separate them mentally: out of mind could now mean out of sight and this nuances the notions of privacy examined above.

Matthew Johnson's description of the way the open hall had constructed relative social status elucidates the significance of spatial change for human relationships. He describes 'those features that stress unequal relations between upper and lower ends – bench fixed against the dais end, wider upper bay, window, positioning of opposed doors at the lower end', and he points out that these are inflexible aspects of a rigid definition of spatialised status. In the new type of house, however, the 'marking of status becomes mobile, through movable goods such as chairs, other furniture and decorative items, and mobile both physically and mentally'.[91] The pragmatism of a changing society, in which status definition was open to subtle negotiations, transferred the method of marking those changes from household spaces to household furnishings. Changing in temporal parallel with the increased specialisation of room use, the relationship between rooms and domestic objects was in flux across society.[92]

Probate inventories, the lists of goods, their value, and the rooms in which they were kept, offer access to the way these status-marking objects were deployed within the house.[93] A quantitative analysis of this material helps to establish the broad outlines of household organisation – the shared meanings of different types of room. But seen in isolation it can be misleading, as it tends to frustrate attempts to understand domestic space as it was *used*. By aggregating data for hundreds of households, the coherence of individual properties, the pragmatic dynamics between the furniture available in a par-ticular hall and the comfort offered by a specific parlour, are lost, along with the qualitative details of the descriptions of objects.[94] The following discus-sion of domestic distinction therefore concentrates on two detailed examples, one of an urban office holder, sometime mayor, and one of a middlingly successful freeman blacksmith. But the descriptions of the rooms of James Nethersole and Richard Moore are situated within a quantitative analysis of the furniture and furnishings in the inventories of their peers, in order to judge their typicality.[95]

The politics of household space
Examining the differences between the households of urban rulers and their subjects offers a different way of understanding how domestic status fitted into the larger political arena of authority outside the front door. Recent writing about Tudor authority has stressed two related aspects, first the fun-damental distinction between administrators of state policy and those to whom they disseminated it, and second the significance of even the most seemingly minor offices in connecting the central administration of the state to each and every one of its subjects. Steve Hindle argues that 'early modern government had a greater social depth than has hitherto been recognised', administered through existing social relationships within communities, to which authority was delegated from the centre.[96]

One of Hindle's central arguments is that those who bore office often appear to be of low social status if that status is measured 'nationally': they might, for instance, be yeomen rather gentlemen. Although inferior in the national hierarchy, they were significant locally: men who took up their position because they perceived themselves as superior within their own communities.[97] In the family, many different kinds of relationship could be reduced to '1. The Governors. 2. Those that must be ruled'. Similarly, Sir Thomas Smith's description of the commonwealth as a four-tiered hierarchy of ranks from gentleman to labourer is crucially undercut, or cut through, by the more fundamental distinction he draws between 'them that bear office, and them that bear none'.[98] Examining communities as a whole, as has been the intention here, is clearly essential under these political circumstances because the dynamic between authority and submission does not always, perhaps does not usually, coincide with national definitions of status. This more fundamental distinction between positions of authority and submission is also a division which helps to unravel some of the problems of seeing domestic tragedies as plays 'about' or 'for' a particular social group.[99]

Recent work has made it increasingly clear that power and authority were not solely expressed through acts of governance but were also conveyed through the complex codings of a politicised elite culture. Anna Bryson argues that 'we need to get to grips with the concepts, values, and codes of conduct which underpinned the power and authority of the elite in early modern England . . . to understand what an aristocratic social order means, culturally and not just in some rather narrow sense of the word, politically'.[100] In a similar way, the daily activities of those who ruled are of central importance to our understanding of the way in which they constructed their authority. For Anthony Fletcher the cultural aspects through which power was articulated include 'Every nuance of daily life and activity – clothes, speech, modes of address, assumptions about social intercourse'.[101]

The lower down the social scale one pushes the dynamic of governance, the narrower the economic distinctions between ruler and ruled are likely to be, and the more important behaviour is likely to become in the marking of superiority. The perceived distance between lawmaker and citizen was necessarily complicated by being personalised through repeated contact, through market transaction, through physical proximity, through the clear and inescapable fact of common humanity with its faults and foibles. Here, opportunities for display of household government must become central to peers' assessment of an individual's fitness to rule.[102] But Fortescue insisted 'that . . . even the smallest of hamlets contained "householders of the sort commonly called franklin, well off in possessions" . . . and "many yeomen, sufficient in patrimony" to bear local office'.[103] If patrimony and possessions, lineage and family wealth are criteria for government, then the household becomes a key arena in which to advertise relative social superiority.[104] The fact that the two inventories analysed in detail here are for households headed by men is in itself instructive. It was between men that social competition grew, but their household stuff was given meaning by behaviour, by reputation and moral honesty: it was women's sexual honesty and appropriate public behaviour upon which their efforts depended.

NARRATIVES OF THE HOUSE

An inventory of the goods of James Nethersole, alderman of Canterbury, was made on 29 October 1582.[105] Nethersole's goods were laid out, inspected, priced, and listed by his peers, men who had been in command of the town at various points over the last twenty years and who continued to hold power and influence. These men included Henry Aldey, whose will was particularly sensitive to the provenance of domestic objects, and who had been mayor in 1560. These were the kind of men on whom the weight of Tudor government rested. Nethersole himself had been mayor three times. He was the man who had slipped on his nightgown and left the comfort of his own house to help a dying man in the night, his deposition employing the trope of good neighbourhood and the permeability of the walls of the home.[106]

He had what was, in many ways, a remarkable civic career in Canterbury. The links he formed through the marriage of his daughters, and the success enjoyed by his son, who became mayor after him, characterise the Nethersoles as one of only a few families to make an impact as a group on urban politics, and this is in itself significant.[107] In a town whose population doubled from around 3,500–3,600 in the 1560s to 6,000 by the mid seventeenth century, families who stayed could really make their mark.[108] He was a prominent businessman with a thriving brewing business, the debts he was owed 'on tales 29 October 1582 for beer' alone amounting to £61 5s 9d. (Tales were credit accounts, often kept by scoring a piece of wood.) Amongst those who can be shown to have purchased their beer from him were a common councillor, and two men who were subsequently mayors of the town, so he was clearly able to develop a mutual connection between his civic and economic successes.[109]

But Nethersole's career was unique also because of the controversy which surrounded it. His rapid promotion to alderman in 1562 was in the context of a major shake-up of the ruling elite which followed a disputed mayorial election. In his first term as mayor he managed to have the previous incumbent Fyssher dismissed and his freedom withdrawn. Fyssher was reinstated in 1570, and it was he who took over when Nethersole himself was removed after only one month of his second term as mayor in 1572, and dismissed from the aldermanic bench in his turn after an accusation of financial irregularity.[110] At the instigation of no lesser person than the Earl of Leicester, Nethersole was reinstated in 1578 and served one final term as mayor the following year.

The political complexities of irregularity and insult are impossible to reconstruct with any certainty from the surviving records. They are distinguished by a recurrent interest in the religious persuasion of the ruling elite on the part of both the town and the privy council. These concerns with a local government of an appropriate spiritual, and therefore moral, character elide notions of urban control with accordance with national politics and the self-conscious shaping of a godly community. The local and the national are made inseparable here, through the dynamic between authority and submission.

Arguably, the particularity of Nethersole's circumstances is extraneous to an investigation of his domestic space, both because this is an exercise in elucidation of the typical through the specific and because I would not argue that either the specifics of his business practice or the scars of his political skirmishes are to be found ingrained in the furniture of his hall or parlour. Nevertheless, Nethersole's precarious political position at various points in his life made the authority of his domestic and personal display even more crucial. It is also significant here that rule in this period was effected through 'personality' in the sense of the convincing dissemination of superiority, and therefore through particularity, through the force of individuality.[111]

The time depth of domestic space too is pertinent to the changing fortunes of an individual career: the construction of a household over a period of time. Reading Nethersole's inventory against the development of his professional career reminds us that objects change meaning in relation to circumstance. To take an obvious example, Nethersole owned a scarlet gown with a velvet tippet, valued at £7. This gown was his aldermanic livery, to be worn on ceremonial occasions when its unparalleled brightness in the public spaces of the town would make a strong visual statement about the unity of the elite and their radical difference from those they governed. We have no way of knowing when he acquired this gown, but, if it dated from the period before his dismissal from the Burghmote, its presence within the house must have graphically symbolised his diminished status within the local community; its reuse six years later a potent mark of reintegration and reinstatement.

Nethersole lived in St Peter's parish, a small parish near to the west gate of the city.[112] Although it is impossible to be precise about the nature of his house, the inventory of his goods suggests a property in several sections on a large site. There was a shop, a hall with its own entrance and a buttery next to it, a little parlour and a study. There was a chamber over the shop and a 'next chamber over the parlour', suggesting that the parlour of this main house was adjacent to the shop, either on the street or behind it. Also below were a separate servants' hall and a great kitchen. Above was a brushing chamber, two maids' chambers, and, presumably the highest, a 'chamber called Jerusalem'. There was also a 'little house' with its own hall, parlour, cellar, kitchen and buttery and yard. There was a little chamber under the buttery, and further chambers over the kitchen and hall. The fact that the upper chambers of the little house were listed sequentially with those of the big house might suggest that it was possible to walk between the two pro-perties.[113] Nethersole also owned a brewhouse and horse mill, a stable, and an oast house with male servants' chambers and a meal loft. Properties with this many rooms, even split across two buildings, were rare within the town. Officeholders' houses had on average between six and eleven rooms (a small number had over twenty), but of those they governed two-thirds lived in seven rooms or fewer and 27 per cent in three rooms or fewer. The larger houses are characterised by a wide variety of chambers, and by several different more public rooms.

Their logic is to be found in the distinct kinds of space offered by each room. Nethersole has, for instance, three halls. The servants' hall was fur-nished with a table and two forms and four stools, at total value of 7s 4d. The hall of the 'little house' had a framed wainscot table, a joined form and two stools, a turned chair and an old dornix[114] carpet, furnishings with a total value of 10s 4d. Finally, the main hall had one long framed table with an old green penistone[115] tablecloth on it and six joined stools around it, valued at 20s for the table and stools and 6s for the cloth. There was also a smaller framed table worth 5s with a 3s dornix carpet on it. A joined form of 2s, and a turned chair and small stool worth 16d between them completed the seat-ing arrangements, softened by cushions 'of sondrye sortes' valued at the huge sum of 23s 4d. The room was hung with 10s worth of painted cloths, and decorated with a table of arms and two other scutcheons[116] worth 2s. Although no cupboard is listed, the objects which usually sat upon one are: a white linen cupboard cloth, fringed, with another red one, also fringed, 'lienge under the whyte' (worth 6s 8d the pair) and four pewter flower pots at 8d.[117] Also kept in this larger hall were a bible 'of the olde translation', a chronicle and a service book, presumably on one of the tables.

The three halls can be seen to offer different and yet related types of space within the properties. The servants' room has the bare minimum of hall furniture: a table, forms and stools. There is no embellishment, the pieces are simply formed and low in value, and no additional objects are kept in the room. The hall to the little house is in many ways just a better-quality version of the same space. The materials and methods of production are listed here, as an inherent part of the value of the pieces: 'wainscot' table and 'joined' form. There is also a chair, offering a way of distinguishing the relative importance of those seated in the room, and there is a carpet on the table, indicating the type of space in which decoration is important, even though little money has been spent on it.

The great hall also has table, form, stools and chair. The major difference in terms of furniture is the cupboard. One of Harrison's key objects, it is richly decorated and embellished and must have provided a focus for the room. And decoration as a whole is what distinguishes this room from the other halls Nethersole owned. The 'tables of armes' display an immediate focus on affiliation and status, and the painted cloths suggest a level of warmth and luxury lacking from the lesser halls. The type of furniture in this hall was typical of Canterbury's elite, particularly the possession of two tables, the long one for dining and an additional smaller one, and the cupboard, although Nethersole's long table in particular was valued comparatively highly.[118] Just under half of his colleagues in local office had a carpet in their hall, and two-thirds of them had cushions. Though rarely worth as much as Nethersole's they were said to be of 'stoolwork', 'churchwork', arras or velvet. Although painted cloths were common amongst his peers, only four other aldermen hung images in their halls. Important men such as the lawyer and common councillor Robert Alcock, father of William who heard Crench's confession in his friend Boys's house, had similar furnishings: four framed story cloths worth 20s.

Around half the civic elite had cupboard cloths on their hall cupboards but, although the hall was the most common place for Nethersole's peers to keep books, only a quarter of them kept one here. His own service book, chronicle and bible spoke to his learning and religious commitment, on display rather than kept in his study. Alcock had a study off his hall containing law books, statutes, chronicles, a bible and 'an old chawcer', but Nethersole's contained only a table on which he presumably conducted his business affairs, as it had a lock and key.[119]

Nethersole's parlours would also have made his house distinctive within the town. Whilst the vast majority of the civic elite had a parlour and several more than one, fewer than two-thirds of the houses in the town as a whole had such a room. In the little parlour was a joined framed table and six joined stools, with a joined form, a joined walnut chair and a further three stools, one with a back, and two 'quisheon [cushion] stools' with padded seats. Eleven other cushions made the remaining seating more comfortable, and a dornix carpet was laid on the table.[120] The presence of a cupboard is once more indicated by a fringed diaper cupboard cloth, and in the fireplace was 16s worth of utensils, including a set of Flanders andirons.[121] The parlour belonging to the little house is inventoried as containing only a joined chair and the furnishings of its fireplace, although the room did have a lock and key. Neither of these rooms contained a bed, although some of Nethersole's peers did sleep in their parlours.[122] And there is no evidence of him playing games there – no set of playing tables 'and their men' as Henry Aldey had, nor did he keep a lute there as William Symes the grocer did.[123] Nethersole's parlour was not hung with painted cloths or pictures, and it does not seem to have been boarded.[124] This sets him apart from his peers – he is unusual in the relative levels of decoration he gave to hall and parlour. Several of his peers had three parlours, and it was these rooms that they decorated with

images and painted cloths. As well as a degree of personal taste, these differences also suggest the changing location of hospitality in Canterbury's elite
houses across the period. If householders displayed their wealth and allegiance
in those rooms where the people they wished to impress were most likely to
see it, then the last two decades of the sixteenth century saw a movement
towards more private, intimate dining in a parlour.

The disparity between the furnishings of different chambers is even more
striking than the diversity of parlours and halls. All contain high-quality
bedding; even the household maidservants in the smaller of the two chambers
set aside for them slept in a featherbed in a bedstead, and there was 2s worth
of fabric hangings in their chamber. The larger maids' chamber contained
two featherbeds, both with coverlets to them, and painted cloths worth
13s 4d. The value for the greater room was £5 7s and 2d, for the lesser 23s 8d.
In contrast however, the most splendid chamber in the house had a total
value of £19 3s 4d.[125]

Like those of his peers then, one of Nethersole's upper chambers was
furnished considerably more sumptuously than the others.[126] This room,
presumably Nethersole's own chamber, was the one over the shop, its windows opening on to the street where he had heard Graves's wife crying for
help.[127] The standing bedstead in which he lay had a tester and valance and
four curtains of red silk around it; inside was a featherbed whose bedding,
including a coverlet of tapestry, was worth £3. The total value of the bed in
which he slept was over £8. This was a room whose surfaces were almost
entirely covered: a little framed table with a dornix carpet on it, a press with
a dornix cupboard cloth and a cushion on top. If he went to the window to
look out into the street, he could kneel upon a long needlework window
cushion to pull back the curtain which hung there. The position of this room
is telling – in terms of access it is deep in the house, upstairs and accessible
from the street only by going through the majority of the house's other
rooms. And yet it has a direct view of the street, making it deep and yet
visibly permeable.[128]

There were four other ordinary cushions in the room, and five needle-
work ones referred to as 'fair', the only time in the inventory that the word
is used. One was perhaps on the joined chair by the table, the others may
have been on the bed. There were only two chests, one a large wainscot,
and between them they contained extra carpets and coverlets. This room
was comparatively warm, lined with painted cloths, each surface softened by
coloured and patterned fabrics whose texture was the smoothness of silk or
the complex roughness of tapestry. Robert Alcock's bed had a tester, valance
and curtains of green taffeta fringed with silk, and was also worth £8, but he
had no carpet on his table and no window curtains or cushions, and both of
these items were unusual in the town as a whole.

The contents of the buttery next to the hall indicates Canterbury's potential for elite dining. The most prestigious pewter was valued together at £6 19s 8d, and there was £6 4s 6d worth of brass. Kept locked away, and therefore priced separately, were four silver salts (£11 17s 4d), a gilt tankard (£4 6s 8d), three stone jugs covered and footed with silver (£6 17s 4d), four white goblets parcel gilt (£14 6s 4d), four covered jugs of silver (37s 4d), and a marvellous array of wrought spoons: twelve with square knops (£3 10s 1d), five with apostle heads (36s 3d), five with lions' heads (35s), five with maidens' heads (28s) and three slip spoons (13s 4d).[129] Clearly linked to Harrison's descriptions of plenty, these items provided for different kinds of dining on different occasions. Only the gentleman Henry Aldey had more spoons than Nethersole, and, although it is hard to calculate because in some inventories silver is priced by weight, they are both among only ten men in Canterbury across the period to own more than ten items of silverware. These individuals tended to own three or four salts as a part of their range of silver goods: Gilbert Penny, Nethersole's son in law, for instance, owned a 'crystall salt, covered in part with sylver, beinge gylt', in addition to his instructively distinguished 'greate sylver salt with a cover, all gylt', 'lesser sylver salt with out a cover' and trencher salt.[130]

The stores of reserved household linen offer important evidence about the way in which the house was used. They were kept in a chamber over the hall in a series of chests: a great old one, three wainscot ones, a dansk,[131] a little cypress and a dansk coffer painted red. One chest was between the chimney and the bed's head, one between the chimney and the door, one at the bed's feet 'next the window' and one between the window and the cupboard: the room was packed with valuable linens and piled with the chests and coffers in which it was kept. There were, for instance, twenty-two tablecloths of various kinds in one of the chests. Three were 'household' ones, in other words day-to-day items, valued at 3s. Five were square (6s), ten long, seven of which were of three ells[132] a piece (15s and 16s), and six 'side', valued at 6s. This range of items underlines the variety of the nine tables kept in the different rooms and used for different purposes.

Ten long tablecloths for three long tables is suggestive of the patterns of laundry in such a house and of the different types of occasion marked by a different quality of cloth. The very use of the word 'household' in relation to three of the cloths, in addition to the identification of 10 pairs of 'course' sheets 'going about the house' underlines the distinction between the everyday and the extraordinary which was marked by the purchase of large amounts of linen.[133]

Nethersole's house shares clear similarities with those of his fellow aldermen. The number of rooms, the specialist functions the rooms fulfil, the variety of goods which they house and the quality of the furnishings are all recognisably similar. Personal choice and changing fashion are also evident, however, in the exact distinctions between hall and parlour and in the aesthetic qualities of cushions, bed hangings and silverware. The complexities of the relationship between rooms affects these men's image within the community. It gave them the material solidity and local stature to be recognised as 'substantial men', capable of exercising authority. Comparing Nethersole's house with Richard Moore's suggests both the similarities and the differences in domestic life in the town.

Richard Moore was a blacksmith and freeman of the City of Canterbury. He had previously lived in Ulcombe, twenty miles west of the city, but he moved to the parish of St Mary Northgate in about 1573 and bought his freedom of the city.[134] He appears to have been one of a number of successful tradesmen who built up businesses in small communities and then moved to the city to try to make more money. They were ambitious and determined men. Richard is interesting in a different way within this argument about drama and social practice, however, because his daughter Ursula was married into the extended family of another immigrant who had arrived in Canterbury over a decade earlier, and was by this time established in his shoemaking business. Some time between early 1576 and late 1581, Ursula married Thomas Arthur, brother to Katherine Arthur and aunt to Christopher Marlowe, around the time that her nephew was arriving at Cambridge.[135] Like Nethersole, perhaps like all individuals, Moore's urban typicality, as a freeman of the town who never rose to officeholding status, is shaded by the individuality of his friends, colleagues and family.

Although Richard Moore died in 1582, the Moores and the Marlowes were involved in the vexed and complex administration of his estate until the 1590s, showing the perceived significance of the goods and money he owned to succeeding generations of his own family, and the close ties which marriage formed between families over many years. In 1582, however, with all this still ahead of him, Christopher's father John Marlowe was one of the appraisers of Richard's inventory.[136] All the evidence suggests that Richard had been a reasonably successful blacksmith, reaping the benefits of being a freeman of the town. His inventory describes the fairly typical household of one of those whom Nethersole governed, and it locates him in that crucial band of urban dwellers above the itinerant workers not free of the City and below those of more substantial wealth who governed it. Richard must have been of a reasonable age when he died in 1582 as his son, Marlowe's uncle Thomas, was forty years old in 1586. It seems likely that by the time of his death he was living in a part of the house only, as his goods are listed in the hall and parlour and in the kitchen.

Richard's hall contained a table, a form and an old chair priced at 3s 6d, a chest of 4s and eight old cushions worth 3s. These furnishings suggest a man with little need, or perhaps capacity, to impress guests, one whose public presence was in decline. There are the cushions which define a more prosperous interior, but they are described as old and there is no cupboard with its cloths in the room. In the parlour were a bedstead worth 12d, a board and a pair of trestles worth 6d which formed a table, and a painted cloth of 2s on the wall. Again, the items are all described as old, suggesting that Richard has not been spending his money on the furniture or furnishing of his household for some time. Nevertheless, both the painted cloths in the parlour and the cushions in the hall have some value; they are not worth only a few pence.

Richard's apparel was kept in two chests. He had four gowns, two of them old, four coats, two old doublets and two pairs of hose. The variety of these clothes is again suggestive of his previous wealth. Nethersole, however, owned five gowns, two cloaks, two coats and three doublets, the gowns alone worth around £20. Moore's gowns are worth a total of 66s 8d – a far cry from Nethersole's clothing, but still indicative of the importance of being able to provide variety in his appearance in order to signify his status. Also kept in Moore's chests were two tablecloths of 4s for use on his two tables, and his reserves of cloth: seven yards of kersey valued at 14s and four ells of lockram worth 3s.

In the kitchen Richard kept his pewter, another symbol of his standing within the community. Hugh Beale, who called Ringer's wife a whore in the street in 1541, had pewter and even eight silver spoons when he died in 1586, although by this stage he lived only in one room.[137] The woman he slandered also owned pewter when she died a widow, and, although she lived in both a hall and chamber over the shop, many of her possessions, like Richard's, were described as old. She owned spinning wheels, hemp and hemp combs, and was obviously making her living with these.[138] Richard too had spinning wheels in his kitchen worth 16d, suggesting that his household, like those of so many of his neighbours, had been involved in multiple employments. Finally, his bedstead of 20s and his two featherbeds with their appurtenances of 40s are listed, again close to the average values for a man of his wealth.[139] Doubtful debts, accumulated over a lifetime of trading, amounted to £24 4s 8d, but he also had an impressive £69 5s of good ones. The total of Richard's inventoried wealth was £110 9s 2d, a staggering distance from the £840 16d of Nethersole's inventory, but also considerably more than that of the majority of his peers who were worth only a few pounds.

When the ownership of goods is treated statistically, it becomes possible to see how Moore and Nethersole fit into the community as a whole.[140] Although the lower section of the social hierarchy possessed the same kind of goods as those just described in some numbers, ownership of a range of 'luxury' items characterises the more prosperous in Canterbury. The 70 per cent of the town's inhabitants whose inventories are valued at under £50 were consistently underrepresented in every category of goods. Those in the next bracket, under £100, were in every case at least equally represented in relation to the proportion of inventories.[141] They owned a larger-than-equal share of Canterbury's jewellery, plate, silver spoons, instruments, window curtains and pictures. Inventories between £100 and £499, the bracket into which Richard Moore's wealth fell, had a larger share of jewellery, plate, playing tables, carpets, curtains and pictures, whereas the highest band, to which Nethersole belonged, had a large proportion of the jewellery, looking glasses, plate, spoons, and nearly every kind of embellishment, especially cushions and curtains for windows. Inventories valued at under £50 in Canterbury share the basics of domestic life, but few of its embellishments, with those in the higher brackets.

The comparisons between Nethersole's and Moore's inventories suggest the significance of the household for two men who had been living on opposite sides of Canterbury to one another for a decade. The former lived in one of the largest houses in Canterbury, the latter in a part of a property. In terms of space and of the complexity of organisation of that space, then, these two men's domestic experience is barely comparable. What makes comparison possible is the similarity of function of the rooms – the logic behind the fact that they share the same essential names of chamber, parlour, and hall. Similarly, although the amount and quality of the furniture the two men possessed is strikingly different, the way domestic objects characterise those rooms underlines the correspondences between the function of their domestic environments. Nethersole's main hall has a table with stools, chairs and a few significant possessions; Moore's hall has table, form, chairs and a few other objects. It is the level of decoration and the presence of items of additional comfort such as cushions, carpets, painted cloths and pictures which makes Nethersole's room into a space for the display of domestic plenty as well as the living of daily life. He has invested a significant amount of his inventoried wealth in this house, considerably more than his neighbour.

Matthew Johnson has argued that the 'idea' of the house undergoes a fundamental shift in meaning around the turn of the sixteenth century. He sees the 'medieval' arrangement of the central hall as 'a statement of affiliation to certain social and cultural values that run up and down the social scale'; a form of building which made it possible for status to be articulated 'in terms of repeated architectural terms of reference'. In a telling example, he speculates that 'A yeoman farmer would understand the basic arrangement of John of Gaunt's hall range at Kenilworth, for all its scale and splendour'. Somewhere around the turn of the century, however, this changes: 'larger and smaller houses are qualitatively different houses; a yeoman farmer would find much that was alien if he were allowed to wander through the corridors of Hardwick Hall'.[142] The nobility and those below them found themselves inhabiting such different spaces that a common notion of 'house' was no longer possible in the seventeenth century as it had been in the sixteenth.

The beginning of the seventeenth century marked the furthest reach of some of the shared meanings of 'house' as a concept, then, as a series of spaces which met the requirements of human beings as a whole, rather than catering differently for individual social groups; as a concept which made sense of Nethersole's house for Moore and vice versa. These were the shared meanings of domesticity on which the stage could draw. In a period in which changing economic structures were polarising wealth, the succession of radical changes to the way houses expressed and defined the social difference between the householder and his family, servants and guests, meant that the connections between household objects, household practice and the physical fabric of the household were freighted with problems of the nature and pace of social change.[143]

Within the significant objects which William Harrison identified as indicating social status lies information about power, administration and government. By defining and expressing wealth and rank, objects become synonymous with capability and with an administrative competence founded on economic and domestic stability. The distinctions which differences in domestic life make between individuals express the hierarchical nature of society; they make manifest the 'unassailable' divide between ruler and ruled in a way which is ultimately conservative. Ten years after Nethersole's death, another erstwhile mayor of a prominent Kentish town was being immortalised in the play which bore his name, placing the relationship between his wealth and his control over his household under intense scrutiny.

NOTES

1 Keith Wrightson, *Earthly Necessities*, London: Penguin, 2002, p. 23; Mark Overton, Jane Whittle, Darron Dean and Andrew Hann, *Production and Consumption in English Households, 1600–1750*, London: Routledge, 2004.

2 For a detailed analysis of the developing significance of the legislation, including its earlier incarnation as the regulation of domestic consumption, see A. Hunt, *Governance of the Consuming Passions: A History of Sumptuary Law*, Basingstoke: Macmillan, 1996.

3 William Harrison, *Description of England*, Georges Edelen ed., Ithaca: published for the Folger Shakespeare Library by Cornell University Press, 1968, p. 200.

4 Turkey work was an imitation of Turkish tapestry work.

5 For details of these changes see Lorna Weatherill, *Consumer Behaviour and Material Culture in Britain 1660–1760*, New York, London: Routledge, 1988; and Overton et al., 2004 where Kent in the subsequent period is examined.

6 See Richardson, 'Domestic objects and the construction of family identity', in Beattie, Maslakovic, Rees Jones eds, *The Medieval Household in Christian Europe, c. 850–c. 1550 Managing Power, Wealth, and the Body*, Turnhout: Brepols, 2004.

7 Catherine Richardson, 'The Meanings of Space in Society and Drama', unpublished PhD thesis, University of Kent, 1999, pp. 58–72.

8 See, e.g., Wrightson, 2000, Overton et al., 2004, where the role of women 'on the intersection of production and consumption' is discussed.

9 As a source they underrepresent, of course, women and those of lower social status. Prioritising a qualitative approach to the language of bequest to some extent circumvents these problems, although it does also necessitate acceptance of the premise that a few particularly articulate individuals express sensibilities which are shared in some form by their peers. For more on these methodological problems see Tom Arkell, Nesta Evans and Nigel Goose eds, *When Death Do Us Part*, Oxford: Leopard's Head Press, 2000.

10 CCAL 39.18 f.116v, 1595.

11 The quantitative evidence for this chapter draws on 546 wills for East Kent towns and villages between 1560 and 1600. The qualitative material is drawn from over one thousand wills, covering the period 1530–1600.

12 This approach is intended to recover the aspects of consumption which have been said to be 'almost impossible to retrieve, such as the moral or ethical meaning of goods and activities, and their use in constructing identities.' Overton et al., 2004, p. 9. Recent work on testamentary discourses, influenced by an anthropological method sensitive to the function of material objects in lifecycles, has done much to increase our understanding of the complex meanings of bequests. See for instance Janet Hoskins, *Biographical Objects: How Things Tell the Stories of People's Lives*, New York, London: Routledge, 1998.

13 A painted cloth for the walls.

14 CCAL 17.40 f.170v, 1567; CCAL 17.43 f.373v, 1581; CCAL 17.40 f.334, 1568; see also CCAL 17.50 f.290, 1595. Katherine also gives her brother George Syer 'my lytell stupnett that was our fathers', demonstrating a similar concept of transmission, but this time within the same generation; see also CCAL 17.43 f.21, 1578, CCAL 17.41 f.100v, 1570.

15 CCAL 17.41 f.311, 1572; CCAL 17.40 f.153v, 1567; CCAL 17.40 f.74v, 1567.

16 See also, for example, CCAL 17.41 f.310, 1572; CCAL 17.43 f.320, 1581; CCAL 17.44 f.45, 1582; CCAL 17.44 f.149v, 1581; CCAL 17.49 f.24, 1593.

17 CCAL 17.49 f.24, 1593.

18 CCAL 17.43 f.440, 1581, see also CCAL 17.51 f.122, 1596; CCAL 17.48 f.220, 1591; CCAL 17.51 f.121, 1597.

19 CCAL 17.40 f.17, 1569; CCAL 17.43 f.21v, 1578; CCAL 17.47 f.375, 1589.

20 CCAL 17.51 f.121v, 1597, my italics.

21 Saucepan.

22 CCAL 17.30 f.80v, 1554; CCAL 17.51 f.236, 1595; CCAL 17.40 f.151, 1567. A jurat was a town officer, holding a position similar to that of an alderman.

23 CCAL 17.48 f.1, 1590.

24 For the distinct meanings of early modern clothing see Peter Stallybrass and Ann Rosalind Jones, *Renaissance Clothing and the Materials of Memory*, Cambridge: Cambridge University Press, 2000; Catherine Richardson ed., *Clothing Culture 1350–1650*, Aldershot: Ashgate, 2004.

25 CCAL 17.42 f.305, 1575; CCAL 17.42 f.168, 1575; CCAL 17.42 f.362, 1576; CCAL 17.44 f.36, 1580; see also CCAL 17.42 f.343v, 1575. For Katherine's connections to Christopher Marlowe see above p. 92.

26 CCAL 17.44 f.154v, 1582; CCAL 17.49 f.445, 1594.

27 CCAL 17.42 f.165, 1575.

28 CCAL 17.43 f.374, 1581.

29 CCAL 17.42 f.169, 1575.

30 CCAL 17.51 f.300, 1596.

31 CCAL 17.51 f.133, 1594. Jose's different cultural background as a Protestant refugee perhaps offers him a vocabulary in translation which, in its striking difference from the words used by those native to Sandwich, gives a unique insight into the issues surrounding the purchase of goods.

32 Stephen Hollinden gives such a bed to his son Laurence, who is at Cambridge learning, CCAL 17.40 f.170v, 1567.

33 CCAL 17.43 f.320, 1581.

34 See for instance Stephen Coppel, 'Willmaking on the deathbed', *Local Population Studies*, 40, Spring 1988, 37–45; Elizabeth Hallam, 'Turning the hourglass: gender relations at the deathbed in early modern Canterbury'. *Mortality*, 1:1, 1996, 61–82.

35 CCAL 39.2 f.8, 1556.

36 CCAL 17.42 f.195, 1575; CCAL 17.47 f.203, 1588; CCAL 17.51 f.181, 1595.

37 Only four chests were left, according to his inventory, CKS 10.8 f.4, 1575.

38 Wooden panelling lining the walls of the room.

39 Obscure, although common, term for a kind of coverlet work, sometimes distinguished from tapestry.

40 CCAL 17.41 f.189, 1571; see also CCAL 17.49 f.286, 1594.

41 CCAL 17.45 f.226, 1583.

42 CCAL 17.42 f.122, 1574; CCAL 17.51 f.299, 1596.

43 John Wybrone of Woodnesborough wills that none of his household goods should be sold if it will be useful to his two daughters when they come of age, CCAL 17.41 f.129v, 1570; see also CCAL 17.42 f.164, 1575.

44 CCAL 17.47 f.3v, 1586.

45 Canopy over a bed.

46 A border of cloth around the canopy.

47 CCAL 17.41 f.301v, 1572; see above p. 42 for the slander.

48 Some items were comparatively frequently given, for instance these testators gave 187 chests, 178 gifts of pewter, 162 featherbeds, 142 bedsteads, 139 spoons, 132 bequests of cookware, 119 gifts of brassware, 108 items of jewellery, 97 cupboards, 95 gifts of linen, 87 of silver plate, 84 of both bedding and tables, 83 divisions of all household goods and 75 tablecloths. These figures are for numbers of bequests rather than numbers of objects; pewter, for instance, which is often given as sets of vessels, would otherwise distort the results. 69 per cent of testators gave domestic items in their wills.

49 In this category are 38 bequests of forms, 31 of chairs, 30 stools, 28 armour or weapons, 24 books, 17 cushions, 16 working equipment, 16 trucklebeds, 14 of both curtains and wallhangings, 13 of both settles and fireplace equipment, 12 of both painted cloths for walls and fixtures and fittings such as windows and wainscot, 11 of carpets, of presses and of other items of storage furniture, 8 coffers, 7 gifts of working tools, 6 cupboard cloths and testers for beds.

50 Respectively 4, 3, 3, 2, 2, 2, 2, 1, 1 bequests.

51 Obviously this approach simplifies and standardises experiences. Perhaps most significantly it has been necessary for the sake of clarity to imagine a woman who was married only once, when this was unlikely to be the norm. But such a narrative offers a standard against which different family circumstances can be seen to produce greater or lesser stores of goods for individual members, and a benchmark in contrast to which even slight differences in status and the size of families and through birth and intermarriage, would produce significant changes in individual domestic wealth.

52 CCAL 17.41 f.293v, 1571. For chests see CCAL 17.42 f.165, 1575.

53 CCAL 17.42 f.46v, 1573; CCAL 17.42 f.279, 1575.

54 CCAL 17.51 f.421, 1597; CCAL 17.30 f.80v, 1554.

55 CCAL 17.42 f.76v, 1574.

56 CCAL 17.41 f.189v, 1571.

57 Trimmed with decorative edgings.

58 CCAL 17.49 f.247v, 1593; Isabel Glover gives her sister Margaret Mund, amongst other clothing, a waistcoat, a neckercher, a yard kercher, her best kirtle, petticoat, kercher, double rayle, neckercher and smock, CCAL 17.30 f.80v, 1554.

59 Henry Aldey gives his sister Margaret Webb 'my playne rynge of goulde which was my wives', CCAL 17.48 f.1, 1590.

60 For analysis of courtship gifts see Diana O'Hara, *Courtship and Constraint*, Manchester: Manchester University Press, 2000, chapter 2.

61 For instance CCAL 17.41 f.215v, 1570.

62 CCAL 17.42 f.165, 1575.

63 CCAL 17.42 f.50v, 1573; CCAL 17.41 f.101, 1570.

64 Edward Philip lays out arrangements for his wife Rose: 'Rose my wyef shall have holde occupye and enjoye durynge the terme of her naturall lyef (yf the sayd Rose shall happen soe longe to remaye sole and unmaryed) the best parlour in the howse where in I doe now dwell with the chamber over the same parlour with one butterye next adyoyninge unto the haule of the same dwellynge howse with free and lawfull entrye ingress egresse and regresse in to from and thoroughe the sayd parlour chamber and butterye bothe for her selfe and her howsholde and famylye', CCAL 17.43 f.217v, 1578. See Judith Roberts, 'Tenterden Houses: A Study of the Domestic Buildings of a Kent Parish in their Social and Economic Environment', unpublished PhD thesis, University of Nottingham, 1990, p. 240. This process helps to explain the small inventories of once-prominent individuals. See also CCAL 17.43 f.363, 1579; CCAL 17.41 f.246v, 1570.

65 For the relationship between widows see P. and J. Clark, 'The social economy of the Canterbury suburbs', in Alec Detsicas and Nigel Yates eds *Studies in Modern Kentish History*, Maidstone: Kent Archaeological Society, 1983.

66 CCAL 17.49 f.162, 1591.

67 For analysis of the differences between women's and men's testamentary practice, see J. S. W. Helt, 'Women, memory and will-making in Elizabethan England', in Bruce Gordon and Peter Marshall eds *The Place of the Dead: Death and Remembrance in Late Medieval and Early Modern Europe*, Cambridge: Cambridge University Press, 2000; Mary Prior, 'Wives and wills, 1558–1700', in John Chartres and David Hey eds, *English Rural Society 1500–1800*, Cambridge: Cambridge University Press, 1990; Martha C. Howell, 'Fixing movables: gifts by testament in late medieval Douai', *Past and Present*, 150, 1996. For the fullest discussion of women's property see Amy Louise Erickson, *Women and Property in Early Modern England*, London: Routledge, 1993.

68 CCAL 17.42 f.335, 1577.

69 CCAL 17.49 f.92, 1592.

70 CCAL 17.47 f.183v, 1587.

71 William Waterman bequeaths his son Edward the trestle table and form in the hall, as well as his best ringlet kettle, CCAL 17.42 f.76v, 1574; Robert Fagg gives his son Henry the cupboard 'or press which standeth in the haule of the howse wherein I now dwell', CCAL 17.42 f.217, 1574; Humphrey Atkinson gives his son William the best cupboard in his hall with a cupboard cloth of dornix, CCAL 17.41 f.323, 1572.

72 See for instance CCAL 17.39 f.277v, 1566.

73 John Alexander, for instance, gives his joined bedstead and featherbed with its bedding to his eldest son Michael after the death of his wife Margaret, CCAL 17.42 f.103v, 1573;

Richard Pysing gives his son John the featherbed and appurtenances after the death of John's mother, CCAL 17.41 f.367v, 1571.

74 John Neame gives his son Richard his best brass pot at marriage or his wife's death, additionally willing that his wife Joan should have all the household goods not willed, and her dwelling in the part of the house in which her husband currently dwells. This kind of provision is suggestive of the complicated strategies employed to provide for both generations at once. CCAL 17.43 f.149, 1535.

75 See for instance the silver spoons which John Neale bought from the heirs of Thomas Gate, CCAL 17.42 f.164, 1575.

76 The identity of appraisers is of considerable interest. Within small towns, several prominent individuals serve in this capacity many times. For instance George Richards, merchant and common councillor of Sandwich, appraises twenty-three inventories over a period of fourteen years.

77 Thomas Crispe's gift to his son Samuel of two spoons, one 'the selfe same spone which his godmother gave unto him', CCAL 17.51 f.121v, 1597, for instance. Fowler Colbrand gives his married daughter Sybil six silver spoons which are in the keeping of her uncle Nicholas, CCAL 17.51 f.414, 1600.

78 This explains the high incidence of beds in downstairs parlours. Richard Wilde leaves his son Thomas the best bed with its appurtenances in the parlour after the death of his wife, which suggests that they had both been sleeping there, CCAL 17.43 f.369v, 1580.

79 Humphrey Atkinson and Richard Laurence, for instance, witness the will of Robert Fale, who describes them as his friends within the document, and asks them to advise his daughter, CCAL 17.41 f.189, 1571.

80 Nicholas Franklyn gives such clothes to his executor George Bigg, along with his best cloak and gown, a satin doublet and half his religious books in Latin, asking him to provide a tombstone for himself, his wife and child, CCAL 17.43 f.41v, 1577; Roger Peake, jurat of Sandwich, gives a turquoise to Sergeant Manwood in the hope of help for his wife, CCAL 17.41 f.101, 1570.

81 Martin Brook gives his son and executor Jarvis his bedstead 'wherein i now lye', CCAL 17.41 f.310, 1572.

82 Henry Aldey refers to '*my* bigger brass pot that is commonly used in the kitchen' and the 'saltseller parcel gilt which *I* commonly use at my orde', CCAL 17.48 f.1, 1590, my italics.

83 Basting ladles, pothangers, toasting irons, trugs, moulding boards and a million 'other things unseen and fogotten', as a 1579 inventory puts it, CCAL 21.3 f.321.

84 Kopytoff's distinction between the commoditisation and singularity of objects, and his distinction between the general and the particular *exchange* of objects can be extended to shed light on the way they enter different *discourses*, changing their meaning as different kinds of attention is drawn to them, Igor Kopytoff, 'The cultural biography of things: commoditization as process', in Arjun Appadurai ed., *The Social Life of Things: Cultural Commodities in Perspective*, Cambridge: Cambridge University Press, 1986.

85 Harrison, 1968, p. 201.

86 Prosperity often permitted new building rather than alteration: see for instance C. Platt, *The Great Rebuildings of Tudor and Stuart England*, London: UCL Press, 1994; W. G. Hoskins, *Provincial England*, London: Macmillan, 1963, chapter 7, 'The rebuilding of rural England 1570–1640', and for detail of local practices Vanessa Parker, *The Making of Kings Lynn*, London, Chichester: Phillimore, 1971; Schofield, *Medieval London Houses*; Matthew Johnson, *Housing Culture*, London: University College London Press, 1993. The rate and extent of change was, of course, very different indeed in different geographical areas.

87 Richardson, 1999, pp. 64–5. See also the distinctions between Appendix, Tables 1 and 2, where distinctions at different social levels can be inferred.

88 John Schofield, 'Urban housing in England 1400–1600', in David Gaimster and Paul Stamper eds, *The Age of Transition*, Oxford: Oxbow Books, 1997, p. 140.

89 See above pp. 53–5.

90 Schofield, 1997, p. 140. For a suggestive aside on this relationship between activity and space see Thomas Tusser's 'Husbandly Poesies', divided into those suitable 'for the hall', 'for the Parler', 'for thine own bed Chamber' etc., and Juliet Fleming's discussion of this and other household writing in *Graffiti and the Writing Arts of Early Modern England*, London: Reaktion Books, 2001, esp. chapter 1.

91 Matthew Johnson, 'Rethinking houses, rethinking transitions' in David Gaimster and Paul Stamper eds, *The Age of Transition*, Oxford: Oxbow Books, 1997, p. 146. See also Johnson, 1993: 'we see a shift away from the idea of house and household as *community* towards the house and household as *society*, in terms of its move towards segregation of social elements rather than unity and its stress on functional differentiation rather than social status', p. 120.

92 See Appendix, Table 1 for differences in the kinds of objects kept in each room.

93 These documents raise many methodological problems, the most significant in this context being their frequently incomplete nature. Bequests, items of little value, particularly ubiquitous ones and items not considered to be 'moveable' may well have been left unrecorded. These problems particularly affect the statistical viability of large-scale quantitative analysis. For more on the use of inventories see Arkell, Evans and Goose eds, 2000; Lena Cowen Orlin, 'Fictions of the early modern English probate inventory', in Henry Turner ed., *The Culture of Capital*, New York, London: Routledge, 2002; Overton et al., 2004, chapter 2. This analysis draws on 1,430 documents for the towns and villages of Kent whose wills were studied above, between 1560 and 1600.

94 Again, the source under represents women and those with few possessions. Of the 1,430 documents analysed here, just under 22 per cent described women's estates. For the social spread of the documents see Michael Zell, 'The social parameters of probate records in the sixteenth century' in *Bulletin of the Institute of Historical Research*, 57, 1984.

95 Appendix, Table 1 sets out the aggregate pattern of goods in the selected towns across the county; Table 2 records all the data for Canterbury; Table 3 extracts the information about officeholders' rooms.

96 Steve Hindle, *The State and Social Change in Early Modern England*, Basingstoke: Macmillan, 2000, pp. 12, 23.

97 Hindle, 2000, p. 224. As different types of community (e.g. urban, rural) were composed of diverse sections of the social scale, so the government of each community could not 'inhere in one class or another but developed from the tension between different groups'.

98 Quoted in Hindle, 2000, p. 23.

99 Writing about the plays as 'middle class' drama throws a wide net over Merry, Arden and Frankford, for instance.

100 Bryson, 1998, p. 23.

101 A. J. Fletcher, 'Honour, reputation and local officeholding', in Fletcher and John Stevenson eds, *Order and Disorder in Early Modern England*, Cambridge: Cambridge University Press, 1985, p. 115.

102 See above p. 33.

103 Hindle, 2000, p. 23.

104 As Weatherill points out for a later period, contemporary commentators 'take it that upper, middle, and lower ranks could be distinguished on the basis of their consumption habits', and the evidence from probate inventories demonstrates that this was the case, although in a different way, for the period considered here. Weatherill, 1988, passim, quotation p. 1. Bourdieu, *Outline of a Theory of Practice*, translated by Richard Nice, Cambridge: Cambridge University Press, 1977: *habitus* dictates 'definitions of the impossible, possible, and the probable', p. 78. For comparative material on the connection between households and social status based on probate inventories see Wallace T. MacCaffrey, *Exeter 1540–1640*, Cambridge, MA, London: Harvard University Press, 1975, pp. 268–70; Margaret Spufford, *Contrasting Communities*, Gloucester: Sutton, 2000, pp. 38–45; V. H. T. Skipp, 'Economic and social change in the forest of Arden, 1530–1649', in Joan Thirsk ed., *Land, Church and People*, Reading: Museum of English Rural Life, 1970; and the wonderfully detailed N. W. Alcock, *People at Home: Living in a Warwickshire Village 1500–1800*, Chichester: phillimore, 1993, part II. For the situation in Scotland see Margaret Sanderson, *A Kindly Place? Living in Sixteenth-Century Scotland*, East Linton: Tuckwell Press, 2002. Ursula Priestly and P. J. Corfield use inventories to talk about room use in Norwich, 'Rooms and room use in Norwich, 1580–1730', *Post-Medieval Archaeology*, 16, 1982, 93–123. See also Garrard, 'English probate inventories and their use in studying the significance of the domestic interior, 1570–1700', in Ad Van der Woude and Anton Schuurman eds, *Probate Inventories: A New Source for the Historical Study of Wealth, Material Culture and Agricultural Development*, Utrecht: HES Publishers, 1980.

105 CKS 10.13.116, 1582; Ralph Baldwin, chamberlain between 1579 and 1581 and shortly to become mayor in 1584, John Semark, mayor in 1569, and a Robert Whithorn were the other appraisers. Nethersole's inventory is one of 3 per cent of the town's inventories to be valued at over £500; Richard's inventory, valued at £110 9s 2d, is one of 15 per cent valued at between £100 and £499; 11 per cent were valued at £50–£99, but a staggering 70 per cent were valued at up to £50.

106 For his description of leaving his house in the night see above pp. 42–3. He became a common councillor in 1559, progressing to alderman in 1562, and mayor in 1567, 1572 and 1579: Graham Durkin, 'The Civic Government and Economy of Elizabethan Canterbury', unpublished PhD thesis, Canterbury Christchurch University College, 2001, appendix 3.

107 In 1570 and 1576 his two daughters were married to men who became aldermen in the early 1580s and mayors later on in the decade. His son Edward Nethersole was himself mayor in 1590; Durkin, 2001, p. 98. As Canterbury was being maintained by immigration, second-generation families were the exception rather than the rule. Amongst the civic elite of Canterbury, 83.9 per cent of common councillors, 71.1 per cent of aldermen and 66.6 per cent of mayors were born outside the city. They came from as far away as Cheshire, Staffordshire, Shropshire, Norfolk, Oxfordshire and Somerset; Durkin, 2001, pp. 79–80.

108 Clark, 1983, p. 66.

109 Robert Railton, Warham Jemett and Thomas Hovenden. The gentleman Christopher Courthop, who gave his son two blankets 'of his mother's spinning', was also a customer, see above p. 69. Nethersole's inventory ends with the cash of which he died possessed: £203 10s, with a further £108 11s of debts due for beer, £30 13s 4d of debts 'on the scores' and a further £36 12s 9d of other debts. An additional £61 5s 9d had been paid in brewing moneys since his death, which could only have been a month or so previously. The £12 19s 4d of hops left in the shop suggest the substantial income generated from such raw materials.

110 Nethersole repaid £30 which he had been given in 1569 in order to provide wheat for the poor: Durkin, 2001, p. 196.

111 Fletcher says, 'In a society where authority was generated by a respect for the honour and reputation of the governor rather than the threat of political force, these aspects of identity were particularly crucial to social order', 1985, pp. 106, 109. For the significance of prominent individuals in urban societies see Robert Titler, *Townspeople and Nation: English Urban Experiences, 1540–1640*, Stanford: Stanford University Press, 2001.

112 Between 1570 and 1599 St Peter's saw 219 baptisms and 214 burials. One of the lowest numbers was recorded for All Saints parish, which saw 161 baptisms, 133 burials; the highest for St Paul's which saw 539 baptisms and 586 burials over the same period: Durkin, 2001, appendix 1.

113 Using inventories to reconstruct relationships between rooms can only ever be an imaginative exercise; see Orlin, 2002, pp. 57–63.

114 A silk, worsted, woollen or partly woollen fabric, originally named after the Flemish town in which it was made.

115 A coarse woollen cloth.

116 Short for escutcheon, the shield of a coat of arms.

117 The cupboard itself is not priced in the inventory, presumably because it had been bequeathed in the will.

118 At 20s with the six stools it was worth more than those of most of his peers (although the habit of pricing tables with stools, forms, settles and wainscot makes the comparison difficult) whose tables and seating ranged between 3s 4d and 20s, with one exceptionally high value of 53s 4d, and a median value of 10s.

119 CKS 10.16 f.517, 1583. Both men also kept weapons there.

120 The cushions were valued at 13s 4d. 36 per cent of the cushions in officeholders' properties were in the parlour, 35 per cent in the chamber and the remainder in the hall.

121 Metal bar on 'fire dogs' to carry the logs.

122 13 per cent of the beds in officeholders' properties were in the parlour.

123 CKS 10.20 f.1, 1589; CKS 10.13 f.349, no date.

124 21 per cent of the painted cloths in officeholders' houses were in the parlour, 58 per cent in the hall. 56 per cent of the pictures were in the parlour, 44 per cent in the hall.

125 The larger maids' chamber also had a chest, a cushion and a close stool. Four aldermen's inventories give individual totals for each room, and the value of one chamber is always significantly higher than the rest. This sum is particularly striking as it does not contain Nethersole's silverware, which was priced separately.

126 John Barker's was called the 'fayrest', CKS 10.20 f.56, 1590.

127 Aldey's main chamber, valued at a comparable £17 17s, was also the 'great chamber next the street'.

128 I am grateful to Jane Grenville for this point.

129 87 per cent of officeholders had pewter, 77 per cent had silver, and 58 per cent had spoons, although these numbers probably under represent spoons, which were often left out of the inventory as they had been given in the will. Several men who owned large amounts of silverware were innkeepers, and it is possible that some of the complexities of Nethersole's household layout relate to innkeeping. If this is the case, the negotiation of more or less public spaces within the house becomes even more complex.

130 CKS 10.21 f.189, 1593. Trencher salts were small ones placed near a person's trencher.

131 A Danish one.

132 A measurement of 45 inches.

133 There were 34 pairs of sheets in all, of varying qualities, and the linen as a whole was worth over £20.

134 Urry, *Christopher Marlowe and Canterbury*, London: Faber and Faber, 1988, p. 16.

135 John Moore's deposition in the court case surrounding Katherine's estate describes her in a 'lower parlor of her saide howse'. Given the will, Christopher Marlowe read it out to the company 'plainely and distinktly'; CCAL 39/11 f.234, quoted in Urry, 1988, p. 128.

136 CKS 10.14 f.70, no date.

137 CKS 10.15 f.165, 1586. For the court case see above pp. 41–2.

138 CKS 10.5 f.279, 1571.

139 Inventories in Richard's band gave values between 5s and £10 for featherbeds (a range expanded by the occasional tendency to amalgamate bedsteads and bedding into one value), median value 26s 8d.

140 See Appendix, Table 4 for the detail of object possession, and Table 5 for the difference in value of the same type of item across different bands of wealth.

141 11 per cent of the sample were in this bracket.

142 Johnson, 1997, pp. 146, 150, 151. For the connections between Wollaton Hall and broad vernacular changes see Alice T. Friedman, *House and Household in Elizabethan England*, Chicago, London: University of Chicago Press, 1989, conclusion. For extended consideration of the differences between 'vernacular' and 'polite' architectural forms see Johnson, 1993, chapter 9.

143 For the growing gap between rich and poor see Keith Wrightson and David Levine, *Poverty and Piety in an English Village*, Oxford: Clarendon Press, 1995, chapter 7; Wrightson, 2000, passim, esp. ch. 8.

3

Arden of Faversham

A RDEN OF FAVERSHAM is a seductive play with which to begin to trace the relationship between images of the household and domestic dramas. It is a strikingly material play, in the sense that it insists upon the significance of its locations, pointedly naming places and linguistically producing spaces on the stage. The place in which events occur generates, shapes, affects or complicates action. Human agency is firmly located in the materiality of its surroundings: individuals are brought face to face with the social forces which shape and control the places in which their lives are lived.[1]

Arden begins with a grant made to its eponymous hero, 'and to thy heirs, / By letters patents from his majesty', of 'All the lands of the Abbey of Faversham' (3–5).[2] His friend Franklin's opening speech explicitly connects Arden's status with his contentment, linking his physical and mental states:

> Here are the deeds,
> Sealed and subscribed with his name and the king's.
> Read them, and leave this melancholy mood.
>
> > (6–8)

But the news does not lift Arden's spirits; he rather continues the investigation of exterior and interior interconnection by pairing Franklin's news of letters with some of his own:

> Love letters pass 'twixt Mosby and my wife,
> And they have privy meetings in the town.
>
> > (15–16)

These opening lines of the play set Arden's authority as a local landowner against his impotence as a husband, through his inability to control his wife's meetings. His statement about 'privy meetings' has obvious connections to the ingrained sins recalled by deponents in the ecclesiastical courts, and carries their weight of the purported attempts to set up an extra-domestic 'house', perversely and dangerously located in the town. But the phrase also casts Arden as a man with a curious kind of knowledge: a man who knows about meetings even though they are secret but who states their priviness, not in the way Margaret Richardson did, to reveal a hidden crime, but in a passive way, as a source of regret.[3] In the communal spaces of the town, Arden's gaze is precise – he sees the passing of letters, he spies his own ring on Mosby's finger – but it does not generate action. In the movement from an insistent extra-theatrical moral need to reveal private sins to the dramatic poetics of interior anguish, culpability becomes confused.

The opening exchange economically sets up the play's main preoccupations. It introduces Arden's significant status and pairs it with his domestic incompetence, and it locates both issues within the topography of Faversham. The town is particularised by the lands of its famous Abbey, and it is characterised by its permeability to the paranoid gaze of the wronged husband. It becomes central as the location within which Arden's status is both expressed physically, in his ownership of land, and undermined through his wife's actions. The rest of the play, then, develops in tension with its notorious denouement, holding up for the audience's scrutiny the inter-relation of status, location and domestic life in relation to the murder.[4] I want to trace the meanings of the household through to their finale as the location of Arden's demise.

The play's geographical specificity is relentless. Arden's organisation of his departure from the town in the first scene deftly spatialises the stage, fixing the house within which they are currently taking breakfast as one of several key points which triangulate Faversham:

> Whilst Michael fetch our horses from the field,
> Franklin and I will down unto the quay,
> For I have certain goods there to unload.
>
> (i.87–90)

Journeys of commerce and service are set up: to the quay which was Faversham's most defining commercial feature as one of the Cinque Ports which served a burgeoning trade provisioning London; to London by road, through Rainham Down, Sittingbourne and Rochester; to the Isle of Sheppey where Arden visits his patron Sir Thomas Cheyney; even the well-worn path to the continent where Black Will has been fighting at Boulogne, and to Flushing whence he boards an oyster-boat after the murder.

These are culturally familiar journeys. They were made by soldiers, merchants, peddlers, men seeking the professional services London offered, groups of travelling players making their circuits around the South East of England. The high geographical mobility which saw individuals travelling the length and breadth of the country for work, moving between the provincial towns of Britain and from the provinces to the capital, ensured that such journeys were familiar to the play's audiences, locating events within a known and imaginable context.[5]

The detail of place in the play is uniformly precise. Will does not take just any boat, he takes an oyster-boat, a reference to a commodity for which Faversham was nationally famous; Alice suggests Mosby slips back to her house by losing Arden in the Fair for which Faversham was known, and which the historical Arden had arranged to house on his own lands for financial gain;[6] Lord Cheyney mentions the precise distance of four miles during which his way and Arden's will converge, before the roads to Sheppey and Faversham part.

Similarly, as the focus of the action switches to London, places and routines are picked out sharply. Arden and Franklin eat at the Nag's Head; the murderers Black Will and Shakebag at the Salutation. The friends walk in Paul's Yard, and Arden's servant Michael trips across the city to find the times of the tides at Billingsgate; Black Will plans an escape by boat from Blackfriars. These details maintain a coherent geography for the play which stretches from Faversham right up to London and gives the exterior scenes a particular kind of physical consistency, a strikingly solid location for the frighteningly open Down, and the broom-closed and ditched road to Sheppey. Such specificity holds together mysterious failures and providential interventions by giving them the coherence of physical connection, but it also indicates their generation by that particular landscape.

'Kentishness' implicitly influences the movement of the narrative, being held responsible for the temperament of its inhabitants. Berating Michael for failing to ensure his entry to Franklin's London home to murder Arden in the night, Black Will tells him, 'Now, sir, a poorer coward than yourself / Was never fostered in the coast of Kent' (iii.148–9). There is an insistence that locality and place affects identity; that the county itself is fertile for the breeding of people and plots. Michael, trying to decide whether or not to leave the doors open in London, sums up the threat he feels from Black Will and Shakebag: 'Two rougher ruffians never lived in Kent' (iv.69). These details work partly to insist that the murder is Kentish born and bred, generated by the nature of its population as well as the specifics of its localities, and such specificity to an extent contains the threat, suggesting that only in this place could such a thing happen. But the realism which it engenders simultaneously insists upon the significance of the narrative for contemporary society, as a series of events which 'really happened' in recognisably recent times.[7]

The specific locations provide the context for a murder narrative which has a strongly episodic structure. The black comedy of the central sections of the play derives from the cumulative nature of the different attempts, and the play makes much of their paradoxical independence and inseparability. They are connected through their status as a trial of Will and Shakebag's professional competence in the art of assassination, through the meditation they offer on the workings of divine providence, and through the way they develop dramatic tension. But they are also cameos of different types of murder, distinct from one another because they take place in different locations.

'We'll have him murdered as he walks the streets', says Alice, 'In London many alehouse ruffians keep, / Which, as I hear, will murder men for gold' (i.443–5). She suggests a connection between particular places and likely outcomes, one which attends to the kind of 'expertise' to be found in such locations and to the way space generates action. This is a particular feature of threatening places such as London, and also the bleak and desolate Down. Will advises Michael that his 'office is but to appoint the *place* / And train thy master to his tragedy' (iii.164–5), and, when Michael tries to extricate himself from his failure to fulfil his part of the bargain, he does so by suggesting the next opportunity:

> . . . with the tide my master will away,
> Where you may front him well on Rainham Down,
> A place *well fitting* such a stratagem.
>
> (vii.17–19)

On the Down, where few people will be passing in the night, it should be easier to finish Arden off. This play, like *A Warning for Fair Women*, suggests but then frustrates a geography of relative threat, where the coincidence of observed routine and unpeopled spaces might produce the ultimate success – the socially invisible murder.

Greene comments twice upon the movement from one failed murder to another: 'Will, make clean thy bloody brow' (iii.84), he instructs after the attempt in Paul's Yard has ended in Will's injury, 'And let us bethink us on some other place / Where Arden may be met with handsomely' (iii.85–6). And then again later in the scene the (vain) hope for a location which will efface the evidence of the deed: 'Let us bethink us on some other place / Whose earth may swallow up this Arden's blood' (iii.117–18). The various connections between place, event, likelihood of success and the physicality of murder seen in the blood which will mark the spot is insistently remarked upon throughout the play. It culminates in Franklin's statement in the Epilogue that 'above the rest' (Epil.9) of his narrative of fitting punishment, one thing in particular 'is to be noted' (Epil.9), that after Arden's discovery on the patch of disputed ground, 'in the grass his body's print was seen / Two years and more after the deed was done' (Epil.12–13).

The fundamental significance of these different locations is the extent to which space can be controlled by the murderers. The progression of the narrative implicitly contrasts outside against inside, domestic against communal, in a way which invites the audience to consider *why* the final attempt within Arden's own parlour was successful, and what might be the implications of the fruitfulness of such a space for murder. The complexities of the household are therefore carefully set up throughout the play as a way of qualifying the final scene. They begin with the implied intimacies of Alice's first line, 'Husband, what mean you to get up so early?' (i.57), a question which retroactively recasts his agonised opening exchange with Franklin as the product of a painful night and focuses audience attention briefly on a shared chamber now left for a more public space. Arden responds with an explicitly poetic evocation of the erstwhile nature of their relationship:

> Sweet love, thou know'st that we two, Ovid-like,
> Have chid the morning when it 'gan to peep,
> And often wished that dark Night's purblind steeds
> Would pull her purple mantle back
> And cast her in the ocean to her love.
>
> (i.60–4)

This description of past joys gives affective force to present circumstances: 'thou hast killed my heart' Arden says, explaining that last night, 'I heard thee call on Mosby in thy sleep.' Having called his name, he remembers, 'you started up, and suddenly / Instead of him caught me about the neck' (i.65–70). This is the start of Arden's potent fantasies of physical displacement, as he imagines himself imagined as his wife's lover. Caught between waking and dreaming, the intimacies of the shared bed suddenly polarise husband and wife as he supposes himself embraced in error.

Alice's resolutely pragmatic reply, 'Instead of him? Why, who was there but you?' (i.71) points up the nature of the spaces the play calls into being. It attempts to limit the meanings of the chamber to a bounded room, a literal physical space like those described in an inventory. But for the audience this exchange opens interpretation up to the possibility of contest in the over-lapping spheres of material and imaginary spaces; of the tensions between this richest room in Arden's house and the possibility that his wife can entertain another man there within the powerful fantasies of her dreams. The brief image suggests a way of reading the play's locations as at once claustrophobically circumscribed and capable of metaphorical expansion; physically intimate and mentally permeable; controlled and uncontainable.

The discussion of the dream is the first of three crucial verbal images of the shared intimate household in which threat is firmly transcribed in the closeness of space. In the second, Alice, in the course of her falling-out with Mosby later in the opening scene, invokes the sensuality of spatial memory,

> Remember, when I locked thee in my closet,
> What were thy words and mine? Did we not both
> Decree to murder Arden in the night?
>
> (i.191–3)

The image plays upon the audience's sense of the relationship between what they see on stage and the private life of the characters which they must imagine, and maps this distance between public action and private intimacy on to the seen and unseen spaces of the household. The imperative to 'remember' is also an irresistible signal to the audience to 'imagine'. The visceral closeness of the recollection invites imagination to enter a morally ambiguous realm of desire, as historical occasions blur with fantasies of spatial and sexual control.

The shock of the speech is partly inherent in its adulterous assertion and partly in Alice's seditious boldness with household space.[8] This is a space over which Alice, like the adulterous wives in the depositions, has total con-trol – locking the doors and separating her passion off from prying eyes.[9] And this control raises insistent moral questions – *when* and *how* did Alice do such a thing? The play's representational realism suggests that we imagine the couple in the physical space of the closet, but the temporally unlocated memory indicates a metaphorical reading which links this smallest household space with Alice's body. At the nexus of these different intimacies, the couple's pledge is a passionate affirmation of their love embodied in a mutual commitment to murder, and recollection of the incident at this point brings them back to their blunted purpose.

The third striking image of the chamber comes further into the play, after several failed attempts to end Arden's life. It is intended to indicate a change in the pace of the plots – a fresh urgency to their need for resolution spurred by Alice's frustration. 'This night I rose and walked about the chamber,' she says to Mosby, 'And twice or thrice I thought to have murdered him' (xiv.86–7). Again, the reported nature of her actions gives the space an off-stage intimacy, and the indication of the duration of her vigil at the bedside is menacing. The chamber, so often called upon in plays to represent physical closeness, is here a polarised space in which Alice's natural sleep is disrupted by thoughts of murder. Watching, normally construed as a position of moral superiority, here becomes one of the authority of strong intent. She suggests a tense space, bounded by the ties of marriage vows which make it like a prison, and she does so in order to prompt a change of plan. All three of these images play with ideas of change through intimacy, casting household space as a catalyst for murder and locating the crime's motivating dynamics in the Ardens' closets and chambers. Description of enclosed spaces which cannot be physically shown underlines forbidden intimacies and private purposes.

These images are strong despite their brevity because they are so freighted with the concerns of domestic authority. They are linked to fantasies of the congruity of physical and mental space, of isolation within the house, and of the establishment of a more permanent control over its spaces. And they connect to the action which the audience actually sees to produce a very particular relationship between domestic space and the social forces which constrain its uses: who, exactly, controls the household? what might Arden's spatial control *mean* in such fractured conjugal and emotional circumstances?

As Alice looks about the chamber in the night, her gaze simultaneously controls the wealth of the room and alters its meaning through the power of her murderous potential. And this wealth generates an intricately woven revenge tragedy in which the numerous actors' vested interests in Arden's death spring mainly from their sense of social competition, of want, and of the inappropriateness of their victim's behaviour for a man of his status.[10] It is these forces, combined with the power of passion, which shape and constrain the use and meaning of the household. Arden develops his initial description of his emotional pain at his wife's infidelity in ways which are perhaps rather surprising:

> Ay, to dote on such a one as he
> Is monstrous, Franklin, and intolerable.
>
> (i.22–30)

The smart of the offence is transferred from the act of infidelity itself to the subject of his wife's affection:

> A botcher, and no better at the first,
> Who, by base brokage getting some small stock,
> Crept into service of a nobleman . . .
> And bravely jets it in his silken gown.
>
> (i.25–30)

In contrast, Arden spells out his own status: 'I am by birth a gentleman of blood' (i.36).[11]

Arden's and Mosby's paradoxical difference and interconnection generates a specific kind of tension, separated as they are by rank, but joined by their shared pleasure in Alice's body. When they meet, Arden frames insults which focus on the gap in status between them, escalating emotions by removing his rival's sword,

> So, sirrah, you may not wear a sword!
> The statute makes against artificers,
> I warrant that I do. Now use your bodkin,
> Your Spanish needle, and your pressing iron,
> For this shall go with me.
>
> (i.310–14)

There is a precision to the weighing of bodkin, Spanish needle and pressing iron against sword, a social exactitude which intentionally replicates the status-conscious language of the statutes. In this context, the speech freights the objects with the symbolic energies of social competition and elevates the pressing iron to its position of emblematic significance in the final revenge of the play.[12] Mosby's reply, 'Ah, Master Arden, you have injured me; / I do appeal to God and to the world' (i.318–19), is nicely ambiguous. By *removing* the sword Arden punctures Mosby's newly acquired status, rather than his person.

The play explores two very different sites of antagonism, then: Arden and Mosby's relative status and Arden and Alice's relative domestic authority. But it almost loses its moral way as first Arden himself, and then the lovers, focus on the wrong of coupling across the classes rather than the more fundamental sin of adultery. When Alice tries Mosby's love in the opening scene, she explores their incompatibility in terms of rank:

> Base peasant, get thee gone,
> And boast not of thy conquest over me, . . .
> For what hast thou to countenance my love,
> Being descended of a noble house,
> And matched already with a gentleman
> Whose servant thou may'st be? And so farewell.
>
> (i.198–204)

The argument between them is most fully developed in the central scene viii, where Mosby too claims to have lost his place in life because of their relationship. In a scene which opens with his soliloquy on his condition ('My golden time was when I had no gold' (viii.11)), he matches her complaints about social denigration:

> if you stand so nicely at your fame,
> Let me repent the credit I have lost.
> I have neglected matters of import
> That would have stated me above thy state,
> Forslowed advantages, and spurned at time.
>
> (viii.81–5)

And the couple are only brought back together with the consummation of Alice's acknowledgement that Mosby's personal qualities are more significant to her than his status:

> Sweet Mosby is as gentle as a king . . .
> So, whatsoe'er my Mosby's father was,
> Himself is valued gentle by his worth.
>
> (viii.140–5)

Throughout the intricate dynamics of this scene, status is repeatedly sexualised as the play develops its interest in the confusion between Alice's body and Arden's property, entangling sexual consummation with possession of the rival's household goods. Lust and domestic authority become part of the same drive, a drive for personal change and for domestic plenty.[13] This fundamentally confuses the object of Mosby's affections, turning what is on one level a scene of argument and reconciliation between man and woman into part of his wider scheme to possess Arden's status as epitomised by his chair and his wife, the key aspects of his household.

Mosby fantasises uneasily about his peers' reactions, not to his continuing relationship with Alice after the murder, but to his intended change in fortune:

> Who, when they shall see me sit in Arden's seat,
> They will insult upon me for my meed,
> Or fright me by detecting of his end.
>
> (viii.31–3)

The chair becomes one of those key objects which Johnson saw taking on the functions of spatial distinction in order to negotiate status in a room.[14] Mosby knows that his 'sufficiency' to occupy it, and with it his ability to govern such a complex household, will be called into question. The precision of its social meanings suggest that he should only ever be able to occupy it provisionally, as a generous gesture of Arden's hospitality.

If sitting in this chair denotes precise qualities of rule and unquestioned control, however, Arden's own title to it is also insecure. Characters repeatedly deny his status: Will refers to him as 'the peasant' (ii.105), and Greene calls him 'churl' (i.488, 509, 513), as do Alice and Mosby (i.574).[15] Mr Bygges, said to be sitting 'churling' by the fire in his chair in the depositions provides a comic analogy – a man whose exercise of domestic authority in the prime position, with a surveying gaze over the hall fire, is in fact undercut by what happens elsewhere, reducing his performance of authority to one of 'churling' rather than 'lording'.[16]

The scene in which Arden is challenged by Dick Reede offers the most subtle and complex depiction of Arden's sense of social responsibility. The sailor with whom Reede initially discusses his suit characterises Arden succinctly: 'His conscience is too liberal and he too niggardly' (xiii.2). This is immediately at odds with the responsibilities of a gentleman, and the conflict between the richer and poorer man is interestingly framed between this unfavourable assessment and Franklin's suggestion that Arden make no mention to his wife of 'the cheer we had at my Lord Cheyne's / Although most bounteous and liberal' (xiii.67–8) in case she should be jealous. In between these two evaluations of munificence comes the vignette of Reede's prior claim to the significant Abbey lands.

Reede's impassioned plea for the land before he goes off to sea is carefully cast to avoid any suggestion of selfish greed.

> Yet will it help my wife and children,
> Which here I leave in Faversham, God knows,
> Needy and bare. For Christ's sake, let them have it!
> (xiii.15–17)

The weight of this oath, however, only provokes a condescending rebuke. Arden himself accuses Reede of 'railing' on him, 'with thy clamorous impeaching tongue' (22); Franklin describes him as 'bitter knave', advising him to 'bridle thine envious tongue' (39), and Arden as 'the railingest knave in Christendom' (54). Both employ the language of public slander in an attempt to contain Reede's plea within a discourse of disordered emotions inappropriately shared between individuals of such different rank. While the sailor's desperation is rejected outright by these men for the unseemly strength of its emotion, for the audience this is a deeply ambiguous and morally ambivalent scene.[17] The security of Arden's position, the play hints, is built on such practices, and his refusal to provide protection for Reede's family reflects interestingly upon the way his own security is stripped away from him at his death. The final plot on his life begins shortly afterwards, and Franklin's closing statement that 'Arden lay murdered in that plot of ground / Which he by force and violence held from Reede' (10–11) insists, of course, upon this end as fitting for his friend, just as the punishments are for his murderers.[18]

The forms which Arden's response to his wife's infidelity takes are also strikingly tangential to early modern ideals of behaviour. Arden's opening speech develops from his assertion of gentle status to offer what should be an appropriately gentlemanly, reasoned response to the problem. What he actually offers, however, is a particularly bloody threat to Mosby, rather than an active plan to chastise Alice:

> And that injurious ribald that attempts
> To violate my dear wife's chastity
> (For dear I hold her love, as dear as heaven)
> Shall on the bed which he thinks to defile
> See his disseuered joints and sinews torn
> Whilst on the planchers pants his weary body,
> Smeared in the channels of his lustful blood.
>
> (i.37–43)

The expected response of dignified chastisement of a woman gives way to the language of competition between wronged men. Arden's image is firmly located within the household – the joints are to be torn on the bed and the body pants on the floorboards – but the playwright, stretching to find an appropriate linguistic register for such a bizarre tragedy, gives Arden, the provincial patriarch, a language of horrific violence reminiscent of the villains of revenge tragedy. This is not, however, Italy, it is Faversham, and appropriate levels of emotional response are therefore governed by different expectations. In the context of this carefully located play of sixteenth-century English provincial life the wildness of his reaction, his lack of self-control, threaten anarchy within the strict codes of appropriate behaviour. The kinds of restraint and reasoned reaction promulgated as ideal male behaviour are in tension with this strikingly 'literary' response in ways which highlight the potential for mimetic tensions inherent in the play's generic novelty.[19]

Arden's role as domestic governor is called into question throughout the play. A time-depth is repeatedly alluded to in Alice's and Mosby's relationship, a temporal space in which it has evolved and altered and which reflects poorly upon Arden's household management. Sending Adam of the Fleur de Luce with a message to Mosby, Alice asks him to 'Bear him from me these pair of silver dice / With which we played for kisses many a time' (i.123–4). Arden himself, when he is reconciled to Mosby in the first scene, justifies the insults he gave him on the grounds of the common knowledge of the affair:

> As for the base terms I gave thee late,
> Forget them, Mosby; I had cause to speak

> When all the knights and gentlemen of Kent
> Make common table-talk of her and thee.
>
> (341–4)

This public circulation of domestic information provides ample grounds for Arden's pain, but does not explain his reluctance to address his concerns to his wife. The subtle negotiations which govern the suppression and dissemination of household knowledge, troubled at by household manuals and foregrounded in depositions, gives greater weight to this statement than might be immediately obvious. When Beatrice Garman's husband followed Mistress Gaunte like an 'Anthony pig', the case came to court when 'the chiefe yomen of the countery talked' about it. Ingrained sins are signalled, as opposed to a possible lapse, and they directly affect Arden's reputation with his peers. His brawl with Mosby in the street, however, rather than closing down such public domestic discussion, merely serves to perpetuate the inappropriately open nature of his actions.

In the opening scene, which sets the tone for Arden's response throughout the play, Franklin makes recourse to aphoristic expressions of 'typical' female behaviour. Advising his friend to 'In any case be not too jealous, / Nor make no question of her love to thee' (48–9), his practical suggestion is that Arden should 'as securely, presently take horse, / And lie with me at London all this term', because, 'women when they may will not, / But, being kept back, straight grow outrageous' (50–3). Physical absence, an occasional necessary evil for which the household manuals discuss contingency plans, is suggested and finally adopted as an almost parodic version of patriarchal control.[20]

Alice's speech of feigned indignation in scene xiii crystallises the suggestions about her husband's misrule. 'Ah me accursed', she begins, and calls him a 'frantic man'. She then employs the moralised binaries of prescriptive literature to characterise her own behaviour:

> Henceforth I'll be thy slave, no more thy wife;
> For with that name I never shall content thee.
> If I be merry, thou straightways thinks me light;
> If sad, thou sayest the sullens trouble me;
> If well attired, thou thinks I will be gadding;
> If homely, I seem sluttish in thine eye.
>
> (106–11)

Typically of the play's criticism of Arden, the speech builds up ambiguity through Alice's charade. She takes the division between public and private behaviour and turns it into a 'no-win situation' in which Arden's interpretation produces emotional and sartorial excess. Her gentlewomanly finery becomes provocation, her housewifely appearance untidiness, and she is caught between her public and private roles. But in her parting shot she offers an explanation for this inappropriateness, locating it in a failure of her husband's authority: 'Thus am I still, and shall be while I die, / Poor wench abused by thy misgovernment' (112–13).

If this charge of misgovernment rings true, it is because of Arden's professed attitude towards the boundary between domestic and communal space.[21] Franklin's logical suggestion that the 'common table talk' of the affair would be best refuted by Mosby 'forbearing' Arden's house provokes the following reply:

> Forbear it! Nay, rather frequent it more.
> The world shall see that I distrust her not.
> To warn him on the sudden from my house
> Were to confirm the rumour that is grown.
>
> (i.349–52)

Arden is clearly represented as misunderstanding the relationship between frequenting the house and the operation of rumour. He also misunderstands the seductive significance of physical proximity, and the ways in which sharing household space necessitates a place within its hierarchies of rule and submission. Mosby's reply permits connections between *Arden* and *A Woman Killed with Kindness* in its identification of the problematic role of the male household guest:

> By my faith, sir, you say true.
> And therefore will I sojourn here awhile
> Until our enemies have talked their fill
>
> (353–5)

Sojourners frequent the house but have no clearly defined place within its patriarchal structures; they occupy a role somewhere between household member and occasional guest. The play gives greatest space to Arden's dealings with men, and that is why the element of social competition is so strong. He 'performs' proscriptive literature backwards, hoping that his public actions will bolster his private authority; finding they do quite the opposite.

For this reason, representations of the Faversham house offer fractured aspects of the hospitality which it would be expected to offer, ones which are frequently sites for a playing out of different kinds of domestic control which questions the householder's overall authority. In the first scene Arden marshals his domestic space: 'Alice, make ready my breakfast; I must hence' (299), but the sustenance which he is about to receive is poisoned. Offering a staged imitation of the obedient wife, she provides as he orders: 'Husband, sit down; your breakfast will be cold' (360). It is Arden who invites Mosby to their table ('Come, Master Mosby, will you sit with us?' (361)), and his rival's partial acceptance suggests the uncomfortable place Mosby occupies in the house, by turns welcome and unwelcome, and privy to a greater knowledge of the diseased nature of its life-threatening routines than its master: 'I cannot eat, but I'll sit for company' (362).[22]

The final meal for which Alice marshals preparations so efficiently nominally forms a celebration of Arden's reconciliation with Mosby and their future friendship, as his attempts to procure a peace-making toast demonstrate. The lover's partial and troubled integration into the house negotiates the complexities of affection and obligation shown in the sharing of food in the depositions. The long sequence of the play's denouement sees domestic authority shift between the characters. In the carefully staged, fatuous struggle over whether Mosby should stay within the already locked doors, Alice and her husband implicitly compete for control over the house. 'I for you, God knows, have undeserved / Been ill spoken of in every place', she says to her lover, 'Therefore, henceforth frequent *my* house no more' (xiv.210–12). Arden, poignantly thinking he is restoring hospitable calm to his already shattered household, insists 'Tush, I'll have no such vows made in *my* house' (217).

But everything changes, of course, when Arden is absent from that house. In the opening scene, Alice's and Mosby's relationship is characterised by their sensitivity to different types of urban privacy. Arden knows that they have 'privy meetings in the town', and Alice says that her lover dares not come to the house because 'my husband is so jealous / And these my narrow-prying neighbours blab, / Hinder our meetings when we would confer' (i.134–6). Space is constricted for them by the immorality of their liaison; having no legitimate business, they have no rightful place in which to meet. The house offers a dangerously secret location, but only in the absence of its male head. Alice comforts Adam, her go-between: 'Be not afraid; my husband is now from home' (i.108) and, as she, Mosby and Bradshaw discuss the letter he brings from Greene, 'let us in to shun suspicion' (viii.166). In the absence of its master, suspicion adheres to meetings outside, rather than inside, the house, and Alice exercises her role as substitute head to its furthest and most frightening extent.

At the end of the opening scene of plotting, Mosby, on completion of his bargain with the painter, suggests celebration: 'Now, Alice, let's in and see what cheer you keep' (636), and Alice herself offers Bradshaw her household hospitality when he delivers the letter from Greene: 'Go in, Bradshaw; call for a cup of beer. / 'Tis almost suppertime.' In each case, the offer of hospitality is linked to 'going inside', as Alice provides the sustenance of the household for those involved in the various plots to murder its head. Stating to Bradshaw that 'thou shalt stay with *us*' (viii.155–6), she is of course referring to herself and Mosby, and the provision of household plenty indicates the extent to which they take over the spaces and stores of the house as their own in Arden's absence.

When he arrives in London, Arden's imagination of the house from which he has exiled himself causes him pain. 'My house is irksome; there I cannot rest', he confides in Franklin, who again gives spatially perverse advice: 'Then stay with me in London; go not home.' But Arden does appear to understand the consequences of such a passive response, 'Then that base Mosby doth usurp my room / And makes his triumph of me being thence' (iv.27–30). The audience has already seen this nightmare played out in front of them in concrete terms. 'I hope', says Mosby when Arden has left for London, 'now Master Arden is from home, / You'll give me leave to play your husband's part' (i.637–8). Both he and Alice seem to envisage a straight swap of one husband for another, in which the lesser man can take over the role of domestic king: 'Mosby, you know who's master of my heart / He well may be the master of the house' (639–40). The rules of affection fundamentally undercut household order in terms which stress the physical replacement of one man with another. The terrifying prospect that a 'botcher' might rule as well as this gentleman is raised.

The two most carefully localised episodes in the play are the scenes in Franklin's London house and the murder itself. The drawn-out intensity of the murder attempts in each, as opposed to the swiftly interrupted efforts made to do away with Arden outside the house, suggest that the household offers a different kind of context for murder. The serious nature of the narrative at these points, in contrast to the black comedy of Will's and Shakebag's behaviour during previous endeavours, additionally alerts the audience to the change of spatial significance.

The routines of domestic life are a strong force in Franklin's London home, where they are constructed as a dynamic of Michael's service to his two masters; a male world of comforts. 'First go make the bed, / And afterwards go hearken for the flood' (vi.3–4), Arden instructs him, and Michael himself explains to the murderers, 'My master hath new supped, / And I am going to prepare his chamber' (iii.126–7). The bedchamber which Arden and Franklin share is a central focus of their life together, a retreat from the complicated affections of Faversham.

The concreteness of Arden's presence in both houses and the full representation of their spaces and routines have the effect of pointing up the competing nature of the personal intimacies of his fractured domesticities. Arden's relationship with his house is troubled in a way which self-consciously reflects the quality of his marital bond. In an impassioned speech to Franklin, he claims 'Here, here it lies . . . That will not out till wretched Arden dies' (iv.32–3), and his assertion underlines the complexities of the location of emotion, and the relationship between rule over hearts and rule over houses. The environments of house and relationship are paired with one another here as they were in the advice literature, but rather than overlapping one another they are painfully split apart.

The murder attempt which takes place in the London house is made possible because of Michael's control over domestic routines. 'This night', he advises Will and Shakebag, 'come to his house at Aldersgate; / The doors I'll leave unlocked against you come' (iii.179–80). He then describes the murderers' route:

> No sooner shall ye enter through the latch,
> Over the threshold to the inner court,
> But on your left hand shall you see the stairs
> That leads directly to my master's chamber
>
> (iii.181–4)

His speech plays out the organisation of the house as an aid to the imagination of both his on-stage and off-stage audiences. The dynamic between seen and unseen is politicised, as the dialogue in which information is exposed suggests a simultaneous violation of space and allegiance. Michael explains the logic of the space to two men who would never be allowed legitimate access to such a house, and in doing so he offers them familiarity with the unseen private space of the chamber. Because such speeches also invite the audience to imagine the scene, imagination becomes a form of entry, and positioning themselves mentally within such a household sharpens their sense of relative status. Michael's directions are supposed to give the killers an understanding of the space which shortcuts experience of it, and which confers on them a freedom to use it as though they were familiar with it. But social propriety dictates that knowledge of an interior comes as a result of closeness to its owner, either parity of social situation or membership of the household as servant. In either case, as shown above, familiarity provides an index of the affective bonds which act as a key to admit the individual. Here, however, Michael trades in his privileged domestic knowledge, signifying the breakdown of the ties of responsibility which the household should generate.

This section of the play is characterised by interiorising soliloquies which stress isolation within the walls of the house. Scene iii ends with Michael's metaphorical consideration of betrayal. He imagines Arden as a lamb feeding 'securely on the down' (191), in verse which casts the victim in an elevatedly tragic role. Calling Arden 'harmless' and mentioning his 'gentle life', against which he sets the 'lawless rage' of the 'slaughtermen', he steps outside the character of illiterate servant to offer the audience a representation of his master as a Christ-like sacrificial figure. Scene iv, which opens with Arden and Franklin's discussion of the usurped house in Faversham, continues after Arden's exit to bed with Franklin's own ennobling soliloquy on his friend's troubles. He too calls him 'gentle gentleman', and describes him casting 'his eyes up towards the heavens, / Looking that ways for redress of wrong' (iv.46–7). He and Michael share a brief exchange, which again stresses the comforts and companionships of sleep ('My master would desire you come to bed.' Franklin: 'Is he himself already in his bed?' (55–6)), and then swap places on the stage for Michael's final discourse upon his loyalties. Having laid out the bonds of his word in his previous speech: 'So have I sworn to Mosby and my mistress; / So have I promised to the slaughtermen' (iii.203–4), Michael now tests their relative strengths. 'My mistress she hath forced me with an oath, / For Susan's sake, the which I may not break, / For that is nearer than a master's love' (iv.64–6). The play exploits the ambiguity of that word 'nearer', simultaneous describer of affection, affiliation and spatial proximity. The conflict between master and lover is a household one, one focussed upon Michael's future domestic location – merely remaining a servant after this night or imagining himself as head of his own household.

His ensuing nightmare of Black Will gives rise to a cry which is a familiar social and dramatic trope: 'help! / Call up the neighbours, or we are but dead!' (85–6). His superiors, presumably in their night attire, enter the stage in a state of confusion: 'What dismal outcry calls me from my rest?' (87), asks Franklin. Such an assault on the quiet senses of the sleeping house is familiar to us from, for instance, *Othello* or *Two Lamentable Tragedies*. But in those plays characters outside try to rouse those within to new and urgent communal knowledge. In the depositions, such a trope calls upon notions of communal responsibility. Here, the discussion is wholly within, a drama played out only for the household itself, and the reworked trope insists upon the paradoxical nature of a rupture created and felt only within the house.

The focus upon the doors throughout the remainder of the scene is suggestive of the metaphorical association between the house and a defensible castle: a private space which can be sealed off from external assault. Roused by Michael's loud waking nightmare, Franklin and Arden return from their chamber through one of the entrances at the rear of the stage. As Arden checks the doors to see whether they are locked, however, he must also be trying one of these doors. Defined by their relationship to the action on the stage, the doors provide not a sustained mimesis of interior versus exterior but rather a focus of attention upon points of access to the house and consequently the possibility of security. Their material protection is in tension with Michael's preceding soliloquy, standing in a space which he describes as 'the threshold, leaning to the stairs' (91), physically in between Arden's and Franklin's chamber and the 'slaughtermen' of the city outside.

Scene iv demonstrates the importance of the doors in keeping the town *out*, and scene v, where Black Will beats upon them trying to get *in*, reinforces this notion clearly. It demonstrates the physically aggressive threat posed by lawlessness within the community, and contrasts it with domestic disloyalty. Between them, the scenes create an interior through entrance, exit and the spatialising qualities of soliloquy, as well as descriptive verse. Unlike the final scene, the focus here is not upon the domestic props which personalise rooms as they define them. Instead, an interior is produced in which the reserved qualities of household space, rather than its nature as a reflection of individual identity, is stressed. To the scene in which the murder finally takes place, the audience bring a conception of the house as a place where, above all, space can be controlled to whatever ends. In order for this restless, peripatetic murder to be accomplished, the narrative suggests, it must find a context which can be 'governed' unproblematically – where governance sets in tension patriarchal control over the household and illegitimate manipulation of space, the locking of doors rather than the exercise of innate authority.

The final murder attempt draws these various meanings of household space into a crescendo of violence. Will and Mosby invent their strategy for the use of Arden's parlour, taking possession of the room by imposing their own image of events upon it. If some spaces are especially conducive to murder, then a parlour should certainly not be one of them. There is an outrageous plausibility in this room as a space for the intended action, one which necessitates a radical reorganisation of its expected use, and especially its careful definition of the importance of the householder. As the parlour of a gentleman, this room has a specific set of meanings revolving around the kind of close relationships which were nurtured within it.[23] Suddenly, the audience's knowledge of the habitual uses of such a room for intimate elite leisure activities is suggestively compared to locations such as Rainham Down. Because space is so often constructed simply through the type of actions which take place on the stage, this type of scene offers a telling paradox. It uses a considerable number of props to construct notions of hospitality and leisure – stools, a chair, playing tables etc. – but the impropriety of the characters' actions, which work against every social and moral precept which governs the room, serve radically to undermine its meanings.

The key to Will's suggestions for the murder bears directly upon Arden's status:

> Place Mosby, being a stranger, in a chair,
> And let your husband sit upon a stool,
> That I may come behind him cunningly
> (xiv.118–20)

His advice is pragmatic, that of the professional killer who weighs space in terms of its potential for smooth and effective action. As Arden is moved on to a stool from his rightful position on the chair, Mosby now, as Arden feared in Franklin's house, physically 'usurps his room', fulfilling the lower-status lover's own dream of being seen 'in Arden's seat' (iv.29; viii.31). The defence offered by status to the threatened assaults of society is now afforded to another who, by replacing Arden in his wife's affections, manages to switch places with him physically. With the chair came the prime position within the room, that around which all other furniture was organised. The privileged view of the house's bounty which it offered was a spatial definition of authority through an all-encompassing perspective, one whose social weight is a part of the meaning of the prop.[24]

The successful plans which are set out for this last attempt demonstrate the domestic as an environment easier to manipulate because familiar and clearly understood. The murderers know Arden's parlour intimately, and they spend enough time within it to plan their actions carefully to take account of its particular logistics. The sureness with which all take up their positions rests upon familiarity with the space of the kind which Michael attempted to give to Will and Shakebag when they plotted the attempt in the London house. There is a palpable impropriety in the familiarity suggested by Black Will's reorganisation of the furniture: he and Shakebag are masterless men without a house of their own and with no connection to one, and it is the only time we see these perpetual wanderers in a domestic setting.[25] They are physically excluded from the London house because Michael shuts the door, but the metaphorical implication of their failure to use its spaces to their purposes is that they are socially and morally inferior to its owner. In Alice's space, however, they are given the keys of the counting house in which Arden's wealth is stored. Again, these questions about admission position the audience socially in relation to a domestic interior. When the mayor enters after Arden's body has been discovered, he reveals Arden's blood 'in the place where he was wont to sit' (xiv.400). His knowledge of Arden's habitual position in his parlour, necessary to the operation of providence, also demonstrates his legitimate familiarity with the dead man's domestic space. A part of Alice's crime, perhaps the most pernicious part, was to allow such men to share a domestic knowledge commensurate with that of the town's highest officer.

The murder takes place just before the friends and neighbours whom Arden has invited to dinner arrive, filling the house with two sets of visitors. Those who initially gather for Arden's final meal are not his close friends, they are his wife's associates. As dining usually defines a network of affection and mutual responsibility, so here it determines the lengths to which Alice has gone to procure her husband's demise. They are a community of murderers, bound to one another through a common aim which cuts across the connections of status, family, and household. If the depositions underlined the vibrancy of narratives which placed unexpected actions within household routines, then surely this murder, substituted for the anticipated binding meal, offers the ultimate affronting shock to domestic meanings.

Once again, doors and locks become significant ways of articulating spatial control. Mosby outlines the physically daring but metaphorically perfect plan for secreting the murderers in Arden's counting house, ensconced with his money as he himself hopes to be as soon as the murder is over. Will asks for clarification: 'But who shall lock me in?', 'That will I do; thou'st keep the key thyself' (106–7), Alice replies. Will's parting line on entering his hiding place underscores the supreme theatricality of the scene, and the effectiveness of its use of stage space: 'When this door opens next, look for his death' (141), and Alice picks up on the door's ability simultaneously to impede and liberate, expanding it into an audaciously poetic description of her desires, 'Ah, would he now were here, that it might open! / I shall no more be closed in Arden's arms' (142–3). In doing so, she points up the tensions between the characters' propensity to dignify their actions by moving into a poetic register, and the insistent 'everydayness' of the setting for a murder which is hardly motivated by lofty ideals.[26]

Michael is to ensure that the street door is locked after Arden's arrival, because 'He shall be murdered ere the guests come in'. The charade which Alice then plays over whether or not Mosby is welcome depends upon a false conception of a permeable house: 'The doors are open, sir; you may be gone', she taunts him. The tension of the stage space at this time, its restricted, entrapping nature, is insisted upon in an aside from Michael which reiterates the preceding exchange, 'Nay, that's a lie, for I have locked the doors' (197–8).

It is not only the repetition but the form it takes, as an aside, fracturing the scene dangerously into an object for audience scrutiny suggestive of ambiguous authority, which intensifies our sense of an interior space. This impression is deepened by Michael's advice to the murderers to 'creep betwixt my legs' as they enter the parlour from the counting house so that they will not be seen from the table (229). His habitual domestic employment, standing on the margins of the room until his service is needed, provides cover for their illegitimate actions. The suggestion works to limit the impression of space, to bring the dynamics of a real parlour, a room crammed with the important and bulky furniture which signifies elite status, to bear upon the wider and less propertied space of the stage.

The murder itself provides an almost welcome relief from the stilted, painfully difficult social interactions which surround it. After the drawn-out tension of the game which Mosby plays to win his fortune in murder, a tension which flirts with an element of chance even in the last minutes of Arden's life, murder at least offers the fevered activity of violence. At the end of such a lengthy build-up, however, the way the audience's desire for a period of relief is thwarted is full of moral significance. The body is barely off-stage when the carefully controlled house is made vulnerable by the sound of knocking without: 'Mistress, the guests are at the doors' says Susan, 'Harken! They knock. What, shall I let them in?' (251–2). Theatrically, what follows is perhaps the most remarkable scene of the play. Susan exits to 'fetch water and wash away this blood' (254), leaving Alice, however briefly, alone on the stage and without dialogue, to survey the house over which she is now sole mistress. On Susan's return, the two of them begin a perversion of a typical female domestic task: 'The blood cleaveth to the ground and will not out', Susan complains, presumably after some energetic trying; 'But with my nails I'll scrape away the blood', her mistress replies, before her efforts are rewarded with the providential supply of proof of her guilt, 'The more I strive the more the blood appears!' (255–7). The action is stark, with little dialogue and an intense and pressured focus on a parody of domestic routine. This silent work creates a space in which the aftermath of murder can be experienced in a symbolism which plays out from the indelibility of the physical stain. Alice, who had previously tied her identity to the house ('If I should go, our house would run away / Or else be stol'n' (x.25–6)), slowly realises that her future is still coupled with its fabric, and that the seemingly final action of murder will not bring about the desired domestic change.

This stage image of servant and mistress scrubbing together signals a break-down in domestic hierarchy which continues within the formal social context of the meal. The suspicious Franklin begins to assert his own authority over the situation, assuming his dead friend's role by telling Alice that she 'may do well to bid his guests sit down' (xiv.284) – attacking her confusion as a lack of the basic skills of hospitality. But on her command 'Master Mosby, sit you in my husband's seat' (287), the servants break into a series of asides which demonstrates dramaturgically the domestic chaos which they discuss: 'Susan, shall thou and I wait on them? / Or, and thou say'st the word, let us sit down too' (288–9). As the guests mime their reception of hospitality, the servants comment upon the emptiness of the gesture, and the result is a kind of mannered domestic anarchy, still retaining the significance of public and private behaviour through soliloquy.

The final competition for authority over the house comes with the guests at last dismissed, and with the Mayor of Faversham approaching the doors. Alice's confident statement, 'My house is clear, and now I fear them not' (356), read in relation to the play's providential scheme, sounds painfully ironic as it clearly misunderstands the nature of the power of the vigilant community. The mayor is the representative of an omniscient justice which cuts across the criminal's supposed distinction between public and private action. Although they locked the doors whilst the murder took place, it was not possible to keep them closed because there is nothing so suspicious as a household closed to the operations of justice: 'Go, Michael, let them in' (361) Alice responds to the play's final episode of off-stage knocking.

Her attempts to deceive the mayor by claiming that her husband has not returned are met with his simple refutation: 'I saw him come into your house an hour ago' (363). The full import of this statement is only appreciated in the context of communal observation of the comings and goings of neighbours and the extraordinary jurisdiction over domestic space which it allowed. The entry of the mayor, appropriately costumed, symbolises the intervention of the community as a whole, and reiterates the conditional nature of domestic authority.

The facility of Arden's property to hold sufficient evidence to reconstitute the event of his death builds upon the perceived relationship between crime and spatial context which has been set up throughout the play. Its significance at this point in the narrative has to be seen in relation to the operation of justice, to its prominence in records of contemporary crimes where material traces provided the most compelling evidence of transgression. The implicit consequences of the failure of the material world to record the sins of mankind would be a social and moral anarchy, and the avoidance of such a state of affairs is an important part of Arden of Faversham's moral project.

Although Arden's body has been removed by the time the mayor and the watch enter, the line of footprints in the snow connects the spaces of murder and discovery, and the various objects which form relics from the site of the murder, the towel and the knife which were used to strangle and stab him, the rushes which stuck in his shoe from the floor of his parlour, and the blood which stained the floor where he sat, provide just enough traces to enable the truth to be discovered. These objects are placed together into an order which is productive of a coherent narrative – read in the right way, they generate a story, the one which the audience has just watched. The discovery of the clues is an immensely satisfying narrative scheme for an audience used to such a process of revelation, and translated into a theatrical device it has the additional power of emphatic reiteration: the understanding of the characters eventually, and against all the odds, becomes equal to that of the privileged audience. By employing such a design as a method of closure, the play borrows a quasi-legal authority from extra-theatrical narratives of the discovery of crime, and simultaneously reinforces the importance of such methods of interpretation for communal harmony.

The house in Arden of Faversham is a space which is 'governed' in the physical sense rather than the patriarchal one. Alice and her co-conspirators implicitly oppose inside and outside in their organisation of the murder, but the connection between such spatial opposites and the moral distinctions of protection and vulnerability becomes confused. At the place where Arden was 'wont to sit', covered by rushes, the patch of Arden's blood which marks the floor is the contrasting pair to the print his body makes in the grass behind his house. A guilty stain, poorly concealed and readable to all with intimate knowledge of the house, is set against the public spectacle of the miraculous image of absence.[27] Between these two impressions of Arden's death there is, of course, a material connection – footprints, a geography receptive to reconstruction. That journey between them means many things: a walk across disputed land; the murderers' bid to banish the ultimate symbol of domestic disease; the climax of the mayor's narrative of revelation; and the epitome of the process by which the death of a householder in a provincial town impertinently enters the national consciousness – a movement from household out to community.

NOTES

1 Criticism of the play has tended to focus on the distinctions and interconnections of public and private actions, but surprisingly little attention has been paid to the ways in which these problematic boundaries are reflected in its dramaturgy. See for instance, Orlin, 1994, chapter 1; Julie R. Schutzman, 'Alice Arden's freedom and the suspended moment of *Arden of Faversham*', *SEL* 36:2, 1996; Garrett A. Sullivan, *The Drama of Landscape*, Stanford: Stanford University Press, 1998, p. 47.

2 All references are to the Revels edition of the play, ed. M. L. Wine, London: Methuen, 1973.

3 See above, p. 36.

4 For the extent of Alice's 'limited realm of freedom and agency, a realm of autonomy made possible by the very fact of its impermanence', which she sees as suspended between Alice's initial declaration of intent and the murder, see Schutzman, 1996, p. 292.

5 See, on movement around the county, P. Clark, 'The migrant in Kentish towns 1580–1640', in Clark and Paul Slack eds, *Crisis and Order in English Towns*, London: Routledge and Kegan Paul, 1972; on routes for travelling players, Siobhan Keenan, *Travelling Players in Shakespeare's England*, Basingstoke: Palgrave, 2002, pp. 8–9; on casual visitors to London, R. Finlay and B. Shearer, 'Population growth and suburban expansion' in A. L. Beier and Roger Finlay eds, *London 1500–1700*, New York: Longman, 1986, p. 46; and the Chamberlain's Accounts for Canterbury, FA 11ff.

6 Holinshed says that Arden altered its location, 'so reaping all the gaines to himselfe, and bereaving the towne of that portion which was woont to come to the inhabitants', quoted in Wine, 1973, p. 157.

7 Of course the play makes reference to the period of Arden's murder, most strikingly perhaps by mention of the King, but the narrative as a whole is intended to signal contemporariness.

8 For a full discussion of 'the play's infusion with political constructs and vocabularies' see Orlin, 1994, pp. 91–8.

9 See above, pp. 51–3.

10 For a subtle analysis of the languages of status in the play see Michael Neill, '"This gentle gentleman": social change and the language of status in *Arden of Faversham*', *Medieval and Renaissance Drama in England*, 10, 1998, 73–97; see also Lake, 2002, pp. 104–6, for the significance of status in the play.

11 Neill's view of Arden as 'an *arriviste*' makes this contest particularly tense and bitter, 1998, p. 82.

12 Neill, however, suggests that 'the pressing iron is given no physical presence, existing instead only as an instrument of lacerating fantasy', 1998, p. 77.

13 Neill's suggestion that rank is 'the primary source of Alice's sexual attractiveness' seems to play down the aspects of their mutual physical attraction which come out in the performance of this scene, 1998, p. 93.

14 See above, pp. 83–4.

15 For further detail of these slurs see Neill, 1998, p. 83, where he says that 'The real significance of such traded insults' is to 'suggest how much any claim to status is dependent on the claimant's power to enforce it'.

16 See above, pp. 47–8.

17 In performance it often hangs on the delivery of Franklin's response to Arden's assurance that 'I ne'er did him wrong': 'I think so, Master Arden.'

18 As many of the play's critics have suggested, the inappropriateness of Arden's dealings with other men intertwines with his domestic control in order to provide the several dynamics of motivation for his tragedy. As Lake points out, 2002, p. 108, 'Arden's failure in the discharge of his public duty to the commonwealth as a landowner and gentleman was paralleled by, was indeed a mirror image of, his private failure as the head of a household and a husband', and 'The play goes out of its way to link the two faults in Arden's character through the nature, place and timing of his death'. See also Catherine Belsey, *The Subject of Tragedy: Identity and Difference in Renaissance Drama*, London: Routledge, 1985, p. 132. Adams points out that as his interview with Reede ends, so does 'divine protection', 1965, p. 106.

19 See, for details of these restraints, Shepard, 2003; Bryson, 1998.

20 As Lena Orlin puts it, 'Arden's absence is Alice's triumph', 'Man's house as his castle in *Arden of Faversham*', *Medieval and Renaissance Drama in England*, 2, 1985, 57–89, p. 77.

21 Lake memorably condemns Arden as lacking 'patriarchal spunk', 2002, p. 110, a phrase which, I suppose, precisely attends to the relationship between the exercise of domestic power and masculine identity! Orlin, on the opposite side of the coin to my argument about Arden's failures, points out that 'The ideological tautology at the heart of *Arden of Faversham* is that Alice's rebellion itself validates her charge against Arden', 1994, p. 97.

22 Comensoli argues that 'The basic role of the economy of feeding is to encode social values and customs' in the play, and points out that even as it 'inscribes' these codes, 'it brings into focus the displacement of desire that underwrites' them, 1996, pp. 85–7.

23 The room is only named in the sources, but it is characterised in performance by the properties required and the nature of the activities which take place there.

24 Although tangential to this argument, it is interesting to note the shift in the narrative at this point. If it is in fact Mosby who sits in Arden's place, then the blood will not be found 'where he was wont to sit'. The providential structure of the Mayor's assertion overrides the change, but if an audience does notice, perhaps the disjuncture itself makes a powerful point.

25 For the striking length of these 'assassins' roles' and the differences between them see Martin Wiggins, *Journeymen in Murder*, Oxford: Clarendon Press, 1991.

26 For a fuller analysis of the uneasy relationship between these different styles see Alexander Leggatt, 'Arden of Faversham', *Shakespeare Survey*, 36, 1983, 121–33; Belsey, 1985, p. 133.

27 For the significance of land in the play generally, and this print in particular, see Sullivan 1998, chapter 1.

4

Two Lamentable Tragedies

THE VISIBILITY OF the print of Arden's body on the land behind his house for 'two years or more' functions, fairly self-consciously in Franklin's Epilogue, as a metaphor for the moral operation of tragedies. It offers the audience a suggestively material example of how they might begin to interpret the significance of the story they have just witnessed: of how individual events gain a wider visibility, how individuals' stories become narratives of public significance.

Although the major source for *Arden* was undoubtedly Holinshed, the play was, as Lena Orlin has shown, also related to ballads of the events of his death. Its narrative bled from chronicle through drama and cheap print, its notoriousness partly defined by the range of genres in which it was significant.[1]

Two Lamentable Tragedies is also linked to the cheaper end of the developing print market. It too is based on ballad narratives, and the salacious goriness of its mode connects it closely to pamphlets about recent shocking crimes.[2] Those pamphlets offered stark sensationalism within a rigid and explicit didactic framework where the 'voluntary confession of the parties' was intended to be used as an 'example to the amendment of [the reader's] life', as Arthur Golding put it.[3] The dramatic genre to which such moralising comes closest is of course that of the Morality play, which focuses the energies of its representation towards a moment of didactic closure. Positioning themselves between Moralities and tragedies proper, domestic tragedies' interests lie both in the psychological effects of crime upon the individual protagonist and in the threat transgression offers to the communities of household and town. They give evidence for the perniciousness of vice and the consequent need for spiritual vigilance for all, and as such both *Arden* and *Two Lamentable Tragedies* gained significant power from their status as stories which had 'really happened'. Their impact was not of the nature of a shocking possibility, but of an appalling actuality; cautionary tales with moral information from the (relatively recent) past, in a present with more than half an eye on the eschatological future.

For the moralist, the potential danger of such historically specific events is their lack of a general applicability, and *Two Lamentable Tragedies* deals with this issue much more explicitly than *Arden of Faversham*. It uses an allegorical framework to mediate between the particular and the general, one which foregrounds the relationship between abstract notions of sin and individual actions. The play is opened by the character of Homicide, who is disappointed because the town is so virtuous that he is not able to 'bath[e]' his 'greedy hands in reeking blood' as he would like. The inhabitants, he says, are 'all bent with virtuous gainful trade . . . And will not soil their well addicted hearts' (A2).[4] Fortunately he meets Avarice, his 'chiefest good', and the two kiss and embrace one another. This structure immediately sets the ensuing action within the context of the malevolent external forces of sin which prey upon the unwary potential sinner.

Truth introduces the play's two stories in distinct terms. The first 'was done in famous London late, / Within that street whose side the river Thames / Doth strive to wash from all impurity'. The location has been perpetually imprinted with the murder, like Arden's field:

> But yet that silver stream can never wash
> The sad remembrance of that cursed deed,
> Performed by cruel Merry on just Beech
> And his true boy poor Thomas Winchester.
>
> (A3)

And the tale is explicitly set up as a well-known one: 'The most here present know this to be true / Would truth were false, so this were but a tale.' The use of the names of the characters instead of any specific details of the crimes emphasises the status of these events as more than just a 'tale', as common knowledge for the audience. In contrast, the other story,

> . . . further off but yet too near
> To those that felt and did the cruelty:
> Near Padua this wicked deed was done,
> By a false Uncle on his brother's son,
> Left to his careful education,
> By dying parents with as strict a charge
> As ever yet death-breathing brother gave
> (A3)

The two plots are connected by the allegorical affinity between Homicide and Avarice and very little else: whilst they use similar imagery to explore related themes, both the pragmatics of their situations and their modes of representation are totally different. One takes place in London, the other somewhere near Padua; one involves the murder of a neighbour and his boy, because the neighbour has money which his less well-off killer wants for himself, the other involves the killing of a young boy for his substantial inheritance by a man who already has enough. Only one is in any sense of the term a domestic tragedy. The decision to represent them in the same play appears to be inspired by the form of pamphlets based on contemporary events: for instance Anthony Munday's *A View of Sundry Strange Examples*, whose eclectic nature Lake describes: 'various murder stories were recounted along with other prodigies and natural disasters (a monstrous birth in Gelderland, the London earthquake of 1580, a freak storm in Prague), all of them designed to show that the times were bad and God's judgement imminent'.[5] Those stories were unified by their pertinent timeliness – the volume as a whole was a collection representative of the particularly virulent texture of the 'now'. *Two Lamentable Tragedies* similarly draws together the near and the far, the young and the old in order to exhibit the diverse ways in which Avarice and Homicide might be connected; in order to suggest the infinite particularities of their general association.

Yarrington uses the two plots of the play to good effect here, patterning different levels of realism in order to make his representation 'lively' for Londoners. Only the local strand of the narrative is interested in the particularising qualities of domestic settings, a feature which is given considerable prominence in contrast to the generalised sparseness of the Italian plot. The first difference one notices between the plots is the distinct languages which Yarrington develops to represent London and Italy. His elite Italians express their intense feelings of affection in protracted verse. The sheer length of their disquisitions upon their feelings, for instance Allenso's final farewell to his cousin, make for a much more static mode of representation in this strand of the play. A part of his speech gives an indication of its style:

> Come hither then, my joy, my chiefest hopes.
> My second self, my earthly happiness,
> Lend me thy little pretty cherry lip
> To kiss me cozen, lay thy little hand
> Upon my cheek, and hug me tenderly,
> Would the clear rays of thy two glorious suns,
> Could penetrate the corners of my heart,
> That thou might see, how much I tender thee.
> My friends behold within this little bulk,
> Two perfect bodies are incorporate,
> His life holds mine, his heart contains my heart,
> His every limb, contains my every part:
> Without his being, I can never be,
> He being dead, prepare to bury me.
>
> (E1–E1v)

The careful rhetorical investigation of feelings is opposed to the suspense of discovery in London. Fallerio's cunning and scheming are contrasted with Merry's hasty and thoughtless actions, with the reactive nature of his plan and his swift lashing out against his victims.

The crashing ironies of Fallerio's cavalier attitude towards God's wrath, for instance his assertion that 'If aught betide him [Pertillo] otherwise than well, / Let God require due vengeance on my head' (E1) as he sends him to his death, are the climax of a string of grim predictions about Pertillo's life which begin at his parents' deathbed with his mother's prophecy that 'His share will be of woe and misery' (B2). Seemingly undaunted by the heavy atmosphere of his predestined early demise, Pertillo's saccharine sweetness forms a total moral contrast to the caricaturedly evil nature of his uncle and the murderers. The latter, like Black Will and Shakebag in *Arden*, express the boundlessness of their appetite for gold in images of passionate lunacy. 'Swones', says the first, 'here's rewards would make one kill himself, / To leave his progeny so rich a prize, / Were twenty lives engaged for this coin, / I'd end them all' (D1v).[6] But whilst this piling up of bodies in an effort to balance desire has a comic energy which the rest of the plot lacks, the intensity of the characters' emotions means that events take place at an almost constant fever pitch.

In total contrast, Yarrington's notion of the English national identity of murder is that of a graphically pared down pragmatic language. It has, to be sure, its rhetorical flourishes, and the characters do share metaphors in their discussion of events. But at moments of pressure the language of emotion is bolder and starker than in Padua, particularly in the tense domestic scenes surrounding the murders.[7] Discussing the plan for removal of Beech's body from the house, Merry says to his sister:

> I'll cut him piece-meal, first his head and legs
> Will be one burthen, then the mangled rest,
> Will be another, which I will transport,
> Beyond the water in a Ferry boat,
> And throw it into Paris-garden ditch.
> Fetch me the chopping-knife, and in the mean
> I'll move the Faggots that do cover him.
>
> (E2)

There is not a word wasted here. The only adjective, 'mangled', in this context becomes merely an accurate description, and 'piece-meal' an emotionless technical term. As Merry removes the faggots, his sister, whose primary dramatic role is to lament his deeds, cries:

> Oh can you find it in hart to cut and carve,
> His stone cold flesh, and rob the greedy grave,
> Of his dissevered blood be sprinkled limbs?
>
> (E2)

But the regularity of lament which is produced by her alliteration only serves to set up his almost comically sparse answer: 'Ay marry can I, fetch the chopping knife.' Material considerations become totally pragmatic and utterly, shockingly, separated from emotion. The language focuses on simple tasks and straightforward solutions to unthinkable problems, and this is at the heart of the domesticity of this strand of the play: it is domestic in the sense of being concerned with pragmatics; it draws its intensity not from rhetorical amplification and escalation but from the mismatch between hideous images and practical solutions, between ghoulish situations and their resolution through an equivalence of 'reassuringly' routine process.

The difference between the narratives is seen also in the way the motivations for the murders are expressed. Fallerio commits murder because, in an explanation which pre-empts the excessive language of his assassins, 'I'd rather lose mine eye, my hand, my foot, / Be blind, want senses, and be ever lame, / Than be tormented with such discontent' (C3). The discontent he dreads is given form as the opposite of his description of his enjoyment of his brother's possessions:

> His tenants pay me rent, acknowledge me
> To be their Landlord, they frequent my house,
> With Turkeys, Capons, Pigeons, Pigs and Geese . . .
> His plate, his Jewels, hangings, household stuff,
> May well beseem to fit a demy King,

His stately buildings, his delightful walks,
His fertile Meadows . . .

(C1)

This 'country house discourse' of an idealised plenty is edged with the
language of authority and governance, and its abundance ennobles Fallerio
socially as it degrades him morally. The concept of discontent also motivates
Merry, but in very different terms. His opening lines appear oddly ambiguous: 'I live in mean and discontented state', he begins, but his physical situation does not, as he acknowledges, bear out his feelings:

But wherefore should I think of discontent:
I am belov'd, I have a pretty house,
A loving sister, and a careful man,
That do not think their day's work well at end,
Except it bring me in some benefit:
And well frequented is my little house,
With many guests and honest passengers,
Which may in time advance my humble state,
To greater wealth and reputation

(A3v)

The problem seems to lie in the necessity for patience, as what might
come 'in time' becomes an imperative present desire. The neighbours who
enter at this point confirm the positive assessment of his situation: 'they
say he is an honest man, / And keeps good rule and orders in his house',
and Beech reproves him for describing his estate as poor, 'For God be
thanked you are well to live'. Merry concludes the discussion of his present
condition by saying he 'would live better if I had the means: / But as I am,
I can content my self' (A3v–A4). 'Living better' suggests an amendment of
domestic circumstances, whilst content is a feature of *response* to environment. The difference between content and discontent shifts throughout the
scene between references to a moral and a material state, an inward perception and an outward estimation. Beech correspondingly describes his own
condition, and it is this rhetorical presentation of his goods, of course, which
expands within the moral cleft of Merry's irrational discontent and fatally
breaks it apart.

Thanks be to God I live contentedly
And yet I cannot boast of mighty wealth:
But yet God's blessings have been infinite,
And far beyond my expectations,
My shop is stored, I am not much in debt . . .
I have a score of pounds to help my need

(A4v)

In the soliloquy which ends the scene, Merry draws attention to the differences which this money would make to him in terms which make reference to the local economic considerations of the 1590s. Because 'I want the coin', he says, 'I cannot buy my beer, my bread, my meat . . .' (A4v) at the best price. If he had Beech's money, however, 'I'd live as merry as the wealthiest man' in London. The motivation for both Fallerio and Merry, then, centres around the sin of covetousness and its discontents, but the way in which they represent the material qualities of desire and unfulfillment are strikingly different. One offers an idealised utopia of plenty, the other a very little more for a fantastically high price.

Although both plots deal dispassionately with their objects of desire and their subjects of murder, they do so within the different registers by which they are characterised. The London strand of the play, in common with *Arden of Faversham* but unlike its Italian counterpart, is intimately, almost myopically concerned with the physicality of death. The play as a whole subtly treats the consequences of murder in its interweaving of two strands whose advancing plots can be measured against one another to suggest the various routes which justice and providence take to reach the same end. But the Merry plot imagines the initial consequences in startlingly practical terms. Not for the innkeeper the luxury of a whole wood in which to lose a body, he has to try to find a hiding place within a vigilant town. The 'problem of Beech's body' works on many different levels. It produces its own curious claustrophobia – whereas other murderers act to rid themselves of cloying spouses and binding contracts, it is the murder itself which seems to fill Merry's home, sending his man from the house wandering and masterless and leaving himself and his sister distracted. 'Exchanged' for a loyal servant, a 'carefull man' as Merry describes Williams, Beech becomes a constant guest, a grimly perverse just desert for the man who tricked him to his death by offering him hospitality. Merry suggests that they move the body 'To the low room', explaining that 'if we keep it longer in the house, / The savour will be felt throughout the street, / Which will betray us to destruction' (D2v). In order that Beech should be prevented from leaving the house as a miasma, Merry is forced to keep humping the unfortunate corpse on the progressive stages of a journey away from the place of murder: first down the stairs, then into the woodpile, then out of the woodpile and all over the town in pieces. As he does so, his sins take on a very tangible weight: the 'heavy burthen' he must carry is one, 'Whereof my soul doth feel so great a weight, / That it doth almost press me down with fear' (E2v).

The different ways the two plots deal with materiality extend to their interest in and representation of physical space. Fallerio's description of the wood to which he is dispatching Pertillo, when compared to the impression of Rainham Down given in *Arden*, demonstrates both the similarity between the two as suitable locations for murder and their difference in relation to a notion of particularity: 'There is a thicket ten miles from this place, / Whose secret ambush, and unused ways, / Doth seem to join with our conspiracy' (D1v). This location is literary, rather than geographical, in heritage: Law points out its connections to the thicket in *King Leir* – 'about some two myles from the Court' – a place whose most fundamental feature is its position away from the location of the rest of the action.[8] Similarly, the Italian plot's unlocalised scenes can be taken to be domestic in nature because they stage exchanges between family members about family issues, but only once, when Allenso is waiting for his arrest, is the space explicitly named: 'I will not stir from out this house of woe' (H2v). Even here, 'house' functions as an idea rather than a location, just as 'wood' merely indicates somewhere remote from the town.

The Merry plot, in striking contrast, works with a firmly localised space in which the stage represents the street and the shops which border it. Dramaturgically, the pace of this strand of the play comes from its large number of entrances to and exits from the houses of its inhabitants, which give a strong sense of the relationship between household and community. The stage represents the inside of Merry's house as the location for his initial exchange with Beech, and then again when brother and sister deal with his corpse, and when they are arrested for the murder. The key points in the murder narrative, then, and the most emotionally intense scenes, take place there, and the characters discuss both the moral and practical implications of a murder within domestic space. Williams, initially believing his master's assertion that he had killed in self-defence, points out the dubiously private, secretive nature of the murder:

> If any quarrel were twixt him and you:
> You should have bade him meet you in the field,
> Not like a coward under your own roof;
> To knock him down as he had been an ox . . .
>
> (B4v)

Aggression should be public so that it can be judged and regulated, and the similarity between Williams's and Mosby's appalled reaction to domestic murder ('then we had been undone' (xiv.93), the latter says to Alice when she recalls her murderous nighttime thoughts) suggests the difficulty of avoiding punishment for a crime whose location is inherently personal, when the walls of the house bound individuality within the community.

Rachel, like Alice Arden and Susan her maid, is given the key task of trying to expunge the physical traces which tie bodies to the location of their murder. Calling her his 'comforter', Merry instructs his sister to 'Wipe up the blood in every place above, / So that no drop be found about the house . . .

/ Then burn the clothes, with which you wipe the ground / That no apparent sign of blood be found' (D2v–D3). The murder becomes subsumed into the routines of the household. Women are given the task of dealing with the after-effects of the crimes, as households work together, but not equally, to suppress their transgressions.[9] When they move him once more, an anti-domestic routine of clearing away the traces of Beech is suggested: 'only dry up the blood, / And burn the clothes *as you have done before*' (E2v). The connection to the ingrained sins of the depositions is clear. But the routine also elucidates the couple's focus on the physical after-effects, rather than the intended material benefits of the deed, and these logistical problems draw attention to the way in which the house succeeds and fails to contain the consequences of Merry's crime.

The most striking feature of domestic representation in this play is the way it locates the house in places other than the main stage. Merry's hastily conceived and brutally executed murder plan is specific about the location of the proposed deed: 'I'll fetch him to my house, / And in my garret quickly murder him' (B3). The stage direction reads: '*Then being in the upper Rome Merry strikes him in the head fifteene times*'. As he picks the pockets of the corpse, his sister, entering below, then exits 'up' to see what he is doing (B4). After a brief wail of horror, Rachel descends again, but the servant Williams, saying 'I'll know the cause wherefore we are undone', insists on seeing what is happening and exits up, followed by Rachel again ('*She goes up*', (B4v)). So the murder takes place on the upper stage, and there is a very stridently orchestrated series of comings and goings in the short space of time after it has happened. The cumbersome nature of the dramaturgy, with its extensive off-stage movements from one level of the playing space to the other, seems to draw attention to its own inconvenience. And in doing so it strongly suggests an everyday spatial pragmatics of small commercial London streets with their living accommodation above shops, focusing the plot's concern with the sheer practical difficulties posed by murder onto the relationship between different areas of the house.[10]

The location of the murder and the body which it produces divide stage space between its upper and lower planes. The upper floor of the house, top-heavy with its weight of actors, appears almost separable from the area below. Although the audience can see it clearly, it has to be accessed via stairs they cannot see. The focus on the stage as street, and the mimetic logic of the upper floor, encourage a reading of the stairs as a part of the private house. This is, of course, very different to the habitual uses of this space in contemporary plays.[11] Action continues on both levels simultaneously for a start, but in a mimetic sense – it is not as though one set of characters is imagined commenting upon the actions of another, thereby providing detachment and space for reflection.[12] We are clearly meant, as an audience, to appreciate both the distance and the connection between the two levels, and to see it as recognisably, generically domestic. Thinking back to James Nethersole's bedchamber in the room over the street, it is possible to see this striking kind of staging as dealing in the same spatial dynamics. Far away from the street access, such rooms were secluded and relatively impenetrable, but the direct visual access they gave on to the street is suggestive of a particular kind of relationship between house and town, perhaps a commercial one, in which attention was always partly turned to the street.[13] One could argue that this distinctive use of the upper stage is a feature of an unembellished translation from the narratives of the event to the play itself. It also, perhaps, offers evidence of a non-professional dramatist and/or a less-than-skilful piece of writing.

But such idiosyncratic dramaturgy also has profound metaphorical implications. The murder room thus staged is comprehensible but unreachable, concealed from the other characters by its distance from the doors of Merry's house. This is reinforced later in the play when the salter's man is sent knocking at all the houses of the street to see if he recognises the person to whom he sold the bag in which part of Beech's body was found. Merry tells Rachel to 'Hide thee *above* lest that the Salter's man, / Take notice of thee that thou art the maid, / And by that knowledge we be all undone' (G3v). In Merry's conception of the situation, the further Rachel can move from the street the less chance there is that the crime will be discovered.

The façade of the house mediates between the domestic and the communal in ways which strikingly recall the depositions' moralised binary between inside and outside. Merry considers physical distance from the street to be synonymous with social invisibility and productive of an inviolable space which can remain unseen. The play's moral project is quite explicitly a refutation of this interpretation. The only other locales which the tiring house represents in this strand of the play are the houses of Beech and his landlord Loney, and the various adjoining shops. The scene in which the murder of Beech's boy is discovered makes the moral 'other' to Merry's notion of the secrecy afforded by the physical house. The murder draws a crowd in its wake when Thomas's cries are heard by a maid who runs to tell her master. He in turn calls to Loney, who appears at a window to answer him, where he is told to 'come down with speed' (C4). Loney is described as 'sleeping' and those entering the stage presumably signal nighttime by the state of their attire and by carrying torches.[14] The dramatic convention is recognisably similar to the scene which takes place in Franklin's London house, where he and Arden run from their bed to Michael's aid. Here, however, the spatial division is between street and window rather than chamber and entry, and the business of the stage underlines the significance of the moment as a construction of a community motivated by threat. It militates strongly against Merry's quest for secrecy by showing the proper prioritisation of personal attention to domestic issues and the overriding importance of the community.

It is the movement between the individual premises, the window above, and the street itself which creates a sense of rupture, marked out against the façade of the house. The commotion here defines communal responsibility as citizens peer from windows and then come to help, rather than the furtive movement which is a feature of Merry's house on almost every occasion. The different levels, rather than representing the less easily accessed areas of an individual house, can here be seen to define the relationship between the personal and the communal. The fact that action outside has implications for those indoors, and vice versa, is emphatically demonstrated by the morally significant appearance of heads and bodies across the wall which divides one from the other.

These meanings are condensed into a strange but telling little exchange which takes place as Merry returns from his second murder sortie. The stage direction, *Enter Merry knocking at the door, and Rachel comes down*, indicates that the dialogue takes place around the door, and it ends with his desperate invitation, 'Come, come to bed, for fear we be descried'. In between, Merry casts the house in terms of refuge from the neighbours who now fill the streets:

> Oh sister, sister, now I am pursued,
> The mighty clamour that the boy did make,
> Hath raised the neighbours round about the street:
> So that I know not where to hide myself
>
> (C4v)

This tiny vignette neatly demonstrates his vulnerability. The scene in which the murder takes place ends as it began, within the house, thereby rounding off an arc of narrative, making it a scene whose subject is departure from and return to domestic space, rather than the event of murder itself. It literally brings the implications of his actions back home. The relationship between the house and the community is uniquely represented here, then, through a mimetic spatial positioning, but it is the moral implications of this 'authentic' representation which define *Two Lamentable Tragedies'* didactic project.

The materiality of this play's staging is significant in other ways too. A series of objects are introduced physically or rhetorically at key points in the Merry narrative in order to set up a sense of the everyday which connects the household to the community. As Merry soliloquises about his need for Beech's goods, he must be holding a hammer, presumably weighing its head in his hands. As he reaches the end of his flawed process of reasoning with the decisive 'They shall die both, had they a thousand lives,' he continues, 'And therefore I will place this hammer here, / And take it as I follow *Beech* up stairs' (B3v). In theatrical terms, this action ensures that the audience understand the full horror of the events which are to be represented 'above', but the placing of the object also represents the mental process of intent, left by the door to mark the entry to Beech's 'last home' as Merry crosses the stage to lure his victim. The hammer reappears, first in a typically bald response to Williams's distracted run of questions about the logistics of the deed, which shows that he is still holding it: 'With what? where with? how have you slain the man?'; 'Why with this hammer I knocked out his brains' (B4v). And when the corpse of Winchester is exhibited the same object is sticking out of his head, drawing gruesomely precise connections between the murders which simultaneously set up the physical brutality and the thoughtless pragmatism of the deed.

Merry urges Beech to 'Come quickly then, they think we stay too long', drawing him into an upper chamber with a promise of drinks with friends of his who await him there. He receives the strikingly mimetic reply, 'I'll cut a piece of Cheese to drink withal' (B4), and Beech presumably crosses the stage to his death holding the piece of cheese. The poignancy of this moment balances Pertillo's childish innocence as he leaves with his assassins, but it is of a different nature – touching because of the prosaic domesticity and simple pleasures it represents in such a fantastic context, the lack of foreboding and the projected routine of dining and friendship which we know will be cut off by his death.

Alongside these telling props, other everyday objects make their appearance in the dialogue. Hearing a cry and having sent his sister downstairs to investigate, Merry asks, 'Why how now Rachel?, who did call below?' The answer is an almost comic deflation of tension: 'A maid that came to have a penny loaf' (C3v). As normal life breaks in upon these edgy scenes it emphasises the distance Merry has travelled *from* that normality in such a very short space of time.

Discovery of Beech's servant gives rise to the sequence mentioned above, a comic one as the local community try to rouse themselves sufficiently to understand events:

> Ho neighbour Loney, pray come down with speed,
> Your tenant Beech's man is murdered.
> > *Loney sleeping.*
> What would you have some Mustard?
> *Neighbour:* Your tenant Beech's man is murdered.
> *Loney:* Who's smothered? I think you lack your wit,
> > *Out at a window*
> What neighbour? what make you here so late?
> > (C4)

The pairing of 'murdered' with the misheard 'mustard' jars the incredible against the familiar. The hammer, the cheese, the mustard, the penny loaf and, finally, the sack which Rachel procures 'To bear hence Beeches body in the night' (E2), provide a narrative thread of daily life. Their conspicuous particularity draws the sheer quotidian prosaicness of life into the play in a way which compliments and balances the more outrageous physicalities of murder. They metonymically allude to a status quo which is ruptured by the murders, and to the proper rhythms of urban transaction by which Merry could eventually have grown rich, had he not lost patience with the pace of honest livelihood.

Merry's desires were located, from the start, within his neighbourhood. Beech's discussion of his contented state is performed within what he takes to be the safety of dependable company in his host's house: 'And here I speak it where I may be bold' (A4v), he says, in secure surroundings of mutual trust. Merry's business is built upon his customers' sense of his integrity – they call him 'honest' and 'plain' in an opening scene which is full of the forms of neighbourly courtesy as they pledge one another with his finest beer, acting out one of those middling definitions of intimacy from the depositions.[15] His murder plot is the antithesis of the slow but steady increase of his fortunes which his courteousness seemed assured to produce, and it is set within the routines of commercial life which his business necessitates. 'I pray you stay not long', says Rachel as he goes to invite Beech to his death, 'Guests will come in, 'tis almost supper time' (B3v).[16] The first murder threw Merry's own house into disarray by fracturing the bonds of service; the second brings disorder to the street which stands for the surrounding community. As murder was antithetical to the protective and nurturing space of the household, so it is in opposition to the ethos of urban life. Loney describes the body of Winchester with the hammer in his head as 'this strange uncivil cruelty' (C4v), and in doing so he characterises its implications for all on the stage. 'Uncivil', meaning 'contrary to civil well-being and civic unity', is a sense contemporary with this play. The new edge to the meaning draws attention to the ways in which the implications of the action stretch beyond the household and threaten an idealised notion of community.[17]

In the aftermath of the murder, Merry and Rachel discuss the threats to their security, and the crude rhyme they share seems to ring out the significance of local knowledge: 'What doth the boy know whereabouts you dwell? / *Merry*: Ay, that torments me worse then pangs of hell' (C3r–v). From this point onwards memory is called upon in a variety of forms by the neighbours to solve the crime. The maid who arrived just after Winchester was attacked is asked 'Did you see any running from the door, / When you looked out and heard the young man cry'. Her reply appears encouraging, 'Yes I saw two truly to my thinking', but her aside in fact reveals a failure of perception: 'By my troth 'twas so dark I could see no body' (C4v). Similarly, although the hammer is known to have been 'borrowed of a cutler dwelling by', 'he remembers not, who borrowed it' (G1v).

The Salter is similarly unable to recall his customer for the bag used to dispose of the body: 'I do not well remember what she wore, / But if I saw her I should know her sure', so a parade of maids is organised by the third neighbour:

> Go round about to every neighbour's house,
> And will them show their maids immediately:
> God grant we may find out the murderers.
> *Go to one house, and knock at door, asking,*
> Bring forth such maids as are within your house.
>
> (G3)

As the party moves across the doors at the back of the stage they describe the small community of Beech's street, but their actions also begin to investigate its limits and boundaries. The point of the performance is, as Rachel describes it, 'To see if he can know the maid again', but he does not recognise her. The limits of urban knowledge are defined, and with them the boundaries of the small communities of street and neighbourhood. At the edge of personal recognition, of knowing individuals by sight, one community becomes another, and the operations of justice are threatened. Merry pins his hopes on this obscurity, 'The hammer is denied, the bag unknown, / Now there is left no means to bring it out, / Unless our selves prove Traitors to ourselves' (G3v–G4). These objects are part of the texture of the community, *familiar* objects which are invested with a history within the narrative; they are recognised physically, but have become divorced from the human interactions which give them meaning. The disjuncture between familiarity and communal knowledge stages a denial of the contemporary meanings of objects suggested above.

But the community challenges Merry's secrecy with their own systems of revelation. The scene in which the maids are sought has clear similarities with the display of Thomas Winchester and, finally, his master's body. The dramaturgy offers a particular kind of 'neighbourhood theatre', in which the commercial street becomes the context for revelation, and where recognition and knowledge are defined both spatially and morally. With Beech laid in front of his own house, the boy finally dies and the neighbours order the women to 'Bring him forth too, perchance the murderers / May have their hearts touched with due remorse, / Viewing their deeds of damned wickedness' (G3). The street which, as the play opened, was a thoroughfare of small commercial ventures open for customers has now become a stage on which to display the maps of cruelty and the plots of wickedness. All who go by (and a street ensures a quantity of 'passengers' (G3) some of whom may have information to give) must read the evidence and either take warning from it or be changed by it and confess. As the night draws in, the third neighbour instructs, 'Bring in those bodies, it grows towards night, / God bring these damned murderers at length to light' (G3v). The shopkeepers treat the corpses almost like commercial goods; sensitive to the local market, they set up their grisly stalls until the purveyors of and customers for knowledge have all gone home.

Arden of Faversham staged the discovery of murder in the theatrically satisfying terms of the providence-inspired reading of clues by a representative of communal authority. In *Two Lamentable Tragedies* the detection is a similarly material process of accretion over time, but the social and communal dynamics are different. The physical nature of the stage-as-house offers a bold visual representation of the possibilities for concealing and revealing, being open and being closed. It is a binary which resonates with the play's emphatic discussion of concealing and revealing motives and actions. From Avarice's opening concerns that company will undermine his 'secrecy' (A2v), the language of murder is dominated by images of the act's suppression which, as they mount upon one another throughout the play, signal the futility of the search for concealment. In the Italian narrative, this is figured in terms of the parity between house and body. Fallerio is aware of the vulnerability inherent in sharing secrets with others: 'I would not ope the closet of my breast, / To let you know my close intention' (Dv). He exhorts his murderers 'First to conceal, and next to execute, / What I reveal, and shall enjoin you to' (D1), and in doing so he suggests the play's bold dynamic between action and revelation. And there is a point of close connection between the two plots as, hearing that the murderers he hired are themselves dead, he says to his son, 'Better and better, then it cannot out. / Unless your love will be so scrupulous, / That it will overthrow your self and me' (H2). Revelation is set in balance against the strength of affective ties within the household. Merry is led from his assertion that 'none can open what I mean to hide' to the need to murder Beech's boy, but despite the second murder, he is faced with further impediments to secrecy: 'But then my sister, and my man at home.' For love and reward respectively, however, he convinces himself that they will conceal his 'close intent' (B3).

Merry's judgement of the loyalty of his household is proved by his sister's statement that others must 'open what I doe conceal'; because 'he is my brother, I will cover it' (F4). But in their less positive moments, both brother and sister are aware of the different types of sight with which the play is concerned. 'Although we hide our sins from mortal men', says Merry, 'Whose glass of knowledge is the face of man, / The eye of heaven beholds our wickedness.' When he asks Rachel whether she can still see the body of Beech under the pile of faggots, she replies 'Not with mine eye, but with my heart I can' (D2v).

Dramaturgically, the most striking way in which the play comments upon the dynamic between concealing and revealing is the scene in which Winchester's body is laid out for all to see. The stage space is divided, the boy *'with a hammer sticking in his head'* is silently inspected by the neighbours whilst, presumably downstage from them, Merry meets with his erstwhile household servant and asks, 'How now good Harry, hast thou hid my fault?' (D3v). Visually wide open, on display for the on-stage and off-stage audiences, the secret remains verbally hidden, festering inside Williams's soul.

But the metaphorical exploration of an idealised secrecy for sinful deeds reaches its height as Williams tries to resolve the dilemma of a loyalty divided between his love for the fallible master of his household and his duty to the instruments of an uncompromising justice which takes no account of circumstance.[18] Williams's dilemma is one at the heart of patriarchal power structures, and it is one which is the subject of considerable debate in household manuals. It provides an additional complexity to the play's representation of the relationship between the particular and the general: the tension between imperfect domestic governance and communal order, and between the personal loyalties and affections which spring from the shared household and the more essential distinctions between good and evil.

With his friend Cowley, Williams travels to 'some unfrequented place, / Where none shall hear nor see my lamentations' (F4v). The spaces inhabited by Williams for the remainder of the play are the only unlocalised places in this strand of the plot. The confining of the rest of the action to the street between Merry's and Beech's shops underlines the perceived connection between Williams's pained countenance and the search for a motive for his emotions on the part of those who observe it. The face, which is in Merry's description the 'glass of knowledge' for others (D2), records evidence of the pain caused by Williams's secret: 'if my eyes bear records of my woe', he says, 'Condemn me not, for I have mighty cause' (F4). Indeed it is Williams's 'heavy looks' and his 'eyes brimful of tears' which have suggested a silence in his friendship with Cowley in the first place as they bear 'testimony of some secret grief' (F4).[19] Williams flees because his friend is 'so curious to intrude / Your self to sorrow, where you have no share'; because he wants to enter the sorrow which is firmly set inside. Cowley, who urges Williams to 'Open this close fast clasped mystery' (H3v), diagnoses 'inward heaviness' and 'secret grief', and he explains the effects upon the body of concealing evil:

> those that smother grief too secretly,
> May waste themselves in silent anguishment,
> And bring their bodies to so low an ebb,
> That all the world can never make it flow,
> Unto the happy height of former health
>
> (F4)

The metaphor of corporeal stagnation is taken up by Fallerio after his conscience has begun to awake itself, 'These are the stings when as our consciences, / Are stuffed and clogged with close concealed crimes' (I1).

Already made homeless by his unwillingness to share a violated domestic space 'With him whose love is dearer than my life' (H3), Williams becomes frustrated with Cowley's attempts to guess the truth which he is trying to conceal: 'No, no', he says, 'your understanding is but dim, / That far removed, cannot judge the fear' (H3v). Williams's connection between the love he feels for his master and the closeness needed for interpretation nicely blurs the affective and the spatial, and suggests the double meaning of household. It acknowledges that domestic experience cannot be entirely understood from the outside as it is impossible to imagine the affective ties which bind individuals together, impossible to imagine oneself inside that space. The particularity of circumstance muddies the clarity of justice seen from outside the context of the crime – it complicates the clean lines of its decisions – and this difficulty generates the bizarre nature of the play's conclusion.

Because each individual household is so complex in its organisation, because there are secrets and suppressions within it, and between it and the outside world, it marks the problematic threshold of communal authority. Although cultural assumptions are easily made about the nature and operation of others' households on the basis of the status and honesty of the householder, the particular nature of the *individual* household is unattainable to the imagination.[20] It is also incomprehensible, in its infinite diversity, to the operations of justice, therefore. Crucial to the moral project of this play is a concept of the policing of the household as a work of co-operation between those within and those without, the former having first to do the work of interpreting interpersonal relations and judging them in general terms, the latter assembling and interpreting the physical evidence.

In line with such a project, the audience are encouraged to read the bodies of Merry's victims as images with a coherent and powerful meaning. Rachel notes the nature of his first corpse as a representation, referring to it as 'This timeless ugly map of cruelty' (C3), an image which plots the nature of his crime. In the extraordinary scenes of stage display in which brother and sister first relocate Beech and cover him in faggots, and then chop him into two more easily manageable halves, the audience is given ample opportunity to observe the consequences of the crime. Merry himself refers to the body as 'The spectacle of inhumanity' (D2v), and the neighbourhood community realise the potential of such a sight to move the guilty to revelation of their crimes. The silent survey of Winchester's wounds, coming just after Merry's own strategy first to cover and then to disperse the remains of Beech, enlarges the metaphorical interest in the relationship between concealing and revealing and its effects upon both individual and community. The 'map' and the 'spectacle' are both ways of quantifying and displaying social information. They demand attention and interpretation.

Indeed the play is littered with references to different kinds of representation and the ways in which they communicate. Merry describes his hammer in terms which make reference to Armenia's will, whose sealing the audience has just witnessed in the previous scene: 'This tool shall write, subscribe, and seal their death' (B3v), he says, drawing attention to a bizarre form of authorship. Rachel refers to Beech's corpse as the 'trumpet' (C3) of her brother's shame; Pertillo calls his murderer a 'map of Butchery' (E4); the Duke addresses the murderer as 'thou sad Anatomy of death' (F1v), refers to the corpses as 'these models of his [Fallerio's] shame' (F2v), and to Fallerio himself as a 'spectacle of shame' (I2v). Allenso, giving his father news of Pertillo's murder, connects speech and writing in a metaphor of admonishment: 'I will not dip my grief deciphering tongue, / In bitter words of reprehension' (H2).

But it is in the Merry plot that the connection between reading, speaking, shame and justice is most fully worked through. Active and passive responses are very carefully connected; display leads to a movement in the viewer. When asked by Williams if he is aware of the murders, Cowley says, 'I heard, and saw, their mangled carcases' (H3v). He has heard the narrative and seen the spectacle and, had he the information, he would 'blaze their shame'. The moral authority of his role introduces a model of seeing, hearing and acting for Williams to emulate.

But seeing does not always lead so unproblematically to understanding. Whilst the bodies are monovalent signs whose wounds perform their own interpretive work of explicating past events, other material objects in the play require a different kind of attention. The irritatingly repetitive second waterman describes the evidence he has literally stumbled upon: 'it is the hang-man's / Budget, and because he thought too much of his labour to / set his head upon the bridge, and the legs upon the gates, / he flings them in the streets for men to stumble at'. But his companion is a more careful observer who does not jump to conclusions:

> Thou art deceived, this head hath many wounds,
> And hose and shoes remaining on the legs,
> Bull always strips all quartered traitors quite.
>
> (G1)

Neighbour 2 is similarly perceptive in his reading of the salter's bag. 'This sack is new, and lo behold his mark / Remains upon it, which did sell the bag', he says, putting in motion another revelatory scheme. His discovery is made after he has firmly set up the relationship between God's providence and man's actions: 'Cease we to wonder at God's wondrous works, / And let us labour for to bring to light, / Those masked fiends that thus dishonour him' (G2v). Wondering is akin to waiting for God to bring justice, whilst labouring, through careful interpretation and busy reading of the physical nature of the evidence, means acting for God in the world.

Neighbour 4 issues a proclamation to the effect that if the watermen see a body 'Floating in any place about the Thames, / That straight they bring it unto Lambert hill, / Where Beech did dwell when he did live in health' (D3). The body is to be returned to his local area because the crime was committed there, and therefore it is there that an explanation for it will be found. This is perceived to be a local issue, engendered by local emotions and perpetrated by local hands. As Neighbour 3 says, 'Me thinks if Beech himself be innocent, / That then the murderer should not dwell far off' (G1v).

The playwright is careful to particularise the places to which Merry takes the parts of Beech's body. Paris Garden ditch and 'some dark place near to Baynard's castle' (F3v) each receive half of the corpse.[21] These co-ordinates on a map of London demonstrate to the audience the distance which the murderer hopes to put between his own street and the evidence, and therefore the limits which he puts upon the authority of his community and the vigilance of justice. Secrecy cannot disguise the fact of murder, only the connection between evidence and perpetrator; the convenient line of footprints in the snow which tied Arden's Faversham house to the place where his body lay can be disrupted, rubbed out by the passage of hundreds of feet in a town the size of London. But the play works to deny Merry's hope that the relationship between crime and context will be confused by the size of the population and the anonymity offered by the breadth of the town's liberties. It stages the dangerous disappointments of a salter who forgets the face of his customer, and a maid whose focus on a corpse with a hammer sticking out of its head distracts her from the perpetrator's retreat, but at the end these mnemonic failures cannot defeat justice.

Rumour and report bring the gentleman, out hunting with his water spaniel, to Beech's community. His landlord confesses that they lack 'half his hopeless body', of which the gentleman brings conditional 'tidings'. It is only if Beech's neighbours 'know his doublet and his shirt' that they will be able to identify him. But here the community-defining physical memory is sound and secure. Loney is categorical in his recognition: 'This is the doublet, these the severed limbs, / Which late were joined to that mangled trunk' (G2).

His subsequent injunction is visually striking and freighted with metaphorical weight:

> Lay them together see if they can make,
> Among them all a sound and solid man.

> *Third Neighbour:* They all agree, but yet they cannot make,
>   That sound and whole, which a remorseless hand
>   Hath severed with a knife of cruelty
>
> (G2)

The Frankensteinian qualities of the relentlessly obvious moralising aside, reconstitution is here represented in supremely physical terms. Beech's murder is implicitly solved the moment his body is brought back together within his community: the assembly of a complete suit of clothes remakes the whole man, and discovery of the murderer must shortly follow. Physical completeness creates the *expectation* of solution through the metaphorical connections between disordered corpses and disordered communities. Different parts of the city, different kinds of men from different walks of life, engaged in labour and leisure, work together to the common purpose of the reconstitution of Beech, and with it the first step towards restoration of a fractured civil order. In the Fallerio plot a Duke intervenes *deus ex machina*, but the conventions of the Merry narrative are of a providential rather than a theatrical nature.[22] Murder and discovery took place within the same scene in Italy, but in London discovery is painful, lengthy and complex.

At the end it must be a combination of the personal and the public which convicts Merry. When the constable arrests him, he tells him that Williams 'hath confessed, / The manner how, and where, the deed was done' (I2). Although the searches of the townsmen produced the evidence, the only way to tie it to the crime itself, the event which took place within the private space of an individual's household, was for the human parts of the domestic whole to display the wrong within to the community. The moral project of the drama, utilising its audience's experience of urban life to play on concerns about urban space, concludes that even the workings of providence can only return the body. Those who understood the human context of the corpse's pitiful state are morally compelled to turn their attentions outward, towards justice.

Several kinds of 'particularity' are crucial to the dramatic structure of *Two Lamentable Tragedies* then: the specific crime as opposed to the general sin; the actual nature of household life behind the door as opposed to a notion of social probability based on status and external signs of temperament; and a theatrical representation which patterns the materially specific against the emotionally general-yet-powerful. Through the material portrayal of the household within a small metropolitan community, the play directs the emotional excesses of its Italian plot into a consideration of London life. The qualities of the staging concentrate attention not so much on domestic space, but on the crucial point of contact between the house and the town.

That focus on community also leads to a self-consciousness about audience response: it is a play concerned with the importance of waking the consciences of the audience themselves, who form, as Londoners, a part of Beech's wider community. It aims to do this through a focus on the expression of strong emotion. Truth, for instance, discusses their response with them, insisting on their sympathy with the stage representation, addressing them as: 'All you the sad spectators of this act, / Whose hearts do *taste a feeling pensiveness*, / Of this unheard of savage Massacre', before she requires them to 'be far off, to harbour such a thought' (E2v). Merry's previous life gave no clue to his sharp departure from honesty, which just goes to show the crucial significance of that one small slip of avarice: 'for where thou art let in, / There is no scruple made of *any* sin' (C3), as Homicide says with approval. The end of the play is relentlessly didactic and admonitory, and it poses a series of questions: what should Merry have done differently, how should his household have responded, how can we tell whether we too will fall in such a way, how can we tell what is happening next door?

NOTES

1 For these different appearances see Belsey, 1985, p. 130; Orlin, 1985, p. 70.
2 For the different forms in which it appears see Orlin, 1994, p. 107.
3 In his *Brief Discourse* on the story of Ann Saunders, quoted in Lake, 2002, p. 13. This is of course to paraphrase a very complicated set of social and cultural relations. For a fascinating study of the 'productive interchange' between elite and popular literature which problematises the social, cultural and gendered divides inherent in the division between different types of literature see Lori Humphrey Newcomb, *Reading Popular Romance in Early Modern England*, New York: Columbia University Press, 2002. For the literary styles employed see Sandra Clark, *The Elizabethan Pamhleteers*, London, Athlone Press, 1983, especially chapters 2 and 3; for the significance of early news pamphlets in forming and informing 'moralised' communities of readers see Joad Raymond, *Pamphlets and Pamphleteering in Early Modern Britain*, Cambridge: Cambridge University Press, 2003.
4 All quotations are from Robert Yarington, *Two Lamentable Tragedies*, London: Printed [by R. Read] for Mathew Lawe, 1601. Spelling and punctuation have been modernised.
5 Lake, 2002, p. 176.
6 For the over-sudden awakening of conscience in the first murderer see Wiggins, 1991, pp. 119–21.
7 R. A. Law describes it, with pitiless accuracy but little eye for its effect, as 'an extraordinary wooden bombast of grotesque commonplace, which it would be difficult to parallel except from some broadside ballads', 'Yarington's *Two Lamentable Tragedies*', *Modern Language Review*, 5, 1910, 167–77, p. 170.
8 Law, 1910, p. 174; Geoffrey Bullough, *Narrative and Dramatic Sources of Shakespeare Vol. 7: Major Tragedies*, London, New York: Columbia University Press, Routledge and Kegan Paul, 1973, p. 370.
9 As Orlin points out, Rachel 'owes her brother the obedience that a married woman would owe her husband', and their relationship reflects that dynamic of submission, 'Familial transgressions: societal transition on the Elizabethan stage', in Carol Levin and Karen Robertson eds, *Sexuality and Politics in Renaissance Drama*, Lewiston, Lampeter: Edwin Mellen Press, 1991, p. 35.

10 Several stage directions refer to characters coming down to the door, e.g., '*Knockes, Rachell comes downe*', and the Constable's 'I must needes go uppe and speake with him'.

11 For a list of these see Alan Dessen and Leslie Thompson, *A Dictionary of Stage Directions in English Drama: 1580–1642*, Cambridge: Cambridge University Press, 1999, p. 1. The 'chess and seduction' scene in *Women Beware Women* provides a representative contrast. It is possible, of course, that there was a way of moving between the stages in view of the audience, but the logistics of the need to carry a body down on some kind of ladder militates against a visible access.

12 See Maus, 1987, p. 564, for examples of jealous men watching their lovers from above.

13 See above, p. 90.

14 See Dessen, 1984, pp. 40–3; Dessen and Thompson, 1999, pp. 149–50, 233–4.

15 See above, p. 49.

16 Comensoli confusingly refers to the location of this strand of the play as a 'village', populated in part by 'smallholders (who owned fields)', an interpretation which confuses entirely the point of the didactic implications of the representation of commercial spaces and relationships for a London audience. She also describes Merry's motivation for murder as the 'despair' of poverty, rather than the greed of impatience, 1996, pp. 103–9.

17 *OED* definition 5 of 'uncivil' gives a first date of 1597 for 'Not in accordance with civic unity; contrary to civil well-being' and takes its example from Thomas Beard's *Theatre of God's Judgements*.

18 Lake reads the play as an investigation of the contradictions inherent between patriarchal allegiance and moral absolutes. He sees Williams's agonies of conscience as part of a wider examination of the problem of the point at which earthly allegiance becomes morally wrong, one which extends to Rachel and to Allenso, 2002, pp. 81–5. For a different angle on these issues of 'Patriarchalism and its discontents', see Orlin, 1994, pp. 105–30. The way these tensions relate to the relationship between household and community seems crucial.

19 For similar reasons, Merry tells Rachel 'To make no show of any discontent, / Nor use too many words to any one' (F3v).

20 As discussed above, the qualitative and quantitative information for household interiors produced differences, Chapter 2, especially pp. 89–90.

21 Paris Garden was on the South Bank of the river close to the Swan Theatre. This puts it slightly to the west of Baynard's Castle, which was on the waterfront below St Paul's, and only two streets to the west of Lambert Hill where Beech lived. These locations are marked on the engraving of the city from Braun and Hogenberg's *Civitates Orbis Terrarum*, 1572, reproduced in Gurr, 2004; the street names and their history can be found in Mary D. Lobel and W. H. Johns, eds, *The British Atlas of Historic Towns, Vol. III, London*, Oxford: Oxford University Press, 1989.

22 For the relationship between the providential scheme here and in murder pamphlets more generally, see Lake, 2002, pp. 28–40.

5

A Woman Killed With Kindness

H EYWOOD'S *A Woman Killed With Kindness* is a very different kind of domestic tragedy from *Arden* or *Two Lamentable Tragedies*. It is not based on a historical narrative and its only gestures towards geographical particularity are a few mentions of York and Yorkshire.[1] There is no murder, and hence none of the accompanying tense frustrations of murder's prelude or aftermath and little of the temporal tightness with which long hours of anticipation are stretched in the other plays.[2] Neither are the social tensions of competition between men quite the same in Heywood's play. It is not only that Wendoll has no need to envy Frankford's wealth because it is freely offered to him, it is also the case that social distinction is differently drawn here – not as the carefully delineated differences between artisan and gentleman, or the exact greed for an extra score of pounds, but as the broad division between penury and plenty, between the security of gentility and the vulnerability of want.

The play opens with a prologue which makes apology for the domestic nature of its tragedy as prosaic fare: 'our muse is bent / Upon a barren subject, a bare scene' (3–4).³ It connects this plainness to the nature of theatrical representation, telling the audience to 'Look for no glorious state' and wishing the things which are to be shown better than they must be: 'Our russet, tissew; drone, a honey-bee, ... / Our course fare, banquets; our thin water, wine' (7–9). This is a twofold desire. On one hand, the audience's imagination must translate the props which stand for objects outside the theatre into their real-life equivalents. But the speech also suggests a wish for the ordinary russet and coarse fare to be socially transformed into the splendours of tissue and banquet. The prologue sets up, in other words, both the strictures of representation and the privations of low status, making suggestive comparison between the way material culture negotiates both types of difference.

The subplot of the play, in which Sir Charles and his sister Susan first lose and then regain their fortunes, picks up on this theme of the physical nature of differences in status. Sir Charles's diminished state is graphically represented in the altered image of his entrances across the play. He appears in the first scene as a gentleman, in the seventh as a husbandman and in the tenth as a prisoner, '*his feet bare, his garments all ragged and torn*', before reappearing in front of Sir Francis's house to offer his sister to him '*gentlemanlike*'. He explains the implications of these changes to his 'false friend' Shafton, who tries to take away the small amount of his patrimony that remains, by stressing the physical nature of a changing lifestyle:

> ... This palm you see
> Labour hath glow'd within; her silver brow,
> That never tasted a rough winter's blast
> Without a mask or fan, doth with a grace
> Defy cold winter and his storms outface
>
> (39–43)

His body has altered in relation to the life of labour he has been forced to adopt, and his concentration on success in this new life has almost erased his former activities and experiences from his memory:

> I have so bent my thoughts to husbandry
> That I protest I scarcely can remember
> What a new fashion is, how silk or satin
> Feels in my hand ... I have quite forgot
> The names of all that ever waited on me;
> I cannot name ye any of my hounds,
> Once from whose echoing mouths I heard all the music
> That e'er my heart desired.
>
> (47–55)

151

The sensory pleasures of domestic comfort and wealth, experiences which made up the texture and quality of his daily life and which were so familiar that he had not been conscious of them, have become noticeable in the breach, where they are replaced with inferior goods and different methods of self-preservation.

These two poles of material comfort and hard physical labour are connected to large family houses and their outlying alternatives: Sir Charles's 'house of pleasure' and the manor to which Anne is banished. Between houses and their lifestyles, a narrative of changing fortunes which questions the essential meaning of status is played out.[4] These are wealthy men – the inheritance Charles loses was worth £2,500 a year – and they are all men of status: Sir Francis's and Sir Charles's often-quoted titles make this clear; Frankford professes himself 'a gentleman, and by my birth / Companion with a king' (iv.3–4) and introduces Wendoll as 'a gentleman / Of a good house, somewhat press'd by want' (32–3). The possibility of social movement is imagined on the wide scale of the Mountfords' fortunes, and it involves the lack of what Frankford, in the soliloquy which lays out his plenty and therefore signals to the audience the impending demise of his content, calls the means 'to maintain a Gentleman' (iv.6).

The opening scenes of the play stage the Frankfords' wedding celebrations in a way which maps these broad divisions of social status on to the spatial arrangement of household entertainment. After an initial discussion of Anne's idealised womanhood, her brother particularises the place in which the elite members of the marriage party are standing by making reference to events which are taking place off-stage:

> We keep you here too long good brother Frankford.
> Into the hall! Away, go, cheer your guests!
> What, bride and bride-groom both withdrawn at once?
> If you be miss'd, the guests will doubt their welcome,
> And charge you with unkindness.
>
> (i.73–7)

'Withdrawn' from the hall with their close friends and family, into a room which therefore fulfils the function of a parlour, the married couple must show appropriate hospitality by returning 'to see the dance within', imagined as taking place somewhere off-stage. Remaining in the parlour, the guests stress their status by planning the fateful hawking and hunting trip for the following day, an archetypally elite pastime. But they also comment upon the scene which the audience cannot see in the hall, making their arrangements while 'the town musicians / Finger their frets within', indicating entertainment of a less sophisticated kind. 'You shall see to morrow', Sir Francis continues, 'The hall floor peck'd and dinted like a millstone, / Made with their high shoes; though their skill be small, / Yet they tread heavy where their hobnails fall' (88–91). As the next scene opens, a third space spreads out from the other two: 'now that they are busy in the parlour', says Frankford's servant Jenkin, 'come, strike up, we'll have a crash here in the yard' (4–5). This comic scene of country dancing is presided over by Frankford's trusted servant Nick, whose elevated role in the household and centrality to the plot of the play is indicated by the slightly more refined nature of his 'crashing'.

Imagining these three spaces, filled with the distinct rhythms of diverse dancing styles, simultaneously sets the celebrations within a complex house in which the contiguity of action indicates interdependency of different social groups and their activities. It demonstrates the complex network of affective and productive relationships which Anne Frankford enters on her marriage, and the ties of mutual responsibility which bind the members of the household to one another.[5] The social distance apparent in the condescension of Sir Francis's descriptions of the dancing in the hall deftly indicates the paradoxical wholeness of complex households, formed through the interdependency of elite householders and villagers, servants and masters.

It is this insistence on the interrelationship of domestic spaces which gives the play its strong sense of a physically coherent household, one which contains and gives significance to the events which take place within it. Up to the point where Frankford returns to his home at dead of night to surprise his wife with Wendoll, the action of the main plot takes place exclusively within the rooms of the house. Anne, coming upon Wendoll in scene vi, says 'We sought about the house, / Hallow'd into the fields, sent every way, / But could not meet you' (70–2), setting up the impression of the wider estate within which the house is positioned. This broad expanse is indicative of Frankford's wealth and influence, but the world off-stage is most often imagined as the intimacy of other rooms within the house, and this impression is crucial to the play's emotional power. As Frankford offers Wendoll the unique position of companion, he seals the bargain by inviting him 'To dinner. Come, sir, from this present day / Welcome to me for ever: come, away' (83–4). The welcome which he extends to Wendoll's person is also a welcome to the house and its provision of hospitality, and their exit to a meal off-stage is physically a movement inside, further into the plenty that Frankford proffers. Staged immediately after the scene in which Sir Charles suddenly faces losing all that he has, the doors which lead to Wendoll's equally unexpected elevation to prosperity associate abundance with a spatial intimacy.[6]

Later on in the play this interest in the rooms which the audience cannot see becomes associated with forbidden intimacies, of course. The tense *double entendres* of the card game between family, companion and guest are eventually cast in spatial perspective by the exchange with which the scene ends. Frankford initially invites Cranwell to leave the room if he wishes: 'Gentle

Master Cranwell, / You are welcome; see your chamber at your pleasure.' But he next *insists* upon his exit: 'Jenkin, some lights, and show him to his chamber' (viii.194–8), followed by the removal of the rest of the party: 'Go, go, to bed', he says to Wendoll, and to his wife, 'prithee wife, into my bed-chamber', leaving himself alone to survey his household under the pretence of 'walk[ing] away my fit' (203–6).

In the first scenes, then, the house is present as a series of spaces which contain the diverse activities of the kinds of people upon which the operation of such an establishment depends. We see parlour and yard, and are given a clear impression of the inclusiveness of the activities in the hall. As Frankford makes his fateful mistake with Wendoll, the domestic spaces which are not seen, most often the parlour, begin to denote the intimate and personal dispersal of bounty as opposed to the open and general provision of hospitality as part of the marriage festivities. The moral weight of the progression to more restricted social occasions within the house which the court deposi-tions evinced is here replicated in the way the narrative is staged. So, how-ever, is the suggestion that such a sudden friendship undercuts the gradual development of spatial intimacy.[7] But as the play moves towards its denoue-ment, the onstage action takes place within the parlour and the characters discuss their movement further inside the house, to the chambers in which the ultimate physical intimacy is enacted, and which the audience never see. This dynamic between seen and unseen, public and private domestic space, eventually expresses the progression of an illegitimate intimacy, one which takes the penetration of household space too far.

While the elite household discuss progression from one room to another, the servants dash between spaces, acting out a relationship of service which demands an awareness of spatial relations. As Jenkin is called for from offstage to pull off Wendoll's boots, Sisly is also demanding that he should 'Come, come, make haste, that you may wash your hands again and help to serve in dinner' (iv.104–5). The dynamic between on-stage and off-stage at these points becomes one of the frantic and the calm, where hard work produces elite leisure. Such interchanges help to draw attention to a domestic experience to which the audience is not privy, a point neatly made in Jenkin's metatheatrically conspiratorial joke about what they imagine to be happening behind the doors through which Wendoll has just exited in scene 4: 'You may see, my masters, though it be afternoon with you, 'tis but early days with us, for we have not din'd yet. Stay but a little, I'll but go in and help to bear up the first course and come to you again presently' (106–10). Setting them up to wait for his return on the stage side of the doors to plenty, he reiterates the significance of the notion of a coherent world off-stage to which what the audience actually sees is always intimately related. But in doing so he also signals its exclusive nature: a series of spaces from which the audience are excluded.

As has often been noted, the stage directions in this play are very detailed, and this is especially so in respect of the activities of service.[8] Scene viii, for instance, opens with this instruction: '*Enter 3 or 4 Servingmen, one with a voider and a wooden knife to take away all, another the salt and bread, another the tablecloth and napkins, another the carpet. Jenkin with two lights after them.*' This procession of servingmen has its own order of provision, marking the transition between one type of activity and another. As Jenkin explains to the audience, employing the metaphor of a line of soldiers sent into battle with the intricacies of complex domestic routines, 'So, march in order and retire in battle 'ray. My master and the guests have supp'd already; all's taken away. Here, now spread for the servingmen in the hall. Butler, it belongs to your office' (1–4). He draws attention to the way the routine moves from the dinner of the master and his guests to provision for the servants, and as he does so we imagine the distinct spaces of parlour and hall behind the two doors between which the servants move. Procession over the stage, a convention often employed to denote displays of martial strength because of its aspects of stately show, is here used to suggest the order proper to status and authority and the stately complexity of the routines of Frankford's household.[9] Procession also indicates military might economically, implying an event which has to be represented metonymically because of its splendour, one which surpasses theatrical realisation.

Once again here, commands from off-stage control the visible action: 'God's light! Hark, within there, my master calls to lay more billets on the fire' (10–11). Shape is given to the unseen celebrations in a way which generates a series of specific instructions: 'One spread the carpet in the parlour and stand ready to snuff the lights; the rest be ready to prepare their stomachs. More lights in the hall there' (13–15). The weight of these details builds into a complex visual and verbal depiction of the routines of consumption, involving carefully chosen props and specified objects which are indicative of elite dining. Although this is clearly a much higher-status house, the salt, the table cloth and the carpet were all prominent items in James Nethersole's inventory, important aspects of the authoritative quality of his household, and they were items specified in Harrison's lists of goods.[10] The audience, however, is once more excluded here, as the parade indicates bounty and is then removed from their sight. The impact of these subtle indications of plenty and exclusion upon the narrative is crucial: they provide the context for Nick's delivery to Frankford of the news of Anne's adultery.

Master and servant's ensuing discussion undercuts the evidence of an ideal, smooth-running house which the audience has been given: it explodes the normality of routine by calling into question the honesty of the household. In this context the symbolic meanings as well as the ritual significance of the meal which we never actually see are brought into play, with their connections to the hospitable bounty which Frankford offered to Wendoll from the start. The function of the judicial trope of dining together, as a definition of friendship and an acknowledgement of common intent and implication, needs to be brought to this scene. In the context of the unselfish provisioning of the domestic environment, and against the bounty of cloths and candlesticks, the play sets the revelation of betrayal. This has the effect of figuring it not only in personal, emotional terms, but also as a sin against the house itself. Problematised here is that richer concept of 'household' as a very intimate connection between properties and people, in which both give definition and meaning to each other. As these two aspects begin to pull away from one another as a result of Anne and Wendoll's sin, the presence of properties associated with household rituals comments ironically upon a disjunction much more fundamental than the interruption of a meal. The information threatens the ability of rich hospitality to reflect an elite status predicated upon moral honesty, and turns it instead into a sham, a theatrical show empty of meaning.

In some ways the foregrounding of household routine in this scene is typical of Heywood's dramaturgy throughout the play. At points of particular tension between Frankford's provision of hospitality and Wendoll's abuse of it, such shows become especially prominent. Later, as Nick and Frankford prepare to enact their charade of the letter which will call them away on the sudden, there is a similar flurry of activity: 'Sirra, 'tis six o'clock already stroke; / Go bid them spread the cloth and serve in supper' (10–11), says Anne. Jenkin looks for 'Spiggot the butler to give us our salt and trenchers' (12–13) and Frankford for 'A stool, a stool! Where's Jenkin, and where's Nick? / 'Tis supper time at least an hour ago' (19–20). Another entry of properties and retainers, '*Enter Butler, and Jenkin with a tablecloth, bread, trenchers, and salt*' builds tension as the audience waits for the arrival of the letter, knowing that the hospitable meal between friends is to be transmuted into the altogether poorer fare of the desperate measures of a cuckolded husband. As in the successful murder scene in *Arden*, representation of the household becomes strikingly detailed at the points where hospitality is being substituted for something radically antithetical to its meanings.

In other ways, however, the location of this crucial news in scene viii is very distinctively handled. The sense of rupture is initially indicated by Frankford's entrance: '*as it were brushing the crumbs from his clothes with a napkin, and newly risen from supper*'. The conventional direction succinctly suggests haste and interstitial action, and Frankford underlines this impression by questioning Nicholas about his own presence: 'Nich'las what make you here? Why are not you / At supper in the hall there with your fellows' (22–3). The audience is asked to question, suddenly, the place which the stage now represents, and it is of course curiously liminal and unlocalised despite the parade of properties which it has just watched moving across; despite the presence of master and servant. Somewhere between parlour and hall, this has been shown to the audience as a space of service, where candlesticks, carpets and voiders move unseen between one room and another, and where the work of organisation can be done.

Master and servant have their crucial, household-shattering conversation in between places, in between rituals, and while the bonding of dining and mutual integration into domestic community and responsibility is happening off-stage. Nicholas makes it clear that he has manipulated household space in order to create an unseen moment, one which no one observes and which no one will know they have shared. He has, therefore, to 'Be brief', as Frankford reminds him, and the scene derives its tension from the painful difficulties of the revelation and the tiny social space they share before others become aware of their absence: 'My wife and guests attend me in the parlour. / Why dost thou pause?' (25–7). The exchange which Nick and Frankford share should not be a part of normal domestic life and its appalling intelligence pushes it to the edges of the house, demanding a secrecy which can be achieved only through a form of deceit.

The news works against the household's rationale of busy production to support the family. It occupies a narrative space similar to those described by deponents as giving room for sexual activity while cakes were baking. Like those acts it is buried so deep within the routines of household production and consumption that it fades from sight, and it similarly undercuts their objectives and meanings. Here, however, it is the victims of the crime rather than its perpetrators who are forced to resort to secrecy, and a duplicity of routines characterises Frankford's actions from this point onwards, in his quest for proof of Nick's accusation.

Initially, Frankford buries his destructive knowledge under a flurry of domestic preparation: 'Lights and a table there. Wife, Master Wendoll, and / gentle Master Cranwell' (112–13). He simultaneously reiterates his now-threatened authority within the house and aims at the presentation of social normality. As Nick and Jenkin enter 'with Cards, Carpet, stools, and other necessaries', as the latter gives another of his busy speeches of preparation, domestic routine covers disjuncture with its reassuring regularity. Concentration upon the daily minutiae gives the illusion that nothing has changed: 'A pair of cards, Nich'las, and a carpet to cover the table. Where's Sisly with her counters and her box? Candles and candlesticks there' (117–19). As 'They spread a carpet, set down lights and cards', the social setting which coheres around the props ensures that the space is once more localised and particularised. But these forms of civil behaviour, no longer underpinned by the crucial prop of Anne's chastity, have become a charade. Frankford states 'For I know nothing', and his statement has a kind of doubleness. It ties the paucity of direct proof to the concealment of knowledge: 'Till I know all', he continues, 'I'll nothing seem to know' (111).

During the fraught scene in which the adultery is explored through the less than subtle subtext of such card games as 'Noddy' and 'Knave out of Doors', Frankford's plan develops further in the direction of domestic sleight of hand. Like Crench, the deponent who caught his fellows in a compromising position within the house, Frankford needs to provide the illusion of licence and spatial control in which intimacy can take place: 'when they think they may securely play, / They are nearest to danger' (218–19). But his own moral authority is similarly threatened by the necessity to be circumspect and to turn his hospitality into a calculated performance, to deal secretly rather than to deal openly."

The couple's illusion of security is to be based around a false sense of control over domestic space, one which is predicated upon an interesting doubleness of authority symbolised by Frankford's instruction to Nick to 'get me by degrees / The keys of all my doors, which I will mould / In wax, and take their fair impression, / To have by them new keys' (214–16). The single set of keys symbolised the married couple's joint domestic purpose, and this second set succinctly expresses divided goals and loyalties. As was the case in the denouement of *Arden*, the different aspects of spatial control which organised the depositions' discussions of authority are set against one another: the functional operation of locks and keys, the patriarchal licence of rule and the moral probity on which it is dependent.

When Frankford initially asked Nick for proof of his outrageous accusation, he was given the much-valorised evidence of 'Eyes, eyes' (viii.81), and although his master replies 'Thy eyes may be deceiv'd I tell thee' (82), his institution of a complex scheme to give himself just such visual confirmation suggests that this was wishful thinking. Nick's ocular proof comes from careful observation of the couples' actions when they themselves are secure in their presumed privacy. The audience's understanding of the relationship comes from the careful construction of scene 6, in which the claustrophobia of household space is staged.

The scene opens with Wendoll '*melancholy*', wrestling with his conscience. He moves from the idea of praying for 'better thoughts' to meditation upon Anne's 'divine perfections' (11), a move in which his intellectual reasoning and his appeal for grace become distracted by the physical image of the woman he is trying to forget. His resolution at the end of the speech gets to the heart of the problem:

> . . . when I come by chance into her presence,
> I'll hale these balls until my eyestrings crack
> From being pull'd and drawn to look that way.
>
> (14–16)

Anne's physical presence offers a constant torment, and the truth of his words is given immediate weight by the ensuing action: '*Enter over the stage Frankford, Anne, and Nicholas*'. In a different kind of silent parade of the house's plenty, the tension between the two parties' close proximity and the fact that there is no interaction between them provides the perfect metaphor for Wendoll's and Anne's unusual position – in close daily contact and yet divided by their loyalties to the man who has brought them together. Wendoll's exclamation 'O, God! O, God! with what a violence / I am hurry'd to my own destruction' (17–18) maps the vehemence of emotion on to Anne's inevitable domestic visibility.

The suggestion of such a daily experience of her, the constant possibility of finding her alone as he enters a room, characterises the intensity of the spatial relations of a household by its stress upon physical presence. Standing on a part of the stage separated from him by their own internalising interest, the self-sufficiency of husband, wife and loyal servant as a household group is both defined and threatened spatially. The temporal priorities which governed Mosby's actions are here reversed: it is Wendoll's location *within* the house which makes possible his intimate lusts for Anne, and she becomes the last rather than the first of the desired fruits of household plenty.

Watching the passing parade of the responsibilities of reciprocity, Wendoll is himself watched by Jenkin. The servant, taking up a position unseen on the edge of the space, gives a perspective on both of the other groups of actors. His entrance is comic – occasioned by Wendoll's anguished outcry of pain at his own disloyalty, which Jenkin takes to be a call to provide a domestic service, but which he turns into an opportunity to overhear domestic anarchy in the making. As the scene opened, Wendoll's soliloquy gave him sole command of the stage, but by this point his introspection has been drawn out into a subject position in relation to his object of desire, as his tragic self loathing is simultaneously undercut by his servant's comic reinterpretation of his every sentence.

Nearest to the audience, Jenkin's physical and 'rhetorical' distance from Frankford and his wife constructs the spatial relationships on the stage as hierarchised removes from authority. As Wendoll explains the relationship between himself and Frankford: 'He doth maintain me, he allows me largely / Money to spend' (27–8), so Jenkin draws parallels to his own relation of service: 'By my faith, so do not you me; I cannot get a cross of you' (29–30). As the curiously voyeuristic staging and the mocking echo of discussions of service and allegiance make clear, Wendoll's household, comprising Jenkin and Sorrel the mare, fits inside Frankford's like a Russian doll: the space in which he watches is watched by the servant and it is finally owned, as Jenkin's eventual loyalty is, by Frankford himself. So although Wendoll can command, he does so within the compass of the other man's authority.

Wendoll and Franklin are implicitly judged by the different qualities of their authority, crucial to their performance of domestic control and demonstrated the moment Jenkin's place on stage is taken by Nick. Similarly unnoticed at his entrance, the strength of his allegiance to Frankford is immediately shown in the violence of his response and his simple binaries, 'I love my master, and I hate that slave' (168), and this sincerity is contrasted against Jenkin's making light of Wendoll's commands. His response, consonant with his initial reaction to the newcomer ('I love my Master – by these hilts I do – / But rather then I'll ever come to serve him [Wendoll], / I'll turn away my master' (iv.92–4)) is crucial to the play's consideration of domestic authority. It proves conclusively that Wendoll could not take Frankford's place within the household; however extensive the qualities which the latter sees in the former, he does not have the virtues necessary for government.

The staging of this scene, with its different spheres of authority and absorption, is the most clearly spatialised expression of the competing households of the play, and it gives physical shape to the preceding action which instituted Wendoll's microcosmic domestic situation. Scene iv opens with a pair of speeches by Frankford, one either side of Wendoll's entry. Frankford first enters 'in a study', wrapped in meditation upon the subject of his own worth, naturally including the 'chief, / Of all the sweet felicities on earth, / I have a fair, a chaste, and loving wife' (9–11). But his claim to have achieved true earthly happiness is interrupted by news of Wendoll's arrival. Whilst the guest is entreated in, Frankford describes Wendoll in a speech which forms a pair to the previous description of his wife:

> . . . his carriage
> Hath pleas'd me much; by observation
> I have noted many good deserts in him –
> He's affable and seen in many things,
> Discourses well, a good companion
>
> (27–31)

As a result, Frankford has 'preferr'd him to a second place / In my opinion, and my best regard' (34–5), second presumably to his wife.[12] The range of gifts Wendoll receives constitute the sustaining aspects of domestic life, lacking only the unique sphere of operation which usually defines household, and the construction of this scene suggests a parity between wife and companion. Later, as he faces betraying all that Frankford has given him by seducing his wife, Wendoll describes their relationship in terms whose employment of the rhetoric of male devotion begin to sound troublingly similar to contemporary discussions of the nature of the married couple as one body: Wendoll asks himself whether he has the power to 'rend his heart / To whom thy heart was join'd and knit together' (49–50).

These two 'marriages' become the subject of Jenkin's relentlessly pointed comic misunderstandings. Finally registering his servant's presence on the stage in scene iv, Wendoll asks him, 'What, Jenkin? Where's your mistress?', to which he gets the smart reply, 'Is your worship married?', and the insubordinately mocking desire to 'like a good servant ... do my duty to' this new wife (57–62). In fact, of course, Wendoll is talking about Anne, and the confusion neatly points up both his obsession with her and his own curious position. His exact standing within the power dynamics of domesticity is very hard to describe, as the Butler explains to Jenkin at a moment of confusion about the identity of Cranwell, 'Master Wendoll, he is a daily guest; I mean the gentleman that came but this afternoon' (viii.8–9) The title of 'daily guest', uncomfortably ambiguous like that of 'sojourner' adopted by Mosby, is also a contradiction in terms suggestive of hospitality, reciprocity, and the tension between visiting and inhabiting a house.

This liminal, patriarchally problematic domestic role is explored in the ideologically fraught transfer of domestic authority as Frankford rides 'out of town'. Significantly, it is Anne who conveys his farewell to Wendoll, speaking for her husband:

> Now in troth my husband
> Before he took horse had a great desire
> To speak with you ... therefore he enjoin'd me
> To do unto you his most kinds commends.
>
> (vi.68–73)

The import of his message is familiar from Mosby's fantasy when Arden has left for London that Alice will give him 'leave to play your husband's part':

> ... he wills you as you prize his love,
> Or hold in estimation his kind friendship,
> To make bold in his absence and command
> Even as himself were present in the house;
> For you must keep his table, use his servants,
> And be a present Frankford in his absence.
>
> (74–9)

Under normal circumstances it would of course be Anne who ruled in her husband's absence, but instead Wendoll's microcosmic household expands to encompass the boundaries of the physical house, and in the process he is invited to usurp not only his patron's position of authority but also his identity.[13] As possessor of half of his heart already, he need only take over the other part to 'become' his absent friend, and this physical mimicry was a familiar trope of advice literature for wives who were to frame their wills, spirits, countenances and actions to match those of their spouse.[14] Wives ruled in stead of husbands because, as part of the same whole, they were expected to desire the same ends, to work towards the same domestic goals. But the bonds between men admit the possibility of a competition between patriarchal equals in an uncomfortably equal pairing.[15]

Wendoll's thought that he should take up the part of husband too leads Anne to choose some potent and pertinent language. 'Are you not well, sir, that you seem thus troubled?', she asks him, 'There is sedition in your countenance' (104–5). But Wendoll makes a distinction between open rebellion and secret insurgence. The solution to his desires which he proposes to Anne is effectively to promise her that if she submits to him her actions need never be known: 'I will be secret, lady, close as night, / And not the light of one small glorious star / Shall shine here in my forehead to bewray / That act of night' (147–50). His disingenuously poetic stellar imagery displaces her resistance to the sin of adultery on to a hesitation predicated on their ability to keep the affair secret, thereby turning sexual sin into an issue of domestic spatial control: 'Your husband is from home, your bed's no blab' (165). Although he can exercise domestic authority publicly, legitimately extending his own command to encompass the whole of Frankford's household, Wendoll's performance of the role of husband must be a tellingly private affair.

And it is at this point that Nick decides to 'henceforth turn a spy, / And watch them in their close conveyances' (175–6). Their illegitimate domestic authority, their search for secrecy within the house, necessitates a careful watchfulness which looks inwards. This is a disturbing image of the household policing itself, its servants using its spaces as a way of investigating its authority figures. The moral probity which Crench insisted upon for his actions hung, of course, upon the fact that his domestic status was slightly higher than that of the couple he watched, as servant with responsibility for locking the doors. Such surveillance is legitimised by the superior hierarchical relationship between watcher and watched, and its representation here in different terms depicts the split between social status and moral hierarchy.

The next time this question of household rule arises is when Frankford leaves to give his wife and his companion space to demonstrate their deception. Now aware of the ironies of the invitation, he suggests that Cranwell 'And Master Wendoll, in my absence use / The very ripest pleasure of my house' (xi.62–4). Despite the fact that the invitation is addressed to both men, Wendoll hears it as exclusive to himself. Using language reminiscent of that which Alice uses about Mosby, he says, 'I am husband now in Master Frankford's place / And must command the house' (89–90). His language exploits the slippery areas of patriarchy, playing on the double meaning of 'husband' as both domestic controller and spouse, and taking Frankford's 'place' in both roles. His performance of the former role, necessitating the exercise of authority, begins with the crucial order to alter the dynamics of the meal which has been so long awaited towards the latter role: 'My pleasure is / We will not sup abroad so publicly, / But in your private chamber, Mistress Frankford' (90–2).

How these lines are spoken seems crucial.[16] Anne replies 'O sir, you are too public in your love', suggesting that Wendoll might speak them openly, as a public announcement to Anne and Cranwell. The latter's role is significant in the play as the representative of community, as a foil to the intensity of the triangular affections of Wendoll, Frankford and Anne, but also as a 'public' in front of whom propriety must be maintained if reputation is to be preserved. If Wendoll does speak those words in front of Cranwell, a seditious change of approach from the value he previously placed upon secrecy is indicated. Anne's explicitly stated motivation for following Wendoll offstage is very telling: 'you plead custom' (111), she says, drawing attention to a sin now ingrained.

Wendoll's specific appeal to the distinction between public and private action destroys, as was presumably intended, any possibility of a regular social occasion. Cranwell immediately dissembles an illness, entreating hostess and lover that he might see his chamber as he 'would be spar'd from supper' (97). Wendoll does not offer hospitality as he should, standing in Frankford's stead; he takes, rather than giving. By the time he and Anne leave the stage to 'sup within', the meanings of the area offstage have changed beyond recognition. No longer representing a space reserved for the elite in which leisured hospitality is given and received, it has now become the site for individual as opposed to social action, imagined as spaces which separate individuals from one another. This surreptitious intimacy suggests activities which are clearly known to all, even though they cannot be seen. Leaving the stage for the chamber, with all its associations of household wealth, Wendoll makes the obvious connection between spaces and bodies: 'I'll be profuse in Frankford's richest treasure' (116).

Because what happens in the chamber cannot be staged, the audience instead witness the disorder which this movement inwards generates in the household's systems of hierarchy and rule. Jenkin tells Sisly that she is 'preferr'd from being the cook to be chambermaid' (xii.2–3), and, as the physical location of their responsibilities changes, so the activities of the servants alter from the general provision of hospitality to the administration of the private rooms of the house. The physical appetites satisfied by cooking and dining are transmuted into their anti-domestic other, the satisfaction of sexual hunger. When Jenkin's role within the house is also altered, 'for this night . . . made the Porter, to see the gates shut in' (20–1), he identifies this as a promotion: 'Thus by little and little I creep into office' (22). In doing so, he indicates that social hierarchies are being shifted by sin, and these changes function similarly to Michael and Susan's discussions after Arden's death about the difference between waiting and sitting at table. As routines are disrupted, so domestic and social confusion are paired.

The relationship between on-stage and off-stage space is as usual constructed by the commands which issue from the latter. Anne exercises her authority remotely, 'sending' that the onstage servants 'should . . . lock up the doors, and see the household all got to bed' (18–19). The couple's location in a space which the audience cannot see, but must nevertheless imagine, is set against the servants' necessary presence within, where they must minister to their mistress's needs. And the prospect of going where the audience cannot, of exchanging imagination for participation, disturbs Sisly. The servant who carries orders between rooms instructs that 'When you have lock'd the gates in, you must send up the keys to my mistress' (24–5), and Sisly urges speed on Jenkin, fearing what she will see: 'I am neither pillow nor bolster, but I know more than both' (27–8). Just as the physical household bears the impression of its inhabitants' actions, so its members carry the imprint of events in their memories and, apart from demonstrating honest squeamishness, we should perhaps see Sisly as indicating awareness that ocular proof demands moral action in a way that suspicion does not.

The dynamic between seeing, knowing and telling is drawn to the audience's attention then and, as was the case in the court depositions, it is a dynamic powerfully sensitive to the relative domestic authority of the parties involved. Anne also commands them to 'make less noise', and this constructs a contiguity of space and action which insists that off-stage actors are close enough to hear the onstage discussions. When Jenkin says he 'smells a rat', Sisly urges him to speak only 'Good words, Jenkin, lest you be call'd to answer them' (8). Their discussion negotiates the idea of slander, trying to find a safe ground between the moral and the loyal. As Jenkin points out, his sentiments are morally unquestionable: 'Why, "God make my mistress an honest woman". Are not these good words? "Pray God my new master play not the knave with my old master". Is there any hurt in this? "God send no villainy intended, and if they do sup together, pray God they doe not lie together"' (9–12). The moral dynamic of the household has changed: the stage now represents a precarious domestic space governed by those unfit to do so. Voicing such straightforward 'good words' here is indeed dangerous.

As the servants leave the stage to 'sleep snug as pigs in pease-straw' in their innocent honesty, 'inside' becomes 'outside' for the first time in the main plot with the return of Frankford and Nick at the opening of scene xiii. The former is forced to enter his own house as a stranger in order to attain proof of the extent of Wendoll's invasion of spaces to which his social and domestic status does not permit him access. The tension of the scene is built by the graded stages of entry through four doors.[17] Only the final one is realised on the stage, but all are symbolically present in the form of the keys which Frankford tells as a narrative progression imitative of the spatial: 'This is the key that opes my outward gate, / This is the hall door, this my withdrawing chamber' (8–9). The visceral nature of the relationship between keys and spatial control is given an added frisson by the audience's knowledge that an exact copy of the set he holds in his hand is currently locked in the chamber with his wife and her lover. His familiarity with the space, and hence its personal, particular relationship to his identity, is signalled by his ability to tell each key from the others, a fact which clearly demonstrates the legitimacy of his jurisdiction.[18]

The carefully constructed tension of this scene, with its ominous nighttime setting and the need for quiet and darkness to cover master and servant's movements, prepares the audience to employ their imaginations. As Frankford names the rooms, the intensification of the mood depends upon their imagining a progression through a house. In a period in which movement within domestic space involved going through one room to reach another, the relative depth of space which penetration involved gave an additional texture to action in the unlocalised space of the stage. The rooms which Frankford describes, as all would know, decrease in size, recede from the external walls, increase in the value of their contents and contract in the numbers of individuals who have experienced events within their interior.

As Frankford brings to mind each room for the audience through the instrument of its security, the mystery of the reserved rooms of the house is reinforced by the disjuncture between his familiarity and their experience. By situating the audience's experience in relation to the progression of rooms, the sequence of Frankford's list demands that at some stage along this journey they must begin to imagine: only the gentlemen and the richer citizens might have experience of a withdrawing chamber separate to a bedchamber. As their imagination is called upon, so their understanding of this space becomes one of their own social exclusion, in addition to their sense of its intimate and personal nature. Unlike Wendoll, those who have no knowledge of such spaces are excluded from their mental visualisation, and this underlines the presumptuousness of his intrusion. For those who can imagine their own withdrawing chamber, the invasion of such a personal space must feel especially threatening.

When Frankford reaches the door at the back of the stage it represents, as he calls it, 'the last door', and the personal and social exclusion which entering necessitates is demonstrated by Nick's presence on the audience's side of it as his master goes in alone. The comedy to which Nick turns at this point accentuates the tension generated by the fact that the audience can see nothing, that nothing will happen until his master returns, and that there is an implicit invitation to imagine what is happening behind the door: 'Here's a circumstance! / A man may be made cuckold in the time / That he's about it' (34–6). Frankford himself, as well as Nick and the audience, is marginalised. Although he can enter freely, he is impotent in the sense of being unable to act within his own innermost space, his authority compromised by his obvious redundancy within the scene he witnesses.[19] The dynamic of the seen and the unseen now takes on the painful weight of shaming revelation, as what happens offstage becomes a private spectacle only for Frankford's eyes. Communal practice suggests that he should broadcast his knowledge of such a sight, but his personal pain and its implications for his authority make that excruciatingly hard to do. Description stops dead at this point in the play, as imagination itself becomes dangerously voyeuristic, forbidden and yet inevitable: 'O, O!'[20]

Frankford's description of his bedchamber as 'polluted' (14) indicates the sense of a violation which is transferred from human interaction to the space in which it takes place. And it is this close relationship between spaces and people which generates the material qualities of the scene of parting between the Frankfords. His solution to the problem of Anne's punishment is a spatial one: he will remove her from his sight. His instructions involve a disinvestiture, a careful removal of the physical objects which defined her role within the household:

> ... Go make thee ready in thy best attire,
> Take with thee all thy gowns, all thy apparel;
> Leave nothing that did ever call thee mistress.
> (xiii.158–60)

Just as Anne acknowledged the fact that she had lost the name of 'wife' by performing acts which explode that role, so here she is required to take away the objects which embodied her performance of household authority. Anne is to make for herself a new household, of just the kind which Wendoll was offered, but without its problematic location within Frankford's own:

> Choose thee a bed and hangings for a chamber,
> Take with thee everything that hath thy mark,
> And get thee to my Manor seven mile off,
> ... Choose which of all my servants thou likest best,
> And they are thine to attend thee.
> (163–71)

A lesson has been learned about the performance of household practices and the uniqueness of household space. When Wendoll sees Anne on her way to this satellite house, he describes the couple as 'the truest turtles / That ever liv'd together', whom he has divorced and therefore 'divided / In several places' where they 'make their several moan' (47–9). Their separation takes away the pain of physical proximity which has been transferred from would-be-lover to husband by Anne's adultery, but it substitutes it with the grief of division, a fundamentally unnatural state for a married couple. The scene is lengthy because it must carry the meaning of the domestic limbo which effects Anne's full penance and makes it possible for her to reclaim her titles of wife and mother at the end of the play. Jenkin's typically comic take on the situation in which they find themselves, watching Anne once more across the stage, but this time outside the house, leads him to ask Wendoll 'What, shall I serve you still or cleave to the old house?' (114–15). As a type of household born out of sympathy for her plight briefly coheres around Anne in her coach, Jenkin's joke about his houseless former master marks the end point of the play's confusions of domestic authority.

But Frankford does not only want his wife to remove all the things which showed her mistress of her household, he also needs her to take away those objects which indicated the joys and comforts of her personal presence, things 'by whose sight being left here in the house / I may remember such a woman by' (xiii.161–2). When Cranwell asks about the reasons for his search for objects left behind, the answer he receives connects the strength of emotion to its material triggers. He explains that he 'lov'd her dearly, / And when I do but think of her unkindness, / My thoughts are all in Hell' (xv.4–6). To avoid this 'torment',

> I would not have a bodkin or a cuff,
> A bracelet, necklace, or rebato wire,
> Nor any thing that ever was call'd hers
> Left me, by which I might remember her.
> (7–10)

These small, personal items connect the couple through memories of her wearing them, and transport his thoughts straight to the hell of her image in his mind.[21] The pain of Anne's presence in the household is as strong for Frankford here as it was for Wendoll at the other end of this anguished narrative of betrayal. In the same way that Frankford's study is used to give him the room to control his passion, so the manor offers the distance necessary to fully work through repentance and to achieve stasis. Emotion and the physical spaces of the household are intimately linked.[22]

Frankford's specificity about the objects which Anne may have left behind is nevertheless far from being particular. They are all items indicative of female beauty, ones which were frequently implicated in discourses of women's moral weakness, and they are therefore of a different order to Mosby's pressing iron, or Rachel Merry's sack.[23] Characterising Anne's presence through such objects makes Frankford's pain potentially ambiguous by suggesting that it is generated by the unstable affections of women in general rather than the particular circumstances of his household. This is a reading given weight by the fact that the play gives so little space to Anne's initial motivations, concentrating instead on Wendoll's confusion.

The lack of a particularity which grows out of the Anne/Frankford relationship in *A Woman Killed* makes it possible for the domestic spaces of the play to take on a broader set of significances much more easily than Arden's parlour or Merry's upper room could. It is in fact at the point at which Frankford stands in front of the final door 'that's Bawd unto my shame' (xiii.10) that the narrative begins to shift in emphasis from the trials of the Frankford family towards the framework of a morality drama.[24] While telling the keys, he conjures up a powerful image of wide cosmography within such a narrow space, describing the room within as 'Once my terrestrial heaven, now my earth's hell, / The place where sins in all their ripeness dwell' (15–16): a 'profaned' holy site. He enters with a prayer, 'O keep my eyes, you Heavens, before I enter, / From any sight that may transfix my soul' (26–7), and when he exits, his language elevates the imagined scene behind the doors from a grubby adultery to an issue of divine judgement and mercy. He would, he says, have killed them then and there, 'But that I would not damn two precious souls / Bought with my Saviour's blood' (44–5); he wishes he could 'Take from the account of time so many minutes, / Till he had all these seasons call'd again, / Even from her first offence' (58–9), making Anne an Eve before temptation, and therefore 'spotless as an angel in my arms' (62) rather than a spotted strumpet in her lover's embrace.

The domestic chaos which follows the eerie calm of Frankford's ocular proof begins as Wendoll enters '*running over the stage in a night gown*', Frankford '*after him with his sword drawn*'. They are followed by '*the Maid in her smock*', who '*stays his hand and clasps hold on him. He pauses a while.*' On one level, this is a familiar scene of domestic disturbance, in which characters running through doors in nightgowns and smocks demonstrate the way immoral actions have disturbed the routines of the household. Frankford's brandished sword underlines his status as a gentleman, drawing attention to the decisive actions which are expected of a man of his status. But the spectacle has equally obvious biblical references to sacrifice and divine intervention. Allusion to the story of Abraham and Isaac, which Frankford underlines to the maid, 'I thank thee, maid; thou like the angel's hand / Hast stay'd me from a bloody sacrifice' (68–9), introduces a complicated set of references which compare Frankford to the tested Abraham, as well as the Christ-like figure of unhasty and compassionate judgement. But Wendoll is not figured as the innocent Isaac of course, and Anne says of herself that she is 'as far from hoping' for grace from her husband 'As Lucifer from Heaven' (80–1). These references shade the rooms of Frankford's house with the tincture of judgement, and in doing so they open out the familial to a much broader set of implications, ones which are explicated dramaturgically in the rest of the scene.

As Frankford, sword still in hand, banishes Wendoll from his domestic paradise, so Anne enters '*in her smock, night gown, and night attire*', her undress clearly signalling the intimate nature of the preceding activities. Her initial punishment is to become a spectacle of sin. Frankford orders the maid to 'Go bring my infants hither' (116), and then instructs his wife to 'Look but on them, and melt away in tears' (123) before he underlines the total contrast between innocence and carnal knowledge: 'Away with them, lest as her spotted body / Hath stain'd their names with stripe of bastardy, / So her adult'rous breath may blast their spirits / With her infectious thoughts' (124–7). When Frankford has left to consider her fate in his study, a parade of servants then enters to look upon their mistress: '*Enter Sisly, Spiggot, all the Servingmen, and Jenkin, as newly come out of bed.*' In chorus, they simultaneously question and accuse, 'Oh mistress, mistress, what have you done, mistress?' (145), and Anne, unable to answer them, instead addresses herself to the audience: 'See what guilt is: here stand I in this place, / Asham'd to look my servants in the face' (150–1).

The staging is powerfully evocative of her translation from Frankford's wife to a negative moral exemplar, a spectacle of guilt and shame, and that movement from the particular to the general is partly effected by her own speeches to the audience. Before the servants enter she addresses the women who watch her:

> Oh women, women, you that have yet kept
> Your holy matrimonial vow unstain'd,
> Make me your instance: when you tread awry,
> Your sins like mine will on your conscience lie.
>
> (141–4)

As an 'instance', an example or illustration, she holds herself up as a representation of a putative future which sin will guarantee – the end point of a narrative which can too easily be begun. In this she resembles Rachel Merry, who as she approaches the scaffold begs 'Let me be mirror to ensuing times, / And teach all sisters how they do conceal, / The wicked deeds, of brethren, or of friends'.

As Rachel Merry is turned off, the officer says 'The Lord of heaven have mercy on her soul / And teach all other by this spectacle, / To shun such dangers as she ran into', and Anne Frankford too understands the way her body functions as spectacle. On her way to the manor, she explains both the image she presents and its import to Nick:

> You have beheld the woefullest wretch on earth,
> A woman made of tears. Would you had words
> To express but what you see; my inward grief
> No tongue can utter, yet unto your power

You may describe my sorrow and disclose
To thy sad master my abundant woes.

(xvi.77–82)

She makes a distinction between her inner emotions, which are personal and particular, and their outward signs, which can be read by all and have a general application. The description of the scene which Nick is to provide for Frankford will necessarily carry with it its own moral implications because spectacle is of itself meaningful, its import transmitted through its affective power.[25]

On her deathbed, Anne is again especially conscious of her own exemplary role. Jenkin tells her brother that 'Many gentlemen and gentlewomen of the country are come to comfort her' (xvii.37–8), and her entrance *'in her bed'* draws her to the centre of both on- and off-stage audiences' attention. Anne makes her death a public scene within which her idealised female qualities can be displayed, and the transformation of her repentance is demonstrated by her progression from the bedchamber in which she offers her husband the ultimately secret spectacle of her infidelity, unstageable and unrepeatable, to this scene in which she opens up her new bedchamber as a space of moral instruction. Having been an exemplary wife, she switches *almost* seamlessly into the role of exemplary penitent, wanting to make sure that her actions have the largest possible audience:

Raise me a little higher in my bed.
Blush I not, brother Acton? Blush I not, Sir Charles?
Can you not read my fault writ in my cheek?
Is not my crime there? Tell me, gentlemen.

(54–7)

Asking her family to read her body as a text of shame, Anne broadcasts the implications of her own good death. And as she does so, she opens up the domestic to communal scrutiny, insisting upon the application of her own situation to wider moral questions. The chorus-like parade of household members and the propensity of the on-stage bed to organise actors for an exhibition to the audience ensures that the dramaturgy of these final scenes forms a striking opposite to the insistence on private spaces with reserved meanings in the episodes leading up to Frankford's shocking discovery.

The meanings of domestic dramaturgy change at the point of ocular proof then, as the house performs the didactic and curative processes of revelation for itself. But the tableau around the bed is instructively different in its make-up to the group who gather in Arden's defiled parlour to apprehend his murderers. This is no display of urban authority in the interests of the maintenance of communal social order. Rather it is the family who gather, representing an alternative stabilising social form which provides continuity.

The stress is upon the essential qualities which have been maintained despite the Mountfords' problems and Anne's disgrace. Despite the move from large houses to humblingly diminished properties on the edges of estates, adherence to a common morality ensures that gentility retains essential meaning. The significance of Sir Charles's small house was not only its sustaining role. As he explains to Shafton, 'this house successively / Hath 'long'd to me and my progenitors / Three hundred year' (vii.15–17).[26] Within the Mountford estate, the several houses offer ways of charting family fortunes: 'my great-great-grandfather, / He in whom first our gentle style began, / Dwelt here, and in this ground increas'd this molehill / Unto that mountain which my father left me' (17–20). The ebb and flow of prosperity is imagined across the scope of generations, and measured in the size of houses within the family-defining contours of land. Identity, for people of such elevated social status, is located within the time depth of a domestic context: 'Where he the first of all our house begun, / I now the last will end and keep this house' (21–2). Maintaining that connection between family and house is worth a great deal. As Charles says, hard physical labour is not too large a price to pay, even for a gentleman whose identity would normally be assured only by his ability to avoid such occupation: 'You see what hard shift we have made to keep it / Ally'd still to our own name' (38–9). Location becomes the central guarantee of identity, the meanings of family preserved within land and house, as individuals imagine themselves as part of a continuum which stretches both far behind and far ahead. 'We lie uneasy', says Susan, 'to reserve to us / And our succession this small plot of ground' (45–6).

As Frankford brings the plot full circle by 'marrying' his wife again he re-emphasises the union of families, although the physical circumstances are both similar and different to those with which the play began. As he points out, 'a cold grave must be our nuptial bed' (xvii.124), and the deathbed, like the wedding party, defines family and household and draws together the narrative's different interests in the strength of human ties of loyalty and the location of family within a particular space. Death too is a rite of passage in which the moral precepts of household life have to be passed from one generation to the next. At Anne's deathbed, alliances are made anew. Acton binds himself to Frankford, the latter offering an honourable replacement for his disgraced sister whose 'kindred hath fallen off', through her actions as well as her death. 'You are my brother by the nearest way' (103), he says, drawing attention to the connection between consanguinity and shared moral values. The location of Anne's death within the lesser household of the manor connects it to the house of pleasure: they are domestic spaces in which kinship has meaning, not in relation to money, or even the customary definitions of status, but to the shared ideals which more properly define true gentility.[27]

NOTES

1 Wendoll admits that Frankford has 'Made me companion with the best and chiefest / In Yorkshire' (vi.39–40), and the letter which Frankford forges is apparently 'sent from York' (xi.47).

2 Unlike the compressed time scales of *Arden* or *Two Lamentable Tragedies*, the time for the birth of two children has apparently passed between the opening wedding and the closing death of their mother. The scene in which Frankford and Nick approach the house does, however, develop this kind of tension against denouement, as I discuss below.

3 All references are to the Revels edition of the play, ed. R. W. van Fossen, London: Methuen, 1961.

4 Diana Henderson, in a reading of the play which shares many concerns with the one offered here, points out the interest of both plots in the significance of houses. She suggests that the play 'is built upon the narrative paradigm of exile from and return to the home', the Frankford plot invoking 'the Christian movement of fall from Edenic bliss into sin, allowing a spiritual homecoming only after sacrifice', the subplot developing 'the cycle of wandering and return in the more material realms of human society', 'Many mansions: reconstructing *A Woman Killed With Kindness*', *SEL* 26:2, 1986, 277–94, p. 277. Although she points to the importance of 'the actual house, represented on stage', she does not go on to discuss the nature of this representation.

5 This is the dramaturgical expression of the process succinctly described by Orlin: 'While betrothal created a couple, marriage inaugurated a household', 1994, p. 143.

6 For a detailed analysis of early modern banqueting and its realisation on the stage see Chris Meads, *Banquets Set Forth*, Manchester: Manchester University Press, 2001.

7 Playing against the welcome is a vague but troubling indication of the kind of illegitimate use of space which Black Will and Shakebag gain in Arden's house. Although the social dynamics are clearly very different indeed, the sense of 'shortcutting' social interaction remains.

8 Dessen, for instance, refers to Heywood as 'the dramatist least inhibited by the limits of the unworthy scaffold', 1984, p. 15; Orlin, 1994, pp. 145–6.

9 For different kinds of 'passing over the stage' see Dessen and Thomson, 1999, pp. 158–9. For more on the relationship between the stage directions here and those at the end of the scene, Richardson in Harris and Korda eds, 2002.

10 See above, pp. 65–6, 88–91. The Frankfords are landed gentry, not urban leaders.

11 Robert Ornstein points out the connection between this kind of behaviour and the actions of the 'sly Italianate intriguer' although, as he admits, 'this deviousness does not square with Frankford's personality'. The conventions of revenge tragedy, here as in *Arden* and to an extent *Two Lamentable Tragedies*, are altered by their presence within an insistently domestic setting because their emphasis is changed from psychological to spatial manipulation. Ornstein, 'Bourgeois morality and dramatic convention in *A Woman Killed With Kindness*', in Standish Henning, Robert Kimbrough and Richard Knowles eds, *English Renaissance Drama*, London: Southern Illinois University Press, 1976, p. 137.

12 Jennifer Panek argues, reading the play in relation to marriage manuals, that 'Frankford fails to grasp the essential concept of the companionate marriage'. She points out the 'deliberateness of his selection' of Wendoll as the opposite of an ordinary friendship 'grown out of long acquaintance and compatibility', 'Punishing adultery in *A Woman Killed With Kindness*', *Studies in English Literature 1500–1900*, 34:2, 1994, 357–78, pp. 364–5. See also Laura Bromley, 'Domestic Conduct in *A Woman Killed With*

Kindness', *SEL* 26:2, 1986, 259–76, pp. 264–5. Lena Orlin provides a fascinating analysis of the tensions between male friendship and developing notions of the household, suggesting that 'In contemporary terms Frankford is implicated in and must accept responsibility for his own undoing' by inviting Wendoll in; Orlin, 1994, pp. 158–81.

13 Leanore Lieblein reads this offer as 'a positive provocation . . . possible only because Frankford does not attribute to Wendoll an independent existence. Wendoll is being invited to do what he will be condemned for doing'. This reading interestingly complicates the apportionment of blame in the play. 'The context of murder in English domestic plays 1590–1610', *SEL* 23:2, 1983, 181–96, p. 191.

14 The wife as image of the husband must provide a perfect representation of him, mirroring his emotions in her body: 'For as the looking-glasse, howsoever faire and beautifully adorned, is nothing worth, if it shew that countenance sad, which is pleasant: or the same pleasant, that is sad: so the woman deserveth no commendation, that (as it were) contrarying her husband, when he is merie, sheweth her selfe sad; or in his sadnesse uttereth her mirth: for as men should obey the lawes of their cities, so women the maners of their husbands.' Cleaver, 1598, p. 229.

15 Laura Bromley's point, in relation to the punishment of the adulterous couple later on in the play, seems to get to the heart of this issue: 'Frankford is Wendoll's social equal, not his master, and he is not expected to impose judgement on him', Bromley, 1986. The power dynamic is totally different, p. 272. Orlin quotes Henry Smith: 'masters should receive none into their houses, but whom they can govern', 1994, p. 179.

16 For instance, van Fossen's Revels edition suggests that both speeches are addressed only between the couple; Sturgess, *Three Elizabethan Domestic Tragedies*, has no asides marked.

17 As Robert Ornstein points out, 'Heywood refuses to exploit the erotic possibilities of an adulterous love', 1976, p. 134. The sexual tensions which are played out in dialogue between Alice and Mosby in *Arden* are here translated into the tense protraction of this scene, and the spatial tensions set up by the use of the stage doors.

18 Orlin says 'Frankford enacts the kind of convergence between self and place that occurs only in one's own home', and deconstructs the way in which the mood of the scene is set, 1994, p. 149.

19 For fascinating discussion of the jealous male's desire for ocular proof in Renaissance drama, and its links to the actions of theatre audiences, see Maus, 1987. Her comment that 'The jealous witness . . . conceives of [the woman's] infidelity as a kind of careless obliviousness to the distinction between man and man', and that 'the notion of friend-as-duplicate-self, taken literally, endangers Leontes's exclusive claim to his wife and to his throne' in *The Winter's Tale* seems particularly pertinent in this context of doubled husbands, p. 570.

20 McClintock's otherwise very useful argument that 'masculine grief in the play is discursive rather than silent, and reflexive rather than affective' does not seem to work here. The fact that representation fails at this point indicates the extent of the problems inherent in translating such a spectacle into emotion. If affectivity has a 'socially reparative power', then this moment is the epitome of social threat, 2002, pp. 111; 113.

21 The lute, a more substantial object, works as a metaphor for the resonance of emotion which has been insisted upon throughout the play. For a detailed discussion of Heywood's use of music see Cecile Williamson Cary, '"Go breake this lute": music in Heywood's *A Woman Killed With Kindness*', *Huntington Library Quarterly*, 37:2, 1974, 111–22.

22 For more on the meanings of the study see Orlin, 1994, pp. 179–89; Comensoli, 1996, pp. 74–8.

23 See for instance Philip Stubbes, *Anatomy of Abuses*, ed. M. J. Kidnie, Tempe: Renaissance English Text Society, 2002. For a reading of the evidence for her costume as characterising Anne as vain (and therefore presumably morally culpable) see Comensoli, 1996, p. 73.

24 Diana Henderson's interesting reading of the play relates the interweaving of sacred and secular language to morality staging, arguing that Heywood avoids the 'parodic disjunction between the style of representation and "larger than life" events' by finding 'serious symbolic resonance through patterns of metaphor, analogy, and narrative movement which for the most part do not clash with his local conditions (as grand passions, intrigue, and spectacle surely would)', 1986, p. 290.

25 For more on this moment see McClintock, 2002, pp. 113–15, where he points out the significance of her body both here and on her deathbed, but does not connect it to the context in which it is displayed.

26 As Dessen points out, the insistent use of 'this' in the scene localises the back wall of the stage as the house itself, 1984, pp. 62–3.

27 Lena Orlin points out the priority of property, which spans the generations, over people 'Because the patrimony is larger and longer-lived than any holder of it', 1994, 156.

6

A Yorkshire Tragedy

THE DEATHBED SCENE which ends *A Woman Killed With Kindness* provides a stabilising image of the continuity of ideals of behaviour within the household and of the families which sustain these ideals. Such endurance is, however, unusual for a domestic tragedy, unique to Anne's distinctively 'natural' death. When Pandino and Armenia enter 'sicke on a bed' in *Two Lamentable Tragedies* the dynamic of intergenerational continuity is suggested by this strong visual symbol, only to be immediately undercut by Fallerio's spoken intentions. The murderous brother has to be taught a more fitting morality by his own son, in a move which neatly reverses the expected progression of family principles. Outside the theatre, early modern men and women concerned themselves with the transfer of possessions and household organisation across the generations, but the characters of domestic tragedy by and large live lives myopically focused on the present, or directed towards an immediate future in which they anticipate the gratification of their desires. Alice Arden's daughter is cut out of the dramatisation of her mother's actions; Pertillo is cut down before he reaches majority; the Frankfords' children appear only to embody the future their mother has jeopardised.[1]

These didactic concerns, which become evident at the end of *A Woman Killed*, are painfully close to the surface of the narrative in *A Yorkshire Tragedy* throughout. As in the subplot of *Woman Killed*, perhaps the overriding meanings of 'household' in the play are family and lineage, and it offers a complex examination of the intergenerational pull of the 'house' as contained by the family seat. It is in the context not only of his role as head of his nuclear family but also as representative of his ancestral heritage that the Husband's actions are judged, resulting in a play whose temporal perspective is as wide as that of *Woman Killed*. It treats familiar domestic themes of the pain of familial rupture and the relationship between household and community, but it does so in a very different theatrical form. The opening scene, in which the servants discuss their London wares, has a familiar social particularity to it,[2] but the rest of the play is totally dissimilar in tone: the physical articulation of rooms and spaces and specifically localised areas of the house are pared down to one significant example.

It is primarily in the curious texture of this play's language, with its modest but strikingly visual descriptions and elaborations, that metaphorical exploration of the relationship between material and human households takes place. Considering the distinctive balance between domestic meanings and domestic spaces in *A Yorkshire Tragedy* therefore offers a way of understanding the effect of the much fuller physical representation of domestic particularity which the other plays studied above have offered; a way of exploring the significance of the presence and absence of the household on the stage. The meanings of the domestic explored in Chapters 1 and 2 seem most distant here, much less insistently called to the audience's mind because their materiality is not tapped into, and only coming into full focus as the play reaches its crescendo of violence.

The majority of the dialogue in the scenes which follow the servants' opening discussion explores the relationship between the house and its head, the Husband. In her opening speech, the Wife explains the misfit between her Husband's status and his behaviour: 'Dice, and voluptuous meetings, midnight revels, / Taking his bed with surfeits ill beseeming / The ancient honour of his house and name' (ii.7–9).[3] The play's insistent message is that this honour, which the Husband has inherited along with his lands, should

steer his behaviour and check his personal desires. Using the lever of tradition
as an intervention in the present, the Wife begs him, 'As y'are a gentleman
by many bloods, / . . . Think on the state of these three lovely boys' (ii.61–3),
his sons. The Gentleman who tackles him over his behaviour echoes, 'Y'are
of a virtuous house; show virtuous deeds' (ii.170), encouraging him to fit his
actions to the aggregate of generations of manners, and to conduct himself
in sympathy with all that the 'house' represents as a moral exemplar for the
local community.

This connection between a history of actions and the materiality of the
house is pushed further by the Gentleman, who also reminds the Husband that

> Thy father's and forefathers' worthy honours,
> Which were our country monuments, our grace,
> Follies in thee begin now to deface.
>
> (ii.137–9)

His social position is such that his family in part define the nature of the
county in which they are based; in the past they have symbolized the county
by expressing its ideals. But their 'monument' here is also necessarily something which is figured physically in the visual impact of the edifice of the
house itself. The Husband's recent actions are deconstructing this representation by severing the link between noble family and proud building, and
as such an unreliable referent the house becomes merely a façade.[4]

Linked to the house itself, the Husband's behaviour is also inevitably
connected to the lands which sustain such a residence. The Wife, having
provided what she thinks will be the answer to all his problems, figures his
proposed career at court as an opportunity to 'redeem / His virtues with his
lands' (iii.22–3). The latter have been lost with the disintegration of the former,
and a recognition of the symbiosis of their relationship appears to be the
only way to rebuild the family. But this offer is spurned, and, in the eerily
prophetic passage with which the scene ends, the wife offers up a vision of
the disintegration of her way of life which takes the widest sense of family
history and converts it to fragile fabric; 'I see how ruin with a palsy hand /
Begins to shake the ancient seat to dust' (iii.90–1).

Sharing his Wife's language in his own soliloquy of developing self-
knowledge, the Husband imagines how 'the gentleman's palsy in the hand'
can 'shake out his posterity' (iv.66–7) in a game of dice. He realises, as Sir
Charles and Susan Mountford did, that his land was not his own but 'Mine and
my father's and my forefathers', generations, generations' (iv.72–3). Without
the substance of his estate, the house in the broadest sense is disintegrated:
'Down goes the house of us; down, down it sinks. Now is the name a beggar,
begs in me. That name, which hundreds of years has made this Shire famous,
in me and my posterity runs out' (iv.73–7). The connection between past and

future is brought to an abrupt halt as the relationship between family and individual patriarchal head is fractured; as custodianship of patrimony turns into the consumption occasioned by personal greed. Such is the metaphorical weight of the domestic environment in this play, freighted with history and circled with land.

This disparity between the solidity of the physical house and the mutability of its current representatives is brought about by their changing reputation, a reputation made at the point of contact between household and community. As the Husband attacks his wife's reputation by accusing her of infidelity, the Gentleman reminds him of the absurdity of his actions:

> Yourself to stain the honour of your wife,
> Nobly descended? Those whom men call mad
> Endanger others; but he's more than mad
> That wounds himself
>
> (ii.106–9)

The body wound of slander is self-inflicted, located within the household rather than offered as a threat from outside, as it was in *Arden*, for instance. The instability of reputation, in which behaviour has to be constantly re-evaluated and is only as sure as its last successful contestation, is set against the longevity of the house. Although slander usually shapes female reputation, as the Husband is aware, it is his own actions which attract the pejorative language associated with moral blemish.[5] It is he who 'stains', he who is 'An *unclean* rioter' (130) whose deeds pollute his ancient stock, and his slander of his wife which damages his public image, as the Gentlemen stress when they call attention to the way in which his words '*soil* his better name' (106). When the madness of the tragedy has finally come to rest, the Knight expresses regret that 'I e'er knew him' because of the way he has altered his 'fair descent, / Till this black minute without stain or blemish', his actions making a 'blot / upon his predecessors' honoured name' (ix.3–5, 33–4).

This discolouring, dishonouring action of reputation upon name is a part of the play's depiction of the material substance of the household as susceptible to physical assault. Because of the Husband's unclean riot, the Gentleman says, 'Thy lands and credit / Lie now both sick of a consumption' (ii.130–1). Early on in her opening speech of lament, the Wife tells the audience that 'My husband never ceases in expense / Both to consume his credit and his house' (ii.2–3), and this image of the house as something which can be expended through unfitting actions continues throughout the play. She offers him her dowry, telling him to 'Consume it, as your pleasure counsels you'. Advised by pleasure and financed by the dissolution of the material substance on which status depends, the Husband is described by the Knight as a 'Ruinous man, / The desolation of his house' (ix.32–3). Unlike his brother, a man 'who profited / in his divine employments' (iv.17–18), the Husband produces nothing, finally admitting that 'I have consumed all, played away long acre' (ix.16).

Gambling provides a perfect metaphor of unpredictability and inequality, one which sets the Husband's self-destruction against the stability of a household of status. The maid, holding one of his sons in her arms and lamenting the boy's fate says, 'Hard when the father plays away the son' (v.5). Gambling necessitates the transformation of all assets into money. The concrete materials of family identity, the house itself and its estates, have to be translated into the universal currency of cash; the particular, distinctive and personal, those things which have history and family connection, are 'played away'. When his wife returns from London, the Husband bombards her with questions in an effort to extract from her what he needs: 'Where's the money? Let's see the money. Is the rubbish sold, those wiseacres, your lands? Why, when? The money, where is't? Pour't down, down with it. Down with it, I say, pour't o'th' ground!' (iii.35–7). His feverish excitement is generated by his wish to see the results of the alchemical transubstantiation of land into something liquid, and therefore malleable and yielding.

In the second scene, the Husband says that the man with no money 'is damned in this world. He's gone, he's gone' (ii.29). He equates poverty with invisibility in a world in which the only visible actions are those made possible by the supply of ready cash. Similarly, when he fights the Gentleman in scene ii, the conclusions he draws from his defeat set money up as his overriding concern; ''tis want of money makes men weak' (185). Money becomes a lifeblood which gives strength because it makes social participation possible. But money in fact, outside the Husband's warped perspective, causes a *loss* of identity. The externally provided credit and the internally generated bounty of the 'house' are eventually to be supplemented by the Wife's dowry, her own defining familial stock, guarded as a separate entity throughout their marriage. The extent to which a sense of self depends upon inheritance is played out here, as it is in *A Woman Killed*, as a loss of identity. 'Yet I'll forget myself to calm your blood' (iii.65), she says, giving up her own family store to her husband. The distinctive qualities of her lands, and possessions such as her jewels which place her family socially and within their own locality, are to be abruptly erased.

The play deals with the abnormal events which are its subject matter through these confusions of form and substance. Most obviously, the murders themselves are figured as bizarre kinds of reckoning, another part of this defacing move towards the anonymity and indistinguishability of money. The husband leaves the Master of the College to find an answer with which his brother will be 'fully satisfied' (iv.51). As he rushes past him in the next scene, *en route* to his last child at nurse, he says 'I want one small part to make up the sum' (vi.5). And the Master picks up on this metaphor as he examines the bodies, 'Has he summed up these / To satisfy his brother?' (vii.8–9), asking 'Was this the answer I long waited on, / The satisfaction for thy prisoned brother?' (viii.22–3). The meanings of 'satisfaction' here bend ironically between the comfort of its ethical and moral closures, and the deathly consequences of these attempts to substitute the human for the physical substance of the household.

The Husband's pun on the word 'angel' provides a particularly resonant image of the disorder wrought by money. At his first entry, he is lamenting his latest loss:

> Pox o'th' last throw! It made
> Five hundred angels vanish from my sight.
> I'm damned, I'm damned, the angels have forsook me
>
> (ii.25–7)

As the Husband leaves to 'provide' for his brother, the Master echoes the earlier play on words: 'Good sir, in that the angels would be pleased' (iv.52). 'Pleased' takes on the full ironies of its meanings of the joys of appeasement only in the Husband's final farewell to the sons who cannot see him because they are, he imagines, 'playing in the angels' laps' (x.40). This move from coins to heavenly messengers makes the same metaphorical point about translation of the material into essence as the other images of coins and summing, but it connects such transformations to a wider, eschatological series of meanings. Faced with the reality of the disparity between knowledge and experience, stating that 'Divines and dying men may talk of hell, / But in my heart her several torments dwell', the Husband asks 'Who in this case / Would not take up money upon his soul?' (iv.85–8). At this crux in his soliloquy of self-loathing, he makes obvious the link between his next series of actions and the extent of his credit, as one who would 'Pawn his salvation, live at interest' (89). When material credit runs out, all that is left for recompense is a man's personal reserves, the first and most important possession of the soul.

Images which connect earth to heaven, soiling money to ethereal purity, set this play firmly within the morality tradition. The Frankfords' household spaces opened out to fundamental moral meanings of sin and judgement at the end of A Woman Killed in a series of biblical metaphors and images, but in A Yorkshire Tragedy the action takes place within such a space from the start. Despite the fact that the play is, as its title suggests, based upon historical events which took place in 1605 near Wakefield, it lacks any kind of particularity, even to the extent that the names of the central characters are abstracted from Mr and Mrs Calverley into Husband and Wife.[6] A Yorkshire Tragedy lies at the furthest possible remove from Arden of Faversham in terms of the relationship between the particular and the general, the domestic and the homiletic, and this fundamentally affects the way in which the household is represented on stage.

Partly, this difference is given shape by the fact that the motivation for this tragedy is different from the impetus for the actions of Mosby, Merry and Wendoll. Rather than being inspired by covetousness, of another's goods or wife, the Husband is apparently possessed by the devil: when he is finally captured he says 'now glides the devil from me, / Departs at every joint, heaves up my nails' (x.18–19). Instead of offering an implicit focus on the social differences between characters then, or even the broad domestic distinctions between plenty and want, the house as figured in the play becomes the hell in which the Husband carries out his vicious plots. It is an environment within which the effects of his intentions can be felt; a space where the extent of his inhumanity can be experienced. As the servant says to the Wife when she tells him of her hopes for her Husband's reformation now that she has secured his position at court, 'If he should not now be kind to you and love you and cherish you up, I should think the devil himself kept open house in him' (iii.24–6). House and individual merge into one here, as they did in the domestic manuals' advice about the seriousness of marriage.[7] This has a strikingly different effect within the narrative, in that domestic space in fact contributes to an examination of *character* rather than *motivation* as was the case in the other plays.

Because the Husband's actions are demonically inspired, they, and the reactions they provoke in others, are represented as 'extra-domestic'. Unlike the characters of *Arden* and *Two Lamentable Tragedies* or the first half of *Woman Killed*, the Wife and her supporters are only too aware of the Manichean stakes attached to their actions. 'I do entreat you *as you love your soul*', she begs her husband, 'Tell me the cause of this your discontent' (ii.32–3). Every conversation is freighted with this level of risk and engagement. The characters' actions are not governed by the logic of aberrant emotions within a routine of domestic behaviour, as is the case in other domestic tragedies, and the daily activities which form a household are therefore of little interest. Actions are rather controlled by the moral absolutes of goodness and evil, heaven and hell; their generation is directed by the need to reveal extremes of character rather than to form a ground against which behaviour can be measured. The Wife describes her spouse in her opening speech, remembering for the audience a series of gestures which simultaneously communicate observed action and the mental and spiritual state it reveals:

> He sits and sullenly locks up his arms;
> Forgetting heaven, looks downward, which makes him
> Appear so dreadful that he frights my heart;
> Walks heavily, as if his soul were earth
>
> (ii.15–18)

This melancholic body language expresses his emotional and spiritual state, and it therefore exists in an unlocated space outside daily life. When the Husband fights with the Gentleman, he conveys similar moral information through his identification of action, in a way which appeals directly to the spatial conventions of the morality play: 'Hard fortune, am I levelled with the ground?' (ii.165).

Because this play represents the relationships between individuals in moral rather than social terms, domestic hierarchies are also very differently depicted. Rather than the investigation of the quality of household governance to which Arden, Wendoll and Frankford are subjected, A Yorkshire Tragedy examines the relative strengths of demonically inspired aggression and honest goodness. The Husband tries his force against his servant in scene v, not as the leadership inherent in his elite position but as the sheer intensity of his verbal onslaught: 'Base slave, my vassal! / Comest thou between my fury to question me?' (33–4). Rather than exercising the unquestioned authority of a naturally gentle mind, he implements his will by force. The careful depiction of the dynamics of service and government is absent here, replaced instead by the combat between good and evil. As the servant says of his battle with his master, 'We struggled, but a fouler strength than his / O'erthrew me with his arms. Then he did bruise me' (vii.27–8). 'Presumption', of which the Husband accuses the Servant, is translated within this power dynamic from a threat to social order into an assertion of goodness against evil. The resolution of the play, therefore, guarantees not the punishment of ineffective patriarchal performance, but the eventual vanquishing of the devil by the forces of providence combined with earthly justice.

The use of the stage in this play interestingly fuses domestic dynamics with the morality tradition in its concern with the spaces between individuals and the moral meanings of their interaction. When the Wife first sees the Husband enter she says, 'Now in despite of ills / I'll speak to him, and I will hear him speak' (ii.22–4). Her intention is to force interaction, to insist upon conversation rather than monologue, but her purpose is frustrated. He is on the stage for only eleven lines, five of which are spoken without knowledge of her presence. When she does address him, it is to receive the 'reply', 'O, most punishment of all, I have a wife' (ii.31). The conversation in which they finally engage fifty or so lines into the scene is characterised by long stretches of abuse punctuated by Grissil-like acquiescence: 'Be it so' (ii.83). The scene offers a powerful evocation of isolation and sets the tone for a lack of contact which characterises the style of the play as a whole. None of the other plays stages scenes solely between husband and wife, and Yorkshire Tragedy is therefore distinctive in doing so. But it gives the couple the whole space of the stage merely to accentuate the distance between them, their lack of contact parodying the unique marriage bond.

The patterning of soliloquy and dialogue reinforces the initial sense of the couple's atomised relationship. The Wife's opening speech is a lament, and it is one of many in the play which give voice to the extent of human impotence in the face of the strength of the evil which has overtaken the house. She opens scene 2 with such a speech, and closes scene 3, demonstrating the extent of her capabilities. When this scene ends, she has done all she can to alter the situation. The Husband has his own laments, first of his situation (iv), and then of his actions to remedy it (viii). And the breakdown of social interaction which this pattern suggests extends beyond the couple, as the master of the College also has cause to lament the fate of the Husband's brother (iv). Other lengthy speeches are spent in admonition, and in the reiteration of the past sins and present state of the Husband's life. These lists have a cumulative effect, and the mounting pressure of their repetition in different mouths as the narrative proceeds is powerful. Between such speeches are the brief snatches of dialogue which the narrative needs to progress, but this static, declamatory style ensures that the plot moves through passion rather than action, dealing with impotence not as a sense of emotional restriction, as is the case in the other plays, but as a personal powerlessness linguistically explored.

The overall effect of this rhetorical construction is to give the impression that characters are acting very much against one another, rather than to the same end. As they speak so often to the audience in soliloquy rather than to their fellows, a strange kind of intimacy is produced. The strength of communication which is developed between character and audience, as one after another they pour out the detail of their emotional states, simultaneously characterises their isolation within the world of the play. The focus upon soliloquy and seclusion is fundamentally anti-domestic, representing a household pulling apart at the seams of mutual purpose.

Partly as a result of this focus, it is perhaps the relationship between public and private action, of all the themes of domestic preoccupation which are present in *A Yorkshire Tragedy*, which is most distinctly handled. In *Arden* and *Two Lamentable Tragedies*, the connections between house and community, and the management of domestic knowledge, were represented as a troubled spatial dynamic. Here, however, the work of rumour is not given a social location, either as the conversations of characters who say too much or as the reported 'table talk' of friends and neighbours. Rather, the assertion of the public knowledge of the couple's problems marks the point at which the emotional energies of their relationship simply cannot be contained within the house. Although they discuss the general knowledge of their financial problems, it is the Husband's unmanageable passions which cause the majority of the comment. As a result, the effects of extra-domestic knowledge are not shocking in the crushing sense of social humiliation, but in the stark terms of the multiplication of pain. 'Why', the wife asks, 'should our faults at home be spread abroad? / 'Tis grief enough within doors' (iii.5–6). When she goes to see her relative in London, he is already aware of a great deal of her story because the work of rumour has been swift and effective, but the audience are never shown how such gossip is spread. The play's moral project is simply to insist upon the inevitability of such a movement of information, and as a result the human processes which lie behind it are left ambiguous.[8] It is not possible, the narrative suggests, to keep the repercussions of actions within the house.

The form which this interpenetration of the domestic and the communal takes is demonstrated in scene ii. The scene has been 'domestic', despite the atomised nature of its dialogue, in the sense that it stages the couple's discussion of the state of their household and family. But as the Husband shouts at his wife 'Strumpet and bastards, strumpet and bastards!' (ii.103–4), so the stage direction reads '*Enter three Gentlemen hearing him*'. In the implicit sense in which the opening of the scene is given any kind of location, it constructs an impression of private space through the painful introspection of its attention to emotional matters. But the arrival of the three Gentlemen shatters this illusion by disregarding any sense of the physical nature of the house as a division between the domestic and the communal. Their entrance demonstrates spatially the way that the domestic operates within the public sphere, and the essential transparency of the former to the latter.

In the pamphlet account of the murders, the argument between the Husband and the Gentleman was settled when 'they both agreed to purge themselves in the field', but in the play the climax of their encounter is relocated to the domestic environment. This has the effect of making it more personal, more meaningful as less encumbered by convention and ritual: 'We are now in private', the Gentleman says, 'There's none but thou and I' (ii.128–9), and their struggle potentially becomes almost intimate for its lack of audience. Their individual combat comes to symbolise the conflict between an exterior sense of morality and justice and the warped rules by which the household operates under the Husband's direction. Like Cranwell in *A Woman Killed*, this Gentleman is a token outsider, a representative of the vigilant community with its stable morality. Unlike Cranwell, of course, he is given no social or characterological particularity.[9]

Partly because this scene is staged in such an unlocalised, non-specific way, it is possible to keep many different meanings of the spatialising word 'private' in play at once. Just as the significance of the Gentleman's explicit identification of the status of the space seemed to pertain not to the visibility of the actions and dialogues they are about to perform but to the frankness and openness which are possible on a one-to-one basis, the Husband reworks the meaning of 'private'. He accuses the Gentleman of having sexual relations with his wife: 'Thou art her champion, thou, her private friend' (ii.151). He returns to the pejorative sense of the word as denoting the secret action, the hidden relationship which acknowledges its own deviation from social norms by concealing itself from public view. Partly, no doubt, the scene is relocated in order to serve the play's economy of representation. With a small cast and a staging which is at all times pared down to its bare essentials, the public spectacle of a duel with its elaborate social forms would be incongruous. But the reworking and questioning of the term 'private' also shows the 'house' acting as a dynamic which governs behaviour, rather than a fully realised physical space. The men perform the multiple and contested significances of 'inside' rather than presenting the audience with the experience of an interior.

London, where the Wife's discussions with her Uncle take place, is the only location where actions integral to the plot occur which are reported rather than represented.[10] Apart from the instances concerned with this journey, the plot unfolds in a linear timescale in front of the audience, structured around the actions of its central protagonist the Husband. The play shows little interest, therefore, in presenting the illusion that anything is going on which cannot be seen on the stage, or that the lives of the characters have any form outside their involvement in the narrative of the Calverley murders. The pamphlet presents the murder scene as both a physical and a mental confusion: 'Some caught up the dead infant, some helped at the maid, all amazed at this tragicke alteration, knewe not what to thinke';[11] actions are frenzied and motives are unclear. In the play, however, this disorder is smoothed out into a stark clarity of uninterrupted purpose as one event moves relentlessly into the next, and where action follows quickly on the heels of motive and neither is at any stage in doubt. The Husband strives with the Maid, then the Wife, then the Servant, and subsequently meets the Master. When the sequence of violence is ended, the reactions of servants, Master and Wife are then dealt with. This logical ordering makes confusion an aspect of comprehension, rather than representation. The full force of the action is set before the audience piece by piece.[12]

As a result, spatial representation is straightforward, as events are seldom distanced from the audience by the mimetic illusion that other actions are taking place elsewhere. Unlike *A Woman Killed*'s location of the domestic space which the stage represents in relation to other rooms, the house in *A Yorkshire Tragedy* exists entirely 'on the stage'. 'Within' in this play means 'off-stage', rather than further into the more private domestic spaces of the house. When the servants tell the wife of the arrival of the doctor, they say 'A surgeon waits within' (v.37), in spite of the fact that she is in her bedchamber, an intimate room deep within the house. There are few calls for servants from off-stage, and the majority of the entrances in the play are either undesired and unexpected, like that of the Gentlemen and the Master, or curious re-entries shortly after exits. The Husband, the Gentleman and the Master all depart only to reappear a few lines later as a further irritant to those on stage. There is, in other words, seldom a sense in which exits are intended to seem productive of an offstage activity which bears upon what the audience see. What we watch is all: condensed and stark action.

Only once does *A Yorkshire Tragedy* stage a recognisable domestic interior, and that is the bedchamber in which the murders take place. The fact that it is at this crucial point that a more fully realised space comes into play is significant, indicating here as it does in the other plays the importance of spatial violation to the full force of the horror of murder. The significance of the Faversham parlour as a location for Arden's death was set up dramaturgically in the preceding scenes as an enclosed space which could be manipulated by the murderers by locking the doors from the inside. The importance of the chamber in *A Yorkshire Tragedy*, however, is set up rhetorically, through the Husband's powerful metaphors of claustrophobia and spatial limit.

The Husband's language encapsulates his sense of the constrictions of the present. Describing his financial constraints, he uses the conventional rhetoric of the bridling of strong emotion and desire: 'That mortgage sits like a snaffle upon mine inheritance and makes me chaw upon iron' (ii.46–8). But it is his penury, rather than his self-control, which restrains him and he remains obsessed with indulgence in the immediate gratifications of action:

> . . . I will not *bate*
> A whit in humour! Midnight, still I love you
> And revel in your company: *Curbed in*?
>
> (ii.77–9)

Although the source of his claustrophobia is financial, his images of want, like his metaphors of entrapment, are ones of physical limit. As he claims that his frustrations stem from his married state, so the oppression which he suffers is partly that of being trapped within a household.[13] In scene 4, in the long speech during which he reasons himself from poverty to murder as its logical consequence, he discusses the fate of his lands in some of the most haunting metaphors of the play. 'What is there in three dice', he asks, 'to make a man draw thrice three thousand acres into the compass of a round little table' (iv.64–6). In this action the past is sacrificed to the present; the context within which life operates and against which the self is defined is gathered into the table, as the focus of the Husband's rapt concentration. 'My lands showed like a full moon about me', he continues, 'But now the moon's i'th' last quarter, waning, waning' (iv.70–1). As part of that unquestionable order of being, the lands' ownership should have been settled for all time, but it has been made mutable through his behaviour. Space is constricting as a gradual process of darkening invisibility.

With the husband's actions, the width and breadth of history and prosperity have become the narrow miserliness of present want. By subjecting the space in which he lives to the roll of chance, he has disintegrated the very ground on which he walks. When his horse trips on the level ground on his way to the town, he once again sees this as a manifestation of the uneavenness of chance; 'a man / May dice upon't and throw away the meadows' (viii.6–7). There is a sense that he gambles as he rides, and his losses take away the land from under his feet. This kind of spatial awareness is a striking aspect of the play's power: the bold distinctions between small and large, between the claustrophobia of need and the broad expanses of plenty. The two poles of domestic life, so clearly represented in *A Woman Killed* as the diverse domestic experiences of Frankford and Sir Charles, here become spatial dynamics in which the constrictions of want are represented by a narrowing of space rather than the altered sensory experience of a different lifestyle. In this shift in ways of representing a change of fortunes, *A Yorkshire Tragedy* denies a place to the subtle gradations of social status which domestic objects bring into play.

As the tension builds towards its climax, the Husband's young son enters '*with a top and scourge*', and metaphors of the contraction of the family estates become a more physical problem of restricted space. The boy complains; 'I cannot scourge my top as long as you stand so. You take up all the room with your wide legs' (iv.92–4). Physically, upon the stage, the small vignette of childhood concerns suggests a narrowing of space by pointing up the magnifying properties of mental absorption. As father and son focus on the top and one another, space appears reduced. But on a metaphorical level, the child's freedom to play, a freedom from care and from want, is compromised by his father's actions. The amount of space which he needs to scourge a top up and down the room literally suggests wealth, and the father's very presence compromises the carefree experience of plenty. Because the imagery the characters employ shines so brightly out of the simplicity of the action, this strikingly specific moment with the spinning top invites connections to the metaphors of the round table and the eclipsing moon in a material representation of the downward spiral of the Husband's fortunes.[14] As he swings the wounded boy around in a distorted echo of the movement of the top, the Husband attempts to take control of the situation by challenging the fates themselves: 'My children's blood shall spin into your faces' (iv.109). The repetition of the circle in visual and verbal images builds to a representation of constriction half-way between the mental and the spatial.

Scene 4 ends with the wounding of the eldest boy and the defiant threats to the fates; scene 5 opens with the maid, also carrying a child, but this time lulling it to sleep with her sibilant speech; 'Sleep, sweet babe; sorrow makes thy mother sleep' (v.1). The intimacy, gentleness and comparative stillness of the Maid's opening speech comes between the previous wounding and the fulfilment of the Husband's threats like the eye of a storm. The Wife, called Mother at this point in the stage directions, is said to be 'by' the maid, asleep like her child but in bed.[15] The tone of the play changes at this point because two female characters and two children are, uniquely, alone on stage together, and the fact that two of them are asleep stresses their vulnerability. It also serves to establish the strikingly different space which a chamber represents, economically signalling calm and security before these habitual qualities are shattered.

The claustrophobic narrowing of context which threatens and enrages the husband in the previous scene is juxtaposed with the small room of the chamber, a female space of nurture and of sleep. The symbolic nature of the representational mode of A Yorkshire Tragedy invites the audience to read the bed on which the Wife lies symbolically, as a soft and yet protective space of nurture. As a space physically marked off from the rest of the stage, it is by its physical presence suggestive of a distinct set of meanings which are gendered by the actors on stage. The male intrusion into this space is harmful; instead of creating it destroys.

The familiar image of the bed in itself alters the tone of this scene, and it is given particular impact as the only piece of furniture for which the play calls.[16] It brings into play simultaneously the two key iconographical manifestations of such an object, the deathbed and the childbed, recalling the rites of passage around which family and household figure and refigure themselves. Involved in birth and death, the bed comes to symbolise the essentially paradoxical nature of the household as simultaneous source of stability and of change. As an image, it carries with it some of the significance of the chamber itself, in a period in which object and room were becoming increasingly synonymous.[17] The meanings of the room as space of safekeeping for the important possessions which both shape and figure identity, and for the members of the household who arrive in and depart from life within it, are brought to mind. Around this organising object, the human household at last arranges itself purposefully. It is, in a pointed irony, this bloodiest scene in which the Calverley house is at last represented as working together, rather than in their habitual atomised isolation. As each character does battle with the Husband on stage next to the bed, its meanings seem to *produce* a household, as a group who cohere to protect its meanings. For the only time in the play, a household as a dynamic of individuals collaborate to defend the Wife and children as the hope on which their future *as* a group depends.

Although the physical presence of the bed is crucial here, the emotional residues of action are in the end the stronger force in this play, both dramaturgically and in the meaning which *Yorkshire Tragedy* makes from its combination of visual and verbal signals. The strength of emotion over-whelms and engulfs the physical space of the chamber. The murders over, the servants invite the Wife to 'leave this most accursed place', which she says she does willingly because ''Tis guilty of sweet blood, innocent blood'. She explains the change which has occurred in the very nature of the room: 'Murder has took this chamber with full hands / And will ne'er out as long as the house stands' (vii.36, 39–40). The image of the permanent association between act and space is partly familiar from *Arden* and *Two Lamentables*, where it is linked to the providential certainty of discovery in a context in which the connections between murderer and crime are threatened by the potential erasure of evidence. Here, however, the significance of the lasting record of the physicality of the assault does not lie in the revelation of the personified murder's greedy grasp. Rather, its endurance is nicely condi-tional: murder will not leave the chamber as long as the physical house stands, but the action of murder has itself threatened the existence of the familial 'house'. As was the case for Frankford, in his several attempts to rid the house of all evidence of his wife in *A Woman Killed*, the connection between spaces, actions and individuals is inseparably, unbearably close.

Because the sense of space in *A Yorkshire Tragedy* is moral rather than domestic, the form which judgement takes is very important to its visual meaning. Towards the end of the play there are scenes of pageant or parade, features to which the play's 'hyper visible' staging is sympathetic, and which have similarities with the scenes of Anne's punishment in *A Woman Killed*. The way in which the pursuit of the Husband is represented continues the representation of his feelings of constricted space, this time in what should be the broadest of environments outside the town: 'Ha! I hear the sounds of men like hue and cry' (viii.10), he says, and then 'O, / . . . My will is bated' (13–15). Those who are chasing him are not seen on the stage, but are heard behind the doors: 'Here, this way' (13), and he notes their ominous presence 'At my back? Oh!' (14), behind him and presumably increasing in volume. In the spatial logic on which the stage operates, he cannot leave it because his pursuers inhabit the place behind the exits, and in front of him the audience forms a boundary which he cannot cross. The Husband is trapped between the two areas which are 'off-stage', and when his pursuers finally enter he is also subjected to the scrutiny of two sets of onlookers, and to their eventual judgement. The sequence lacks the sense of a household opened up to the display of sin in front of a judging audience, which is so prominent a feature of the moralised dynamic between the domestic and the homiletic in *A Woman Killed*, but it retains the visual impact of judgement which forces the audience to objectify the scene in front of them, and to take up a moral position in relation to it.

In Scene x, where the Husband is given the morally and didactically significant opportunity to express his remorse, a similar dynamic is employed. Crucially, however, the tiring house wall is this time employed to represent the ancient seat of the Calverleys. The opening stage direction suggests that the '*Husband with the officers, the master and gentlemen*' enter, '*as going by his house*', and this is stressed rhetorically in the opening words of the accused: 'I am right against my house, seat of my ancestors' (x.1). As he moves across the stage from one side to the other, from the apologies to his wife to the embrace of his dead children, the Husband moves in fact towards judgement as he is on his way to prison. But once more he is moving between two 'juries'; between those whom he has wounded and those who have witnessed his actions. He is forced, by his progress across the stage, to confront the family he has wronged, and the audience is compelled to see him in physical and interpretative relation to his crimes. What the latter see is a 'double ground', a rich context which sets him in relation to the various meanings of household which the play has developed. Forming a backdrop to the action the tiring house, as a stately edifice punctuated with doors, comes to represent the house as monument to the family past. Ranged in front there is the particular present of the Calverley family, the nuclear unit of this specific generation of Calverleys. The permanence and stability of the former contrasts sharply with the physical decay and death of the latter, and it is in the light of these two images that the audience judges the Husband.

At what are arguably the two most emotionally intense moments of the play, the murder in the chamber and the complete acceptance of culpability which is necessary to repentance and forgiveness, the house is present on the stage as a physical context which gives meaning and shape to events by according them the full force of their implications. But there is no tension, in *A Yorkshire Tragedy*, between the force of emotion and the appropriate forms of social intercourse; no friction between the routines of domestic life and the aberrations of murder. The dynamics of the Calverley household are for the most part pared down to the intense feelings of the Husband and Wife for one another, admitting none of complicated, comparative hostilities of domestic jealousy or suppressed desire. In this play, murder seems inevitable and it is shown openly, boldly; performed comparatively artlessly with no thought of concealment. The excessive violence of the crime and the comparative insignificance of its motive diminish the significance of the domestic setting. The careful enumeration of those objects and spaces which are threatened by the humiliating power of sexual dishonesty and the contest between men are extraneous to the more fundamentally destructive murder of the next generation of the family.

A Yorkshire Tragedy is a play curiously caught between the force of example offered by its particularity and the stark moral framework of its generality.

In eschewing a closed mimetic representation of domesticity it aims at a very different effect to the other tragedies. The Arden, Merry and Frankford households tend towards the separation of audience and narrative, arguably working towards sympathy rather than empathy with the characters through the construction of an intimacy and privacy which by their nature exclude. Such a separation fosters a sense of satisfaction on the part of an audience who are bound, in their anticipation of the development of the narrative, to know better. Heightened in their awareness of the 'mistakes' which the characters make in their exercise of authority and their performance of obedience, attention to domestic detail cultivates moral superiority. Here, however, in the extreme actions and reactions of the Calverley household, didacticism has the upper hand. The Husband draws an explicit moral from his actions: 'Let every father look into my deeds, / And then their heirs may prosper while mine bleeds' (x.59–60). He draws attention to possible relationships between the narrative and what might happen subsequently outside the theatre; how the play might be relevant to fathers in the audience, no matter how unlikely the recurrence of such a situation might seem. Because of the sparseness of physical representation and narrative particularity, the play has a timelessness despite its topical subject matter. What it lacks as a result, however, are the recognisable domestic elements on which identification can begin to build its sense of familiarity.

NOTES

1 Randall Martin uncovers some of the significance of these disjunctures when he states that 'Gentle status and paternal authority are only authentically established by transference of family wealth to an heir'; 'Arden winketh at his wife's lewdness, & why!': a patrilineal crisis in *Arden of Faversham*', *Early Theatre* 4, 2001, 13–33, p. 16.

2 It also evinces, as Lena Orlin has shown, a marked interest in material culture, 1994, pp. 253–5.

3 All references are to the Revels edition of the play, ed. A. C. Cawley and Barry Gaines, Manchester: Manchester University Press, 1986.

4 In Dolan's compelling phrase, the house 'forms a collective subject out of the dead, the living, and the anticipated', 1994, p. 157.

5 Dolan argues that both '*Two Most* and *A Yorkshire Tragedy* . . . link Calverley's prodigality, slander against his family, and murder of his children as *self*-destructive acts', 1994, p. 155.

6 For details of the lives of the historical Calverleys see Orlin, 1994, pp. 229–34.

7 See above, pp. 45–6.

8 Only in the stylistically different opening scene are such social interaction and the movement of knowledge and individuals suggested.

9 Comensoli calls the Gentleman a 'choric' figure, a description which usefully draws attention to his dramatic, as opposed to social, function; 1996, p. 100.

10 For the differences between this arrangement of the narrative and the one presented in *Two Most Unnaturall and Bloodie Murthers*, see Cawley, '*A Yorkshire Tragedy* and

Two Most Unnaturall & Bloodie Murthers', in D. W. Jefferson ed., *The Morality of Art*, London: Routledge & Kegan Paul, 1969, pp. 106–7.

11 Cawley and Gaines eds, 1986, p. 107.

12 As Adams says, 'The power of the play lies, not in the characterization, but in the rapidly developing dramatic situation, as the action speeds quickly to the catastrophe', 1965, p. 132.

13 For a reading of the source of the Husband's torments as located in his inability to cope with his patriarchal role see Orlin, 1994, pp. 234–5; Comensoli, 1996, p. 101.

14 The detail comes, of course, directly from the source: see Cawley and Gaines eds, 1986, p. 106.

15 For the significance of the role of the mother in domestic tragedies see F. Dunworth, 'Motherhood in Elizabethan Drama', unpublished PhD thesis, University of Kent, 2004.

16 For a fascinating discussion of the stage bed as 'like a stage-within-a-stage, an intense and compelling visual and symbolic arena for acting out powerful passions and transgressions', see Sasha Roberts, 'Lying amongst the classics: ritual and motif in elite Elizabethan and Jacobean beds', in Lucy Gent ed., *Albion's Classicism: The Visual Arts in Britain, 1550–1660*, New Haven, London: Yale University Press, 1995.

17 See above, p. 83.

Conclusion

I N T H E F I R S T major book on these plays, Henry Hitch Adams argued that
the realism of domestic tragedies 'made the moral lesson effective by
illustrating, directly in terms of the experiences of the audience, the punishments for sin'.[1] This book has been an attempt to unpick the ways in which
that realism might have engaged the experiences of the plays' first audiences,
through a reconstruction of attitudes towards house and household and an
extended consideration of staging practices.

In part at least, this has necessitated an argument about theatrical absence.
The opening chapters have reconstructed the extra-theatrical significance of
domestic spaces and the meanings of their contents. Part of the point of this
exercise has been specific to domestic tragedies. Didactic drama necessarily
presents things as they should *not* be, and domestic tragedy by and large stages
the denial, undermining and downright disregard of the generally accepted
significances of the household. Throughout these plays, the progression of
property and family values which smoothes the disjunctures of death is pointedly interrupted. Silently marginalised in domestic tragedy is any notion of a
longer view, of a future beyond the individual and a perspective wider than

the house. Characters are isolated by their preoccupations and lusts, and generations are fractured by their actions. Domestic space is violated by individuals who cannot relinquish their own physical purchase on what they see around them in favour of guaranteeing a future for their families. Curiously then, it is the lack of representation of one important strand of extra-theatrical thinking about the household which is particularly significant in understanding the impact of these plays.

Over the course of the first two chapters I have made several claims for the nature of domestic perception. Fundamentally, I have argued for the materiality of a contemporary understanding of the domestic, and for the sensory qualities of memories of the household. All the different types of evidence studied have suggested that individuals understood there to be a close interaction between the 'household human' and the 'household physical', one which was negotiated both ideologically and in practice through objects and spaces. And the evidence has also shown just how pervasive these ideas were: articulated through many different discourses for a variety of purposes, the meanings of the household were both common and important; both widespread and high-profile.

Being part of a household was always shaped by the distinctions and inequalities of status and gender because it was defined by ties of respons-ibility within spatial proximity. Such differences were worked out in relation to objects and the daily routines in which they were employed. Early modern men and women understood the uniqueness of objects as comparable to the individuality of human beings, and they found in the particularity of their goods a potential for the articulation of a symbolic language of human inter-action. Inherent in the distinctiveness of every domestic thing was a history of its temporal and affective connection to the household. But because of this capacity to focus meanings, objects also functioned particularly effectively as metonyms, representative elements of the rooms in which they were kept or all the goods which individuals owned. They were paradoxically valued as both whole and fragment. This dynamic between the part and the whole, the one and the many, negotiated the importance of the coherence of space. Particularly amongst the urban elite, for whom goods were especially signific-ant in reflecting status, the way in which rooms were decorated made them important in their totality, and individuals went to great lengths to preserve their unity. Domestic plenty, in goods for comfort and complex routines, and a diversity of household spaces, offered a central way of expressing authority within the local community. Cushions, carpets, pewter and silverware literally marked the difference between being 'anybody' and being 'somebody'; they gave individuals identity within the power structures of the town.

Several aspects of the relationship between houses and households seem to have had a particularly pervasive power. The evidence studied here repeatedly addressed the contest of different kinds of authority over the household, ones which set physical control against patriarchal or moral management. The dialectic between 'inside' and 'outside' was carefully deployed for moral purposes; a rhetoric of neighbourhood and community employed or denied in the 'closed' or 'open' house. There was a complex grammar of the legitimacy of actions which was grounded in identification of their physical location, and events which were fundamentally opposed to the ideologies of household life tended to be represented as taking place within anti-types of domestic space. The domestic produced its others as distorted but recognisable mirror images of itself.

In this period, in which the pattern of analogous thought was so central to thinking about the house, attention was bound to be drawn to the connection between public and private spaces. But there was also, as a result, an interest in their boundedness. It was the essential physical separability of inside and outside, despite the impossibility of similarly dividing individuals' actions, which allowed meaningful ideological connection to be made between them. The idea of the boundary was physically important, therefore, because it marked the limits of individual household spaces, and ideologically significant in managing both shame and judgement. But within the close and emotionally loaded spaces of the house, the relationships between knowing, seeing and telling were markedly different. In the performative scenes in depositions, in which illicit sexual encounters were observed, relationships between watcher and watched were complicated by the discrete nature of the spectacle and the entanglements of partiality which household ties produce.

The way the house contained individuals, the physical closeness in which it kept them, was central to its meanings. Above all other spaces, the rooms of the house make prominent the meanings of tangibility and of intimate contact, and this physical closeness, not least between men and women, must have been particularly striking in such a highly stratified society. For these reasons, emotion is closely linked to the spaces of the household. Intimate actions and strong emotions are domestic in the sense that they have no place outside the doors of the house; their only legitimate location is inside, where they will not disrupt the proper course of social life.

Household spaces are by definition familiar ones; rooms seen daily, objects used regularly. But the duration of this familiarity also had its moral aspects in early modern England. As the evidence of wills and depositions in particular showed, association with a household was given value by the fact that it was never an instantaneous situation, but rather one characterised by accretion and gradual maturity: a series of associations which developed over time. These connections, between individuals and between individuals and houses, have an essential time-depth to them, one which operates in a cycle of forgetting and remembering: the state of a kind of hyper-awareness, where spaces are so familiar that they are no longer noticed, and the ritualised moments at which they come to the forefront of memory, as friends and neighbours visit and share food, and as marriage and death alter the dynamics of the household.

Domestic space has also been seen to be governed by the dynamics of command and subservience, in ways which are in potential tension with its intimacies. Domestic actions are ones which perform these power relations, ones which exercise the differences between authority and subjection within a bounded space. As Natalie Zemon Davis puts it, the world of the family is one of 'conspicuous tension between intimacy and power',[2] and therefore one where authority must uniquely be negotiated through, rather than outside, intimacy, and where the individuality (with all its particular strengths and weaknesses) on which patriarchal structures tend to flounder cannot be avoided. In the household, the disparity between role and character is potentially at its height.

All of these meanings of the household were articulated in the way domestic tragedies were staged. The crimes which they portray are crimes of familiarity, as Frances Dolan has suggested.[3] They are born out of constant presence and its erosions of humanity and their consequences are dealt with within these bounds. Tragedies which take place within the household have the specific intensity which accompanies small spaces, with their concentration upon action and reaction. Interpersonal dynamics have traditionally been seen as shaping the genre, but it is the way those dynamics play out within the confined rooms of the house which gives the dramas their compelling power. These plays have been compared unfavourably to 'tragedy proper'. The 'domestic' as a setting has been taken to mean 'reduced' – the tragic universe of Lear scaled down from the broad heath under the broader sky to the walls of the house; the disintegration of the individual spirit condensed into, rather than expanded out of, human surroundings.[4] This diminishing has, understandably, been read in relation to the plays' own protestations of limited representation: the 'barren subject' and 'bare scene'. In other words their scale has been seen as a paucity of both imagination and representation; the former too prosaic and the latter too concrete. But thinking about them spatially suggests instead that the condensed world they offer is one intensified by its restrictions. Adams argued that the most powerful of these plays present to the reader 'people who, for a time, transcend their petty existences through the terrifying power of their ruling passions', but for early modern men and women this seems to outline a wrong relationship between daily life and emotion.[5] The terrifying power of passion was the very reason for domestic organisation, and the mismatch he suggests between the magnitude of emotion and the scale of its context misunderstands the moral status of the bounded nature of the household. It was surely because emotion was seen as being in regular danger of exploding the primacy of the communal over the individual that the containing system of analogous spheres came about. In a period in which the ceiling over of halls brought the house down to size, Lena Orlin suggests that it 'scaled itself to, echoed, and reassured' the human figure of 'his own significance and centrality', and this reading is partly borne out by the developing levels of comfort which it offered.[6] But it is only half of the story. As it was for the Husband in *A Yorkshire Tragedy*, the house might be a space which bates the will as it comforts the body, its physical shape scaling back, rationalising, the potentially spiralling lusts of its inhabitants. The explosions of emotion which threatened the fabric of the household had a cultural power in early modern England which they have perhaps lost, as we have moved from concern with the claustrophobic to interest in the agoraphobic; from fear that the house will not contain, to fascination with illimitable human emotion.

All the plays examined here, by their nature as 'domestic' tragedies, offer their audiences a position with Marleton, out on the stairs to the yard, or in their stockinged feet with Crench, just inside the entry to his master's house.[7] The realism they offer might 'bring the moral home', but this didactic intent is all the time in competition with the urge to imagine which comes from the various invitations to believe that what is staged is 'real'. William West's description of Augustine's *curiositas* as 'the lust of the eyes, the sin in particular associated with the watching of theatrical shows and *the observation of the things of the world as if they were shows*' gives a shrewd indication of the conflicting pleasures these plays offer. 'To stop at observation and never proceed to action', West continues, 'is to remain merely within the realm . . . of the theatre', but it also goes against morally appropriate action outside the theatre.[8] The moralised rules which should relate observation to intervention were in themselves under unbearable pressure within household space. As an audience, watching Nick waiting for Frankford to cease watching his wife and her lover shows just how blurred the clear distinctions between actors and audience can become. It demonstrates the extent to which the plays consider domestic surveillance a part of their moral project, as well as an important aspect of their representation – what they expect from their audiences as well as how they stage their narratives. The similarities and connections between the forms of domestic representation across these very different types of evidence is striking, and suggestive of the closeness of theatrical spectacle and domestic life in areas such as material culture and models of 'audiencing'.

Outside the genre of domestic tragedy, the household is often staged impressionistically, economically, through the kind of interaction characters share. *Romeo and Juliet*, for example, opens with the brawl between the two houses, continues with the formal marriage negotiations between Capulet and Paris in I.ii, but changes register in I.iii when three women gather on stage to discuss Juliet's age and potential nuptials. Their gender, the nature of their discussion and the language in which it is cast – particularly the folksy details of the Nurse's recollections: "Tis since the earthquake now eleven years, / And she was weaned – I never shall forget it' (25–6) – all insist upon a particular kind of gendered domesticity for the scene. Domestic tragedies, however, focus the intensity of human interaction into depiction of adulterous liaisons, and their dialogue concerns itself with plans for deceit and murder rather than with marriage negotiations. In other words they need to find an alternative to the subject matter of their narrative if they are to indicate domesticity, because that subject matter is fundamentally anti-domestic, intent on undercutting all the meanings of house and household upon which other plays depend. And it is partly for this reason that the physical house is so important to their dramaturgy. In setting up a mimetic representation of an interior through properties, through the identification of different rooms, and through domestic routines such as dining, they bring into play the moral and political implications of the household. Properties and routines, as metonyms for the household, provide a setting-off point for imagination, somewhere to focus meanings and a prompt for audiences to begin to consider the ideologies associated with domestic space. They invite consideration of allegiance, and of the fundamental dynamic between governors and those they govern, with their associated proscriptions for behaviour. In order to demonstrate abuse fully, the particularity of domestic detail becomes especially insistent when the ideals of domesticity – hospitality, the authority of governors over governed, and female chastity – are being corrupted by inappropriate behaviour. The physical household is put on stage at such points to stand silent witness to the complexities of emotion described in the opening chapters of this book. In these plays then, action is set in tension with location, and that focus on the interaction between the two sets domestic tragedy apart in a developing theatrical taste for character, interiority and interpersonal exchanges.

The four plays studied here represent very different kinds of household. Arden is a member of the urban elite of a small town; Merry a minor metropolitan tradesman; Frankford and Calverley inhabit the main houses on their estates as country gentlemen. One of the crucial issues to arise from Chapter 2 was the establishment of the basic elements of the different rooms of the house, and their congruence across at least the broad middle of the social scale. When Frankford's domestic plenty is paraded across the stage, it is possible to approximate such finery using the 'universal' properties of a theatrical company, because the forms of objects have a general currency, and audiences can then read from narrative situation to prop and back again.

But the meanings of these objects are also general enough to have a more personal impact on the audience. Such an impact, as I have discussed it here, is not only about making theatrical sense – there seems little doubt that audiences would understand the meanings of a carpet and candlesticks – it is also a part of the sensational-didactic project of making those who follow the narrative consider its possible relationship to their own domestic practices. The threats and disasters befalling the staged household are given material connections to domestic spaces outside the theatre. Because the meanings of the household were ideologically prominent and still broadly similar across different social groups in this period, a shockingly realistic English tragedy was particularly timely.

The chapters of this book have been concerned with a limited number of plays, but, if the analysis of the particular kind of domestic representation offered here is to have any real meaning, it is necessary to make some brief comments about the typicality of the form which it takes, taking as read the fact that the level of such representation in domestic plays is abnormally high. If we divide the form of domestic representation into its constituent parts, it is clear that the use of domestic properties, the verbal description of domestic objects, the identification of different rooms within the house, the interest in exits, entrances and the controllability of space, and the staging of detailed domestic routines such as food preparation and lifecycle moments such as deathbed scenes are, to a greater or lesser extent, common to many different kinds of play of the period. All plays which stage a domestic scene use similar theatrical forms, and as they do so they make simultaneous reference to extra-theatrical ideologies of household and the audience's own domestic experience, to a greater or lesser extent. The factors governing the extent of that audience engagement are the final points demanding consideration here.

First, it is possible to draw some very broad generic outlines, because genres have their own distinct interests, and a bed appearing in a history play will inevitably mean differently from one placed in a comedy. In romantic comedies, domestic representations are keyed to the tension between intimacy and patriarchal marriage. Lovers are divided between upper and lower stage, or united in secrecy, but they will eventually form a household rather than seeking the privacy of an interior, as the intensity of their passion is transmuted into the stability of marriage. In the histories domestic issues comment on affairs of state, offering their diminished scale as a response to state policy and its implications within the family. The boundedness of rooms suggests personal and family space in opposition to the battlefield, with its needs and priorities often at odds with the 'national good'. The meanings of household in tragedies are considerably more recognisable from the domestic plays. They tend to focus on one very intense interior scene – the bedchamber in *Othello*, the closet in *Hamlet*, for instance. They use the idea of bounded space to intensify emotion and, as they are interested in disjuncture, to call to the audience's mind the disparity between a bedchamber and a wife-murder; the singleness of a closet and the doubleness of sibling husbands. In general, then, early modern plays use the conventions of domestic representation to explore the particular significance of the household which is central to their generic form. They generate meaning from the contrasts between the domestic and the non-domestic, be it town, battlefield, street or stateroom: in other words the household is only one element of their meaning and they therefore have little interest in the illusion of a coherent domestic space.

Despite the flexibility of these forms of representation across genres, however, it is not *only* the prominence and frequency of their use which marks domestic tragedies out. Other plays' interest is in the domestic as a concept, rather than a location. In direct ways, the high level of representation in domestic tragedies is extraneous – it does not further the development of character, nor is it directly a part of narrative progression. It provides an interpretative ground for these developments though, one which is intended to be recognisable to the audience in its level of particularity in a way that is simply not the case in, for instance, the plays of Shakespeare. A domestic scene in the commercial streets of London and one in the palace of Elsinore will necessarily call upon different levels of audience engagement. But explicitly domestic scenes do occur in his work, although they mainly take a comic form. Act I scene v of *Romeo and Juliet*, for instance, has a level of particularity in its depiction of servant banter which could come directly from a domestic play:[9]

> *Peter:* Away with the joint-stools, remove the court-cupboard, look to the plate. Good thou, save me a piece of marchpane, and as thou loves me, let the porter let in Susan Grindstone and Nell-Anthony, and Potpan!
> *Second Servant:* Ay boy, ready.
> *Peter:* You are looked for and called for, asked for and sought for, in the great chamber.
> *First Servant:* We cannot be here and there too. Cheerly, boys! Be brisk awhile, and the longer liver take all.
>
> (6–15)

The reasons for this sudden imposition of particularity in the swift progression of death-marked love are instructive. The vignette carries, in its extraneousness, the complexities of an elite house and the tensions of preparation, but it does so by demonstrating the myopic concerns which are seen to accompany the outlook of less-than-noble status, thereby neatly fusing the two central meanings of 'domestic'. This suggests that particularity, as a mode of representation, is an integral part of social comment and the formation of social distinction. Given the connections between local plays and ones which revolve around social difference it is not surprising, then, that the other genre which comes closest to domestic tragedy in its form of representation is city comedy. Up-to-date and rawly satiric, it exhibits some generic differences, as might be expected, but also instructively points up the variations which satire imposes on household representation.

City comedies stage a fundamentally different relationship between inside and outside. It seems impossible to keep anything under personal control, to keep it physically within the house, in these plays – private ownership of possessions, even wives, is often denied. But it is also impractical to keep communal life out, as is amply demonstrated in the course of Morose's unsuccessful quest for a quiet life in *Epicene*.[10] Instead, the household is incorporated into the representation of urban life as a part of its patterns of consumption and production, and 'identities, norms and rationality are pulled into the maelstrom of economic circulation'.[11] The plays map models of commercial interaction on to social intercourse, and antisocial behaviour is synchronised by the rhythms of the city's commercial life. This offers an immoral regularity which is analogous to the ingrained sins of the tragedies, but instead keyed to extra-domestic processes and pressures, making the domestic urban. Here, 'outside' does not represent the pressure of good neighbourhood and the need to ensure that domestic behaviour conforms to communal ideals. And city comedies explicitly do not share domestic tragedies' high levels of interior action. The social diversity upon which the immoral prey and on which satire feeds would not be available within a single house; the slight acquaintances which provide the narrative dynamic for confusion and farcical humour can be generated only in the distinctions between households.

In some ways it is precisely because the household is given meaning by the impossibility of separating it fully from the streets of the town that these plays stage complex representations of domestic interiors; because domestic space is opened up to communal display. One obvious example is *Volpone*, in which a large proportion of the play is set in the eponymous character's bedchamber, where suitors to his wealth approach his bed to offer presents.[12] Such scenes are socially self-selecting – only those of sufficient wealth can gain legitimate access (producing the material proof in the form of their gift). Like the tragedies' competitions between men, therefore, these domestic scenes are ripe grounds for social competition, always most acute amongst the *nearly* equal. Staging an event in a domestic interior always offers the potential for social comparison between different households; in city comedies that comparative process takes place between characters, in domestic tragedies more markedly between characters and audience.

In comedies and tragedies alike the bed itself produces intimate space by focusing the audience's attention. In Act III scene ii of *A Chaste Maid in Cheapside* the gossips gather in Mistress Allwit's lying-in chamber following the christening of her latest child.[13] They are all provided with 'low stools' (7) around the bed, business which functions to suggest a bounded space. So far so similar to the dramaturgy of Anne's demise in *Woman Killed*. But Allwit's comments following the departure of his wife's gossips retrospectively insist upon intimacy and give it a satiric slant: 'How hot they have made the room with their thick bums, / Dost not feel it . . . How they have shuffled up the rushes too . . . / With their short, figging, little shittle-cork heels!' (201–12). Here, the chamber becomes a space for outrageous female consumption, as the gossips devour as much of the wine and as many as possible of the celebratory sweetmeats. Its intense confinement sets up the disgraces of gendered overindulgence which are judged in retrospect, rather than insisting openly on the obligations of domesticity. Anne Frankford's chamber defined family and lineage, opened as a spectacle addressed to all those (on- and off-stage) who had seen her fall; Allwit's and Volpone's chambers are explicitly open to people they hardly know, in order to facilitate the flow of resources in and out of the household.

The concerns of the narrative in city comedies characterise physically intimate spaces as controllable, then, but often to the comic ends of fleecing guests or gulling husbands with outsiders rather than sorting out the emotions of family affairs. Domestic interiors become tools for managing personal advancement in city comedies, and as such they carry on the negotiation of public concerns around status. This comparison makes clear the complicated connections between status and erotic motivations which domestic tragedies develop, in which men often seek to advance their standing by *replacing* other men in the latters' domestic spaces, rather than taking their wealth away to improve their own situation.

A great deal of detail is given about household matters in city comedies, although it is mainly given verbally. As is the case in domestic tragedies, such detail evokes interiors by the naming of representative items. In Act II scene ii of *A Mad World, My Masters*, for instance, Sir Bounteous Progress, a man whose generous hospitality is constantly mocked, plays out his domestic plenty in the linguistic detail of false modesty for Lord Owemuch, actually his nephew Follywit in disguise:[14]

> and now I am as like to bring your lordship to as mean a lodging – a hard down bed i'faith, my lord, poor cambric sheets, and a cloth o'tissue canopy. The curtains indeed were wrought in Venice with the story of the prodigal child in silk and gold; only the swine are left out, my lord, for spoiling the curtains. (II.ii.2–7)

The comedy is generated by the social precision of such speeches, but also by the interplay between the presence of bounty in both the audience's and the characters' imagination: the way the descriptions provoke a detailed imagination of the objects aids the characters' almost tangible dreams of future plenty, but simultaneously stresses its contested physical ownership in the present of the play's representation. There are similarities here with Frankford's soliloquy of content just before Wendoll's arrival in the house, and with Beech's description of his domestic sufficiency before the attentively impatient Merry. In both comic and tragic modes, domestic descriptions act as a display of plenty which invites comparison and, almost inevitably, jealousy.

In order to stress the undermining of regulatory household ideologies, both genres are interested in particularity then, indeed they rely upon it. But despite the dramaturgical similarities, there are substantial differences between the operation of domestic interiors in these two genres, and some of those differences are particular to the distance which satire establishes between audience and representation. It offers, as Brian Gibbons puts it, 'astringent critical discrimination and the pleasures of glee, disgust, intellectual exercise of wit, rather than sympathetic identification with character, scene and experience'.[15] The kind of imaginative enterprise in which the audience is involved is correspondingly different: an objectifying, evaluating exercise in terms of broad social categories rather than a real engagement with the connection between unique identities and the physical and emotional spaces which shape them. In satire the domestic is marginalised to a role in epitomising behaviour, but in tragedy the material qualities of the household become much more central, and they bear a greater weight of the meaning of the play. City comedy offers a *social* particularity: the pretension-puncturing satire of social foibles and indicative, exaggerated behaviour; domestic tragedy offers *personal* particularity, a consideration of the extent to which domestic practice and household space generate tragedy, and how individuals' very distinctive actions lead to adultery and/or murder.[16]

In the tragedies, objects and settings become more 'realistic' the more specific they are to a particular household: owned and used within a unique space, they offer comparison to other unique objects outside the theatre. Gibbons's assessment of city comedy's mode of representation is equal and opposite: 'It is a kind of paradox,' he says, 'that the more a playwright stylises character and setting... stressing underlying patterns in the seemingly contingent circumstances of everyday city life, the more closely he is likely to engage contemporary issues'.[17] The more condensed individuality is into the stylisation of telling details, the more it brings issues outside the performance into play. But those issues address social status, not domestic life. Household tragedy and satiric comedy, then, appear to develop different kinds of mimesis around their employment of domestic objects and interiors, the former personally specific, the latter socially precise.

Finally, though, it seems possible to argue that not all the differences between these mimetic modes are generic. Across the course of the plays studied in the chapters above, with the one exception of the moment of murder, the particular has developed towards the general, the domestic in the direction of the eschatological. In addition to his notions of the function of realistic representation, Henry Hitch Adams also argued that, unlike early dramas, 'wilder and more extravagant crimes' characterise seventeenth-century plays, and Frances Dolan too makes an argument for a temporal development towards the depiction of murderous husbands, rather than wives.[18] Most pertinently, Leonore Lieblein explains the failure of *The Miseries of Enforced Marriage* to 'develop into domestic drama' as part of a movement towards city comedy: 'its economic realities have ceased to provide the context for domestic strife and have become instead the subject'.[19]

That shift of interest, from *Arden*, to *Yorkshire Tragedy*, to *Miseries*, can be seen as a relocation of focus outside the household. In the first instance, the distance between the full representation of *Arden* and *Two Lamentable Tragedies*, and the theological dimension of *A Woman Killed* and the metaphorical household spaces of *Yorkshire Tragedy*, represents a movement away from synchronic interests towards the diachronic ones of the wider meanings of 'household' as lineage and patrimony. And the social competition which gives rise to such a blinkered focus on the present, the selfish immediacy of desire, demands of course a more detailed kind of domestic representation. In a period when household objects were so alive with meanings about social status, they offered an important way of reflecting an emphasis upon the material present, and this emphasis continues in city comedies in rather different terms. In domestic tragedies, objects reflect more than status. The comforting ground of normality which they are also required to hold up as backdrop for adultery and murder is lost when houses are wide open to the schemes and routines of the city.

NOTES

1 Adams, 1965, p. 142.
2 Davis, 1975, p. 127.
3 Dolan, 1994, passim.
4 McClintock, for instance, though with only the least taint of pejorative intent, argues that 'Grief in *A Woman Killed with Kindness* operates in the domestic sphere rather than in the cosmic realm of tragedy like *King Lear*', 2002, p. 117.
5 Adams, 1965, p. 187.
6 Orlin, 1994, p. 34.
7 See above, pp. 52–6.
8 West, 2002, p. 51, my italics.
9 William Shakespeare, *The Complete Works*, ed. Stanley Wells, Gary Taylor, John Jowett and William Montgomery, Oxford: Oxford University Press, 1988.
10 Ben Jonson, *Epicene*, ed. Richard Dutton, Manchester: Manchester University Press, 2003.

11 Mehl et al. 2004, p. 18.
12 Ben Jonson, *Volpone or The Fox*, ed. R. B. Parker, Manchester: Manchester University Press, 1999.
13 Thomas Middleton, *Five Plays*, ed. Brian Loughrey and Neil Taylor, Harmondsworth: Penguin, 1988.
14 Thomas Middleton, *A Mad World, My Masters and Other Plays*, ed. Michael Taylor, Oxford: Oxford University Press, 1995.
15 Gibbons, Brian *Jacobean City Comedy*, 2nd edn, London: Methuen, 1980, p. 6.
16 For a fuller exploration of these differences see Catherine Richardson, 'Early modern plays and domestic spaces', *Home Cultures*, 2:3, November 2005.
17 Gibbons, 1980, p. 118.
18 Adams, 1965, p. 126; Dolan, 1994, chapter 3.
19 Lieblein, 1983, p. 195.

Appendices

STATISTICAL INFORMATION ON THE MATERIAL CULTURE OF THE HOUSEHOLD

The following tables are based on the 1430 probate inventories from the Archdeaconry and Consistory courts of Canterbury analysed for this project.[1] These represent extant sixteenth-century inventories for the towns of Canterbury, Tenterden, Faversham and Sandwich, and for the villages of Bethersden and Woodnesborough. The documents are divided as follows: Canterbury 582; Tenterden 173; Faversham 215; Sandwich 288; Bethersden 128; Woodnesborough 44. The goods of households headed by women are listed in 286 of these documents: just under 22 per cent of the total. The earliest inventories were made in the 1560s, when the registers begin, and they have been analysed up to 1600.[2] Canterbury was the largest Kentish town, with the closest links to the capital; Faversham, just off the main London road, was growing prodigiously in the second half of the sixteenth century as a result of thriving trade with the capital through its port; Sandwich and Tenterden are in two very different agrarian regions and had distinct economies: a fishing port on the coast and a Wealden clothmaking town on the edge of Romney Marsh respectively. The two villages lie close to them, but were separate enough to retain a rural identity.[3]

The choice of which items to record has been dictated by the focus of this project on the material culture of the domestic interior. All 'stored goods' such as plate, brass, pewter, linen and apparel, have been recorded, as have all instances of furniture for seating, sleeping and storage, and all tables. This was vital in order to gauge the relative function of rooms in terms of their provision of surfaces and spaces for use. Fixtures and fittings have been recorded for the information they give about relative levels of comfort and about the improvements made to a house.

All embellishments to rooms, such as painted cloths, hangings and curtains, have been listed and, in order to identify those rooms in which leisure time was spent, playing tables, books and musical instruments have been recorded. In order to glean the greatest amount of information about the use, as opposed to the construction, of houses from inventories, the tools, equipment and raw materials necessary for other processes have been recorded. Stables, work houses, shops, kitchens, barns and other outhouses have been recorded in name only, to indicate the relative size of houses, as have lofts solely for the storing of consumables.

The first three tables treat the distribution of items between the rooms of the early modern house. Table 1 considers all urban houses in the sample, and Tables 2 and 3 look in detail at the effects of status on the composition of rooms in Canterbury, the town with the largest number of surviving documents. The differences between urban and rural houses were of several types.[4] Urban domestic space was more likely to be used for a narrower range of activities, and there was a clearer separation between areas used in the daytime and at night. Spatial relocation as opposed to the reorganisation of rooms marked different parts of the daily routine and different activities in the towns. In addition, some items were simply not available in the villages: rural houses contain no looking glasses and no pictures. Clearly, the larger rural houses were not dissimilar to urban properties, suggesting that considerations of status combine with the different requirements of agrarian and urban lifestyles to produce such variations.

The first column in Tables 1 to 3 lists the total number of goods found in the chambers, halls and parlours of the houses in question. The following three columns list the percentage distribution of these items amongst the three different rooms, with the total number found in each type of room in brackets – so for instance in Table 1 86.85 per cent of all bedsteads listed in either chamber, parlour or hall in the urban inventories were kept in the chamber, 2,233 objects in total. The final column lists the number of objects found within the inventory sample on which the table is based which were not listed in parlour, chamber or hall. This column refers primarily to inventories where items are not divided between rooms, and it provides useful additional information on numbers of goods in the area as a whole. The objects have been grouped for ease of reference into the categories of bedding, 'leisure' items, wheels and trendles (wheels), tables, storage items, stored valuables, embellishments and seating. Beds, spinning equipment, storage, embellishments and seating have been totalled to give an immediate impression of the form and function of the different rooms, and the figure given for apparel indicates the sum of all pieces listed.

Tables 4 and 5 show the distribution of key domestic items within four bands of inventory totals in Canterbury.[5] The top band, over £500, represents 3 per cent of the sample, £100–499 inventories make up 15 per cent, £50–99 11 per cent, and those inventories valued at under £50 correspond to

70 per cent of the documents studied. The goods chosen fall into two basic categories of non-essential household items and interior furnishings and embellishments.

Table 4 shows percentages with numbers in parentheses, and reflects only the presence of items in each inventory, rather than the quantity of each type of object which individuals possessed – for example 8 per cent of all the armour and weapons to be found in Canterbury inventories was to be found in those documents with a total over £500, representing 28 items or groups of items. (Figures for armour include all weapons.) Inventories in the lowest band of wealth, although they represent 70 per cent of the total sample, contain only between 11 per cent and 54 per cent of the total number of goods. They list comparatively high numbers of books, tablecloths, instruments and painted cloths. The band between £50 and £99 includes larger amounts of jewellery, plate, silver spoons, instruments, window curtains and pictures. Inventories between £100 and £499 have a larger share of jewellery, plate, playing tables, carpets, curtains and pictures, and the highest band has a large proportion of the jewellery, looking glasses, plate, spoons, and nearly every kind of embellishment, especially cushions and curtains for windows. Although the lower section of the social hierarchy possessed all goods in some numbers, ownership of a range of 'luxury' items appears to characterise the more prosperous in Canterbury. Whereas those whose inventories were valued between £0 and £49 were consistently under-represented in every category, even those in the next bracket were, in every case, at least equally represented.

Table 5 uses the same data for Canterbury, but selects only those goods for which an individual monetary value was given. The range of values given for the objects in each category is shown first, followed by the number of items in parentheses. The subsequent figure in square brackets is the median amount, giving an especially valuable sense of distribution in the case of large groups of items. In other words the 18 individually valued occurrences of armour and weapons in inventories valued over £500 were priced between 12d and £4, with the median value being 26s 8d.

Some of the highest values are undoubtedly a result of a generic price being given, for instance to all the armour in the house. A few items appear to have a set price, with which all instances roughly coincide, for example playing tables and curtains. The majority, however, show a steady rise in both the range of values and the median value in each ascending category of total inventoried wealth. The painted cloths which were most prevalent in the lower band of inventories, for instance, can be seen to be cheaper versions of those higher up the scale, worth a median of 2s, rising to 5s in the next band, then 6s 8d, and finally 10s in the highest bracket. Differences in domestic environment for the heads of these typical households were not only those of the range of objects, but also the numbers of items and the type and quality of the materials of which they are made. Moreover, several qualitative shifts appear within the evidence between the extremes of upper and lower values. While inventories valued at under £50 in Canterbury appear to share few characteristics with those in the other brackets, those from £50 upwards share aspects of the wealthiest estates while retaining an identity of their own.

TABLE 1 OBJECTS IN ALL URBAN ROOMS

Object type	Total in rooms	In chamber	In hall	In parlour	Not in named rooms
Bedstead	2571	86.85 (2233)	1.94 (50)	11.20 (288)	576
Bed	325	86.46 (281)	2.77 (9)	10.77 (35)	115
Trucklebed	734	80.65 (592)	3.13 (23)	16.21 (119)	114
Total beds	3630	85.56 (3106)	2.26 (82)	12.18 (442)	805
Book	483	32.30 (156)	47.62 (230)	20.08 (97)	535
Instrument (playing)	38	18.42 (7)	44.74 (17)	36.84 (14)	15
Tables (playing)	116	6.03 (7)	59.48 (69)	34.48 (40)	21
Looking glass	70	42.86 (30)	32.86 (23)	24.29 (17)	14
Trendle	58	58.62 (34)	32.76 (19)	8.62 (5)	77
Wheel	200	65.00 (130)	31.00 (62)	4.00 (8)	303
Trendle & wheel	258	63.57 (164)	31.40 (81)	5.04 (13)	380
Table	2429	37.26 (905)	41.46 (1007)	21.28 (517)	739
Storage[6]	440	71.14 (313)	16.82 (74)	12.05 (53)	195
Cupboard	1432	27.93 (400)	49.30 (706)	22.77 (326)	462
Coffer	177	75.14 (133)	8.47 (15)	16.38 (29)	63
Chest	3680	82.17 (3024)	4.38 (161)	13.45 (495)	1269
Press	319	53.61 (171)	32.60 (104)	13.79 (44)	99
Total Storage	6048	66.82 (4041)	17.53 (1060)	15.66 (947)	2088
Spoon	813	61.50 (500)	13.16 (107)	25.34 (206)	1768
Table cloth	3340	82.75 (2764)	2.99 (100)	14.25 (476)	1838
Plate	267	63.30 (169)	10.86 (29)	25.84 (69)	604
Apparel	3043	73.25 (2229)	7.30 (222)	19.45 (592)	4484
Painted cloth	1191	55.33 (659)	27.62 (329)	17.04 (203)	237
Hangings	411	60.83 (250)	19.22 (79)	19.95 (82)	35
Sum of cloths	1602	56.74 (909)	25.47 (408)	17.79 (285)	38
Picture	357	26.61 (95)	35.01 (125)	38.38 (137)	112
Cupboard cloth	853	43.49 (371)	34.11 (291)	22.39 (191)	211
Total embellishments	2812	48.90 (1375)	29.30 (824)	21.80 (613)	595
Bench	92	32.61 (30)	54.35 (50)	13.04 (12)	25
Chair	2426	30.54 (741)	50.12 (1216)	19.33 (469)	678
Form	1602	36.33 (582)	43.32 (694)	20.35 (326)	410
Stool	4103	21.96 (901)	45.09 (1850)	32.95 (1352)	825
Settle	440	28.64 (126)	46.36 (204)	25.00 (110)	95
Total seating	8663	27.47 (2380)	46.33 (4014)	26.19 (2269)	2019

TABLE 2 OBJECTS IN ROOMS IN ALL CANTERBURY HOUSES

Object type	Total in rooms	In chamber	In hall	In parlour	Not in named rooms
Bedstead	1153	85.52 (986)	2.25 (26)	12.23 (141)	261
Bed	124	83.87 (104)	3.23 (4)	12.90 (16)	43
Trucklebed	372	79.84 (297)	2.69 (10)	17.47 (65)	61
Total beds	1649	84.11 (1387)	2.43 (40)	13.46 (222)	365
Book	260	41.54 (108)	42.31 (110)	16.15 (42)	354
Instruments (playing)	26	15.38 (4)	50.00 (13)	34.62 (9)	11
Tables (playing)	56	5.36 (3)	66.07 (37)	28.57 (16)	8
Looking glass	26	46.15 (12)	26.92 (7)	26.92 (7)	4
Wheel	104	60.58	33.65	5.77	167
Trendle	13	69.23	23.08	7.69	13
Wheel & trendle	117	61.54 (72)	32.48 (38)	5.98 (7)	65
Table	1174	40.37 (474)	38.67 (454)	20.95 (246)	377
Storage	204	71.56 (146)	14.7 (30)	13.72 (28)	113
Cupboard	759	31.36 (238)	46.77 (355)	21.87 (166)	261
Press	156	61.54 (96)	24.36 (38)	14.10 (22)	58
Coffer	94	77.66 (73)	7.45 (7)	14.89 (14)	43
Chest	1558	82.35 (1283)	4.62 (72)	13.03 (203)	595
Total storage	2771	66.26 (1836)	18.12 (502)	15.63 (433)	1070
Spoon	323	57.28 (185)	17.65 (57)	25.08 (81)	908
Table cloth	1193	82.65 (986)	3.02 (36)	14.33 (171)	973
Plate	107	54.21 (58)	16.82 (18)	28.97 (31)	356
Apparel	1142	77.23 (882)	5.60 (64)	17.16 (196)	71
Painted cloth	671	56.93	27.27	15.80	119
Hangings	179	56.42	21.79	21.79	15
Sum of cloths	850	56.82 (483)	26.12 (222)	17.06 (145)	134
Picture	153	23.53 (36)	27.45 (42)	49.02 (75)	85
Cupboard cloth	373	40.21 (150)	36.19 (135)	23.59 (88)	134
Total embellishments	1376	48.61 (669)	28.99 (399)	22.38 (308)	353
Bench	51	35.29 (18)	49.02 (25)	15.69 (8)	12
Chair	1121	35.15 (394)	44.69 (501)	20.16 (226)	339
Form	842	36.94 (311)	42.16 (355)	20.90 (176)	205
Stool	1915	23.34 (447)	43.24 (828)	33.42 (640)	434
Settle	234	31.20 (73)	44.02 (103)	24.79 (58)	54
Total seating	4163	29.86 (1243)	43.53 (1812)	26.62 (1108)	1044

TABLE 3 OBJECTS IN CANTERBURY OFFICE-HOLDERS' ROOMS

Object type	Total in rooms	In chamber	In hall	In parlour	Not in named rooms
Bedstead	126	88.10 (111)	–	11.90 (15)	16
Bed	5	80.00 (4)	–	20.00 (1)	–
Trucklebed	49	85.71 (42)	–	14.29 (7)	3
Total beds	180	87.22 (157)	–	12.78 (23)	19
Book	40	5.00 (2)	80 (32)	15.00 (6)	55
Instrument (playing)	2	–	50 (1)	50.00 (1)	–
Tables (playing)	5	–	40 (2)	60.00 (3)	–
Looking glass	3	33.33 (1)	33.33 (1)	33.33 (1)	–
Trendle	–	–	–	–	1
Wheel	12	75.00 (9)	25.00 (3)	–	11
Trendle & wheel	12	75.00 (9)	25.00 (3)	–	12
Table	142	40.14 (57)	35.21 (50)	24.65 (35)	26
Storage	5	80.00 (4)	20.00 (1)	–	3
Cupboard	98	39.80 (39)	32.65 (32)	27.55 (27)	23
Coffer	3	100.00 (3)	–	–	1
Chest	195	92.31 (180)	0.51 (1)	7.18 (14)	19
Press	29	82.76 (24)	10.34 (3)	6.90 (2)	3
Total storage	330	75.76 (25)	11.21 (37)	13.03 (43)	49
Spoon	43	44.19 (19)	13.95 (6)	41.86 (18)	216
Table cloth	198	93.94 (186)	0.51 (1)	5.56 (11)	78
Plate	29	44.83 (13)	13.79 (4)	41.38 (12)	112
Apparel	149	85.91 (128)	0.67 (1)	13.42 (20)	153
Painted cloth	73	54.79 (40)	24.66 (18)	20.55 (15)	1
Hanging	31	64.52 (20)	12.90 (4)	22.58 (7)	5
Sum of cloths	104	57.69 (60)	21.15 (22)	21.15 (22)	6
Picture	27	–	44.44 (12)	55.56 (15)	5
Cupboard cloth	75	49.33 (37)	32.00 (24)	18.67 (14)	18
Total embellishments	310	50.65 (157)	25.81 (80)	23.55 (73)	35
Bench	–	–	–	–	–
Chair	139	46.04 (64)	27.34 (38)	26.62 (37)	23
Form	83	38.55 (32)	39.76 (33)	21.69 (18)	17
Stool	340	22.35 (76)	37.65 (128)	40.00 (136)	24
Settle	39	33.33 (13)	38.46 (15)	28.21 (11)	8
Total seating	601	30.78 (185)	35.61 (214)	33.61 (202)	72

TABLE 4 PERCENTAGE OF ITEMS IN EACH BRACKET OF TOTAL INVENTORIED
WEALTH (NUMBER)

Object type	Percentage in inventories over £500 (3% of sample)	£100–499 (15% sample)	£50–99 (11% sample)	£0–49 (70% sample)
Armour	8 (28)	33 (121)	16 (59)	43 (159)
Books	7 (16)	23 (51)	15 (33)	54 (118)
Featherbed	9 (69)	33 (262)	14 (115)	44 (349)
Jewels	12 (11)	40 (36)	18 (16)	29 (26)
Looking glass	16 (4)	32 (8)	12 (3)	40 (10)
Plate	17 (49)	48 (140)	22 (64)	14 (41)
Spoon	14 (18)	37 (47)	21 (27)	27 (34)
Table cloth	7 (38)	26 (132)	16 (81)	51 (264)
Instrument	3 (1)	28 (8)	21 (6)	48 (14)
Playing tables	6 (3)	40 (21)	17 (9)	37 (19)
Cushion	9 (51)	37 (199)	15 (84)	39 (210)
Window cushion	28 (10)	39 (14)	11 (4)	22 (8)
Cupboard cloth	12 (38)	38 (120)	16 (50)	34 (105)
Carpet	13 (36)	47 (130)	16 (43)	24 (65)
Curtain	11 (34)	45 (134)	45 (134)	30 (90)
Curtain window	23 (20)	47 (41)	18 (16)	11 (10)
Painted cloth [hangings]	6 [5] (42)	27 [38] (173)	11 [16] (71)	56 [42] (363)
Picture	10 (7)	46 (31)	21 (14)	24 (16)

TABLE 5 VALUES OF ITEMS IN EACH BRACKET OF INVENTORIED WEALTH
(NUMBER) (MEDIAN)

Item	Total	Range over £500 [median]	£100–499	£50–99	£0–49
Armour	200	12d–£4 (18) [26s 8d]	4d–£4 13s 4d (64) [11s]	6d–£3 10s (30) [9s 6d]	2d–50s (88) [3s 4d]
Books	121	2s–30s (9) [5s]	6d–£20 (17) [8s]	2d–£20 (17) [6s 8d]	4d ob.- £6 (78) [2s 2d]
Featherbed	182	3s 4d–£7 (17) [26s 8d]	5s–£10 (45) [26s 8d]	10s–£2 (15) [26s 8d]	2s 6d–£2 13s (105) [20s]
Jewels	32	3s–£3 (2)	18d–£30 (22) [20s]	3s–50s (4) [26s]	3s 4d–£4 1s (4) [12s 8d]
Looking glass	12	20d–5s (2)	18d–5s (6) [3s]	6d–12d (2)	6d (2)
Plate	107	13s 4d–£14 10s (14) [3s]	12d–£23 5s 8d (51) [50s]	8d–£7 4s 4d (25) [30s]	8d–£10 9s 2d (17) [32s]
Spoons	69	13s 4d–£9 9s (13) [£3 15s 10d]	7s–£6 (20) [48s]	3d–£4 9s 4d (17) [30s]	2d–37s 11d (19) [18s]
Table cloth	103	6s–26s 8d (6) [13s 8d]	6d–53s 4d (23) [5s]	5s–£5 2s 4d (9) [10s]	3d–£3 5s 3d (65) [5s]
Instrument	18	13s 4d (1)	20d–20s (4) [13s]	2s–26s 8d (4) [5s 6d]	12d–23s 4d (9) [8s]
Playing tables	23	3s–3s 4d (2) [3s 2d]	8d–3s (8) [14d]	2s–2s 6d (4) [2s 3d]	6d–12s (9) [16d]

TABLE 5 (*cont'd*)

Item	Total	Range over £500 [median]	£100–499	£50–99	£0–49
Cushion	29	3s (1)	6d–5s (9) [20d]	6d–5s (5) [3s 6d]	1d ob.–10s (14) [8d]
Window cushion	6	2s–16s (2)	12d (1)	6s 8d–10s (2)	20d (1)
Cupboard cloth	46	20d–6s 8d (4) [5s]	4d–33d (21) [19d]	10d–2s (4) [1s 6d]	6d–6s 8d (17) [12d]
Carpet	66	3s–50s (5) [8s]	12d–43s 4d (34) [6s 8d]	8d–13s 4d (8) [3s]	6d–40s (19) [2s ob.]
Curtain	20	8d–2s (3) [2s]	10d–40s (6) [2s]	6d–11s (3) [2s]	4d–16s (8) [2s 6d]
Window curtain	19	4d–2s (4) [13d]	8d–3s 6d (9) [12d]	4d–2s 6d (4) [16d]	6d–8d (2) [7d]
Painted cloth	336	8d–53s 8d (22) [10s]	12d–8li 5s 6d (80) [6s 8d]	6d–13s 4d (42) [5s]	4d–13s 4d (192) [2s]
Picture	13	3s 4d (1)	4d–6s (4) [1s 10d]	6d–6s 8d (3) [8d]	3d–2s (5) [12d]

NOTES

1 See Bibliography for full details of the register books.
2 In practice, this has meant stopping at the end of PRC 10.28, as the registers are not organised by year. Details of each item have been recorded in a relational database using Microsoft Access.
3 Criteria used in the selection process in addition to geographical distribution were numbers of extant wills and inventories, surviving churchwarden's accounts and parish registers, the extent of available secondary research, extant early modern buildings and instances of deposition material relating to the places under consideration.
4 For more information on these differences, including the full range of statistical data see C. Richardson, 1999.
5 The usual provisos about inventory totals apply. They are of course notoriously inaccurate indicators of total wealth, particularly as a result of the way debts and leases were recorded. However, that perhaps makes the striking patterns in the distribution of goods in a sample of this size even more interesting. For a summary of the problems see Cox, 'Probate inventories: the legal background, II', 1984.
6 Any receptacle other than those listed separately.

Bibliography

MANUSCRIPT PRIMARY SOURCES

Deposition Books:
CCAL X.10 vols. 2–21
CCAL X.11 vols. 1–3
CCAL PRC 39 vols. 1–24

Registers of Wills:
CCAL PRC 17 vols. 17–51
CCAL PRC 32 vols. 29–38

Inventory Registers:
CCAL PRC 21 vols. 1–15
CCAL PRC 28 vols. 1–3
CKS PRC 10 vols. 1–28

Chamberlain's Accounts for Canterbury:
CCAL FA vols. 11–17

PRINTED PRIMARY SOURCES

A Warning for Fair Women, Charles Dale Cannon ed., The Hague: Mouton, 1975
A Yorkshire Tragedy, Cawley, A. C. and Barry Gaines eds, Manchester: Manchester University Press, 1986
Arden of Faversham, M. L. Wine, ed., Revels Edition, London: Methuen, 1973
Ars Moriendi . . . the helthe of mannes sowle, Amsterdam, New York: Theatrum Orbis Terrarum: Da Capo Press, 1970
Aughterson, Kate The English Renaissance: An Anthology of Sources and Documents, London: Routledge, 1998
Beard, Thomas Theatre of God's Judgements, London: Printed by Adam Islip, 1597
Brathwaite, Richard The English Gentleman, London: John Haviland, 1630
Calvin, John A commentarie upon S. Paules epistles to the Corinthians, translated by Thomas Timme, London: [By Thomas Dawson] for John Harrison, and Georgey Byshop, 1577
Calvin, John Sermons of M. John Calvin, on the Epistles of S. Paule to Timothie and Titus, translated by L. T., London: Imprinted [by Henry Middleton] for G. Bishop and T. Woodcoke, 1581

Cleaver, Robert *A godlie forme of householde government*, London: Thomas Creede for Thomas Man, 1598

Coke, Sir Edward *An Exact Abridgement in English . . .* , London: M. Simmons for Matthew Walbancke, and H. Twyford, 1651

Davis, Lloyd ed., *Sexuality and Gender in the English Renaissance: An Annotated Edition of Contemporary Documents*, New York and London: Garland Publishing, 1998

du Bosc, Jacques *The Complete Woman*, translated by N. N., London: Thomas Harper and Richard Hodgkinson, 1639

Fenner, Dudley *The Order of Houshold, in Certain godly and learned treatises*, Edinburgh: Robert Waldegrave, 1592

Gataker, Thomas *A good wife Gods gift and, a wife indeed. Two mariage sermons*, London: John Haviland for Fulke Clifton, 1623

Gouge, William *Of domesticall duties*, London: John Haviland for William Bladen, 1622

Harrison, William *Description of England*, Georges Edelen ed., Ithaca: published for the Folger Shakespeare Library by Cornell University Press, 1968

Heywood, Thomas *A Woman Killed With Kindness*, Brian Scobie ed., New Mermaid Edition, London: A & C Black, 1985

Heywood, Thomas *A Woman Killed With Kindness*, R. W. van Fossen ed., London: Methuen, 1961

Heywood, Thomas *An Apology for Actors*, 1612, London: reprinted for the Shakespeare Society, 1841

Jonson, Ben *Epicene*, Richard Dutton ed., Manchester: Manchester University Press, 2003

Jonson, Ben *Volpone or The Fox*, R. B. Parker ed., Manchester: Manchester University Press, 1999

Loengard, Janet Senderowitz *London Viewers and Their Certificates, 1508–1558: Certificates of the Sworn Viewers of the City of London*, [London:] London Record Society, 26, 1989

Middleton, Thomas *A Critical Edition of Thomas Middleton's Your Five Gallants*, Clare Lee Colegrove ed., New York: Garland Publishing, 1979

Middleton, Thomas *A Mad World, My Masters and Other Plays*, Michael Taylor ed., Oxford: Oxford University Press, 1995

Middleton, Thomas *Five Plays*, Brian Loughrey and Neil Taylor eds, Harmondsworth: Penguin, 1988

Shakespeare, William *The Complete Works*, Stanley Wells, Gary Taylor, John Jowett and William Montgomery eds, Oxford: Oxford University Press, 1988

Stubbes, Philip *Anatomy of Abuses*, ed. M. J. Kidnie, Tempe: Arizona Center for Medieval and Renaissance Studies in conjunction with Renaissance English Text Society, 2002

Sturgess, Keith *Three Elizabethan Domestic Tragedies*, Harmondsworth: Penguin, 1985

The Tragedy of Master Arden of Faversham, M. L. Wine ed., London: Methuen, 1973

Tilney, Edmund *A briefe and pleasant discourse of duties in mariage, called the flower of friendship*, London: Henrie Denha[m], 1568

Two Most Unnaturall and Bloodie Murthers, London: V. S[immes] for Nathanael Butter, 1605

Vives, Juan Luis *The Office and Duty of an Husband*, London: John Cawood, 1555

Whately, William *A Bride-Bush: Or, a Direction for Married Persons*, London: Felix Kyngston for Thomas Man, 1619

Yarington, Robert *Two Lamentable Tragedies*, London: [R. Read] for Mathew Lawe, 1601

Yarington, Robert *Two Lamentable Tragedies*, Students' Facsimile Edition 153, Amersham: John S. Farmer, 1913

SECONDARY SOURCES

Abate, Corinne S. ed., *Privacy, Domesticity and Women in Early Modern England*, Aldershot, Burlington: Ashgate, 2003

Adams, Henry Hitch, *English Domestic or Homiletic Tragedy 1575–1642*, New York: B. Blom, 1965 (originally published 1943)

Agnew, Jean-Christophe, 'Coming up for air: consumer culture in historical perspective', in John Brewer and Roy Porter eds, *Consumption and the World of Goods*, London: Routledge, 1993

Agnew, Jean-Christophe, *Worlds Apart: The Market and the Theatre in Anglo-American Thought, 1550–1750*, Cambridge, New York: Cambridge University Press, 1986

Alcock, N. W., *People at Home: Living in a Warwickshire Village 1500–1800*, Chichester: Phillimore, 1993

Amussen, S. D., 'Gender, family and the social order, 1560–1725', in Anthony Fletcher and John Stevenson eds, *Order and Disorder in Early Modern England*, Cambridge: Cambridge University Press, 1985

Amussen, S. D., *An Ordered Society: Gender and Class in Early Modern England*, Oxford, New York: Basil Blackwell, 1988

Appadurai, Arjun ed., *The Social Life of Things: Cultural Commodities in Perspective*, Cambridge: Cambridge University Press, 1986

Archer, Ian, *The Pursuit of Stability: Social Relations in Elizabethan London*, Cambridge: Cambridge University Press, 1991

Ardener, S. ed., *Women and Space: Ground Rules and Social Maps*, London: Croom Helm, 1981

Arkell, Tom, Nesta Evans and Nigel Goose eds, *When Death Do Us Part*, Oxford: Leopard's Head Press, 2000

Atkinson, David, 'An approach to the main plot of Thomas Heywood's *A Woman Killed With Kindness*', *English Studies*, 70:1, 1989, 15–27

Attwell, David, 'Property, status and the subject in middle class tragedy: *Arden of Faversham*', *English Literary Renaissance*, 21:3, 1991, 328–48

Baldwin, F. E., *Sumptuary Legislation and Personal Regulation in England*, Baltimore: Johns Hopkins Press, 1926

Barish, Jonas, *The Antitheatrical Prejudice*, Berkeley: University of California Press, 1981

Barnwell, P. S. and A. T. Adams, *The House Within: Interpreting Medieval Houses in Kent*, Royal Commission on the Historical Monuments of England, London: HMSO, 1994

Barry, Jonathan ed., *The Tudor and Stuart Town: A Reader in English Urban History 1530–1688*, London: Longman, 1990

Barry, Jonathan and Christopher Brooks eds, *The Middling Sort of People, Culture, Society and Politics in England, 1550–1800*, Basingstoke: Macmillan, 1994

Beier, A. L., *Masterless Men: The Vagrancy Problem in England 1560–1640*, London: Methuen, 1985

Beier, A. L. and Roger Finlay eds, *London 1500–1700: The Making of the Metropolis*, New York: Longman, 1986

Belsey, Catherine, *The Subject of Tragedy: Identity and Difference in Renaissance Drama*, London: Routledge, 1985

Blair St George, Robert, *Conversing by Signs: Poetics of Implication in Colonial New England Culture*, London and Chapel Hill, NC: University of North Carolina Press, 1998

Blench, J. W., *Preaching in England in the Late Fifteenth and Sixteenth Centuries: A Study of English Sermons 1450–c. 1600*, Oxford: Basil Blackwell, 1964

Boase, T. S. R., *Death in the Middle Ages: Mortality, Judgement and Remembrance*, London: Thames and Hudson, 1972

Bolton, Jeremy, *Neighbourhood and Society*, Cambridge: Cambridge University Press, 1987

Bonfield, Lloyd, Richard M. Smith and Keith Wrightson eds, *The World We Have Gained: Histories of Population and Social Structure*, Oxford, New York: Blackwell, 1986

Bossy, John ed., *Disputes and Settlements: Law and Human Relations in the West*, Cambridge, New York: Cambridge University Press, 1983

Bourdieu, Pierre, *Outline of a Theory of Practice*, translated by Richard Nice, Cambridge: Cambridge University Press, 1977

Bourdieu, Pierre, *Distinction: A Social Critique of the Judgement of Taste*, translated by Richard Nice, London: Routledge, 1984

Bowers, Rick, 'A Woman Killed With Kindness: plausibility on a smaller scale', *Studies in English Literature 1500–1900*, 24:2, 1984, 293–306

Breen, John M., 'The carnival body in *Arden of Faversham*', *Cahiers Elizabethians*, 45, April 1994, 13–20

Brewer, John and Roy Porter eds, *Consumption and the World of Goods*, London: Routledge, 1993

Brewer, John and Susan Staves eds, *Early Modern Conceptions of Property*, London and New York: Routledge, 1995

Bromley, Laura G., 'Domestic conduct in *A Woman Killed With Kindness*', *Studies in English Literature 1500–1900*, 26:2, 1986, 259–76

Brown, Frank E., 'Continuity and change in the urban house: developments in domestic space organisation in seventeenth-century London', *Comparative Studies in Society and History*, 28:3, 1986, 558–90

Brown, Pamela Allen, *Better a Shrew Than a Sheep: Women, Drama, and the Culture of Jest in Early Modern England*, Ithaca: Cornell University Press, 2002

Bryson, Anna, *From Courtesy to Civility: Changing Codes of Conduct in Early Modern England*, Oxford: Oxford University Press, 1998

Bullough, Geoffrey, *Narrative and Dramatic Sources of Shakespeare Vol. 7: Major Tragedies*, London, New York: Columbia University Press, Routledge and Kegan Paul, 1973

Burgess, Clive, '"By Quick and by Dead": wills and pious provision in late medieval Bristol', *Economic History Review*, 405, October 1987, 837–58

Burgess, Clive, 'Late medieval wills and pious convention: testamentary evidence reconsidered', in Michael A. Hicks ed., *Profit, Piety and the Professions in Later Medieval England*, Gloucester: Alan Sutton, 1990

Butcher, Andrew, 'Oneley a boye called Christopher Mowle', in D. Grantley and P. Roberts eds, *Christopher Marlowe and English Renaissance Culture*, Aldershot: Scolar, 1996

Capp, Bernard, *When Gossips Meet: Women, Family, and Neighbourhood in Early Modern England*, Oxford: Oxford University Press, 2003

Carlson, Eric, 'Good pastors or careless shepherds? Parish minister and the English reformation', *History*, 88:291, 2003, 423–36

Cary, Cecile Williamson, '"Go breake this lute": music in Heywood's *A Woman Killed With Kindness*', *Huntington Library Quarterly*, 37:2, 1974, 111–22

Cawley, A. C., 'A Yorkshire Tragedy and Two Most Unnaturall & Bloodie Murthers', in D. W. Jefferson ed., *The Morality of Art*, London: Routledge & Kegan Paul, 1969

Cescinsky, Herbert and Ernest R. Gribble, *Early English Furniture and Woodwork Vols. I & II*, London: Routledge, 1922

Chartier, Roger ed., *Passions of the Renaissance*, A History of Private Life, general eds Philippe Ariès and Georges Duby, Cambridge, MA, London: Harvard University Press, 1989

Chartres, John and David Hey eds, *English Rural Society 1500–1800*, Cambridge, New York: Cambridge University Press, 1990

Chaytor, Miranda, 'Household and kinship: Ryton in the late sixteenth and early seventeenth centuries', *History Workshop Journal*, 10, Autumn 1980, 25–60

Clark, Peter, 'The migrant in Kentish towns 1580–1640', in Peter Clark and Paul Slack eds, *Crisis and Order in English Towns 1500–1700*, London: Routledge and Kegan Paul, 1972

Clark, Peter, 'The ownership of books in England 1560–1640: the example of some Kentish townsfolk', in Lawrence Stone ed., *Schooling and Society*, Baltimore: Johns Hopkins University Press, 1976

Clark, Peter, *English Provincial Society from the Reformation to the Revolution: Religion, Politics and Society in Kent 1500–1640*, Hassocks: Harvester Press, 1977

Clark, Peter, 'The social economy of the Canterbury Suburbs', in Alec Detsicas and Nigel Yates eds, *Studies in Modern Kentish History*, Maidstone: Kent Archaeological Society, 1983

Clark, Peter ed., *The Early Modern Town*, London: Longman, 1976

Clark, Peter ed., *Small Towns in Early Modern Europe*, Cambridge: Cambridge University Press, 1995

Clark, Peter and Paul Slack eds, *Crisis and Order in English Towns 1500–1700*, London: Routledge and Kegan Paul, 1972

Clark, Peter and Paul Slack, *English Towns in Transition 1500–1700*, London and New York: Oxford University Press, 1976

Clark, Sandra, *The Elizabethan Pamphleteers: Popular Moralistic Pamphlets 1580–1640*, London: Athlone Press, 1983

Clay, C. G. A., *Economic Expansion and Social Change: England 1500–1700, Volumes 1 & II*, Cambridge: Cambridge University Press, 1984

Cohen, Anthony P., *The Symbolic Construction of Community*, London: Routledge, 1993 (originally published 1985)

Comensoli, Viviana, *Household Business: Domestic Plays of Early Modern England*, Toronto, London: University of Toronto Press, 1996

Cook, Anne Jennalie, *The Privileged Playgoers of Shakespeare's London 1576–1642*, Princeton: Princeton University Press, 1981

Coppel, Stephen, 'Willmaking on the deathbed', *Local Population Studies*, 40, Spring 1988, 37–45

Corfield, P. and N. B. Harte eds, *London and the English Economy, 1500–1700*, London and Ronceverte: Hambledon Press, 1990

Cox, John D. and David Scott Kastan eds, *A New History of Early English Drama*, New York: Columbia University Press, 1997

Cox, Nancy and Jeff, 'Probate inventories: the legal background, Part I', *The Local Historian*, 16:3, 1984, 133–45

Cox, Nancy and Jeff, 'Probate inventories: the legal background, Part II', *The Local Historian*, 16:4, 1984, 217–28

Cox, Nancy and Jeff, 'Valuations in probate inventories: part I', *The Local Historian*, 16:8, 1985, 467–78

Cox, Nancy and Jeff, 'Valuations in probate inventories: part II', *The Local Historian*, 17:2, 1986, 85–100

Davis, N. Z., *Society and Culture in Early Modern France*, Stanford: Stanford University Press, 1975

Davis, N. Z., *Fiction in the Archives*, Cambridge: Polity Press, 1987

Dawson, Giles E., 'Records of plays and players in Kent', *Malone Society Collections*, Vol. VII, Oxford: Oxford University Press, 1965

Dawson, Anthony B. and Paul Yachnin, *The Culture of Playgoing in Shakespeare's England*, Cambridge: Cambridge University Press, 2001

de Certeau, M., *The Practice of Everyday Life*, Berkeley, London: University of California Press, 1984

de Coppet, David ed., *Understanding Rituals*, London and New York: Routledge, 1992

de Grazia, Margareta, Maureen Quilligan and Peter Stallybrass eds, *Subject and Object in Renaissance Culture*, New York, Cambridge: Cambridge University Press, 1996

de Vries, Jan, 'Between purchasing power and the world of goods: understanding the household economy in early modern Europe', in John Brewer and Roy Porter eds, *Consumption and the World of Goods*, London: Routledge, 1993

Dessen, Alan, 'Interpreting stage directions: Elizabethan clues and modern detectives', in G. R. Hibbard ed., *The Elizabethan Theatre IX*, Port Credit: published in collaboration with the University of Waterloo, 1981

Dessen, Alan C., *Elizabethan Stage Conventions and Modern Interpreters*, Cambridge: Cambridge University Press, 1984

Dessen, Alan and Leslie Thompson, *A Dictionary of Stage Directions in English Drama: 1580–1642*, Cambridge: Cambridge University Press, 1999

Detsicas, Alec and Nigel Yates eds, *Studies in Modern Kentish History*, Maidstone: Kent Archaeological Society, 1983

Dinn, Robert, 'Death and rebirth in late medieval Bury Saint Edmunds', in Steve Bassett ed., *Death in Towns, Urban Responses to the Dying and the Dead 100–1600*, Leicester: Leicester University Press, 1992

Dolan, Frances E., *Dangerous Familiars: Representations of Domestic Crime in England 1550–1700*, Ithaca, London: Cornell University Press, 1994

Dollimore, Jonathan, *Radical Tragedy: Religion, Ideology and Power in the Drama of Shakespeare and His Contemporaries*, Brighton: Harvester Press, 1984

Dollimore, Jonathan and Alan Sinfield eds, *Political Shakespeare: Essays in Cultural Materialism*, Manchester: Manchester University Press, 1985

Doran, Madeleine, *Endeavours of Art: A Study of Form in Elizabethan Drama*, Madison: University of Wisconsin Press, 1954

Douglas, Mary, *Purity and Danger*, London: Routledge, 1966

Dubrow, Heather, *Shakespeare and Domestic Loss: Forms of Deprivation, Mourning, and Recuperation*, Cambridge: Cambridge University Press, 1999

Dunworth, F., 'Motherhood in Elizabethan Drama', unpublished PhD thesis, University of Kent, 2004

Durkin, Graham, 'The Civic Government and Economy of Elizabethan Canterbury', unpublished PhD thesis, Canterbury Christchurch University College, 2001

Dyer, Alan D., *The City of Worcester in the Sixteenth Century*, Leicester: Leicester University Press, 1973

Erickson, Amy Louise, *Women and Property in Early Modern England*, London: Routledge, 1993

Fisher, F. J., 'The development of London as a centre of conspicuous consumption in the sixteenth and seventeenth centuries', in P. Corfield and N. B. Harte eds, *London and the English Economy, 1500–1700*, London and Ronceverte: Hambledon Press, 1990

Fleming, Juliet, *Graffiti and the Writing Arts of Early Modern England*, London: Reaktion Books, 2001

Fletcher, Anthony J., 'Honour, reputation and local officeholding', in Fletcher and John Stevenson eds, *Order and Disorder in Early Modern England*, Cambridge: Cambridge University Press, 1985

Fletcher, Anthony, 'The Protestant idea of marriage in early modern England', in Fletcher and Peter Roberts eds, *Religion, Culture and Society in Early Modern Britain*, Cambridge: Cambridge University Press, 1994

Fletcher, Anthony and John Stevenson eds, *Order and Disorder in Early Modern England*, Cambridge: Cambridge University Press, 1985

Fox, Adam, *Oral and Literate Cultures in England, 1500–1700*, Oxford: Clarendon Press, 2000

Foyster, E. A., *Manhood in Early Modern England: Honour, Sex and Marriage*, London: Longman, 1999

Friedman, Alice T., *House and Household in Elizabethan England*, Chicago, London: University of Chicago Press, 1989

Fumerton, Patricia and Simon Hunt, *Renaissance Culture and the Everyday*, Philadelphia: University of Pennsylvania Press, 1999

Garrard, Rachel, 'English probate inventories and their use in studying the significance of the domestic interior, 1570–1700', in Ad Van der Woude and Anton Schuurman eds, *Probate Inventories: A New Source for the Historical Study of Wealth, Material Culture and Agricultural Development*, Utrecht: HES Publishers, 1980

Gibbons, Brian, *Jacobean City Comedy*, 2nd edn, London: Methuen, 1980

Gibson, James M. ed., *Records of Early English Drama, Kent: Diocese of Canterbury*, London: British Library and University of Toronto Press, 2002

Ginzburg, Carlo, *Ecstasies: Deciphering the Witches' Sabbath*, translated by Raymond Rosenthal, Harmondsworth: Penguin, 1990

Goodman, Nelson, 'Twisted tales; or, story, study, and symphony', in W. J. T. Mitchell, ed., *On Narrative*, Chicago and London: University of Chicago Press, 1980

Goose, Nigel, 'Household size and structure in early-Stuart Cambridge', in Jonathan Barry ed., *The Tudor and Stuart Town: A Reader in English Urban History 1530–1688*, London: Longman, 1990

Gowing, Laura, 'Gender and the language of insult in early modern London', *History Workshop Journal*, 35, 1993, 1–21

Gowing, Laura, ' "The freedom of the streets": women and social space, 1560–1640', in Jenner and Griffiths eds, *Londinopolis*, Manchester: Manchester University Press, 2000

Gowing, Laura, *Domestic Dangers: Women, Words, and Sex in Early Modern London*, Oxford: Clarendon Press, 1996

Greenfield, Peter H., 'Touring', in John D. Cox, and David Scott Kastan eds, *A New History of Early English Drama*, New York: Columbia University Press, 1997

Gurr, Andrew, *Playgoing in Shakespeare's London*, Cambridge, New York: Cambridge University Press, 3rd edn, 2004

Hallam, Elizabeth A., 'Turning the hourglass: gender relations at the deathbed in early modern Canterbury', *Mortality*, 1:1, 1996, 61–82

Halliwell, Stephen, *The Aesthetics of Mimesis: Ancient Texts and Modern Problems*, Princeton, Woodstock: Princeton University Press, 2002

Halpern, Richard, *The Poetics of Primitive Accumulation: English Renaissance Culture and the Genealogy of Capital*, Ithaca: Cornell University Press, 1991

Harbage, Alfred, *Shakespeare's Audience*, New York: Columbia University Press, 1961

Harris, Jonathan Gil and Natasha Korda eds, *Staged Properties*, Cambridge: Cambridge University Press, 2002

Harris, Olivia, 'Households and their boundaries', *History Workshop Journal*, 13, Spring 1982, 143–52

Hasted, Edward, *The History and Topographical Survey of the County of Kent, Vol. XI*, Wakefield: E P Publishing Ltd, 1972

Hattaway, Michael, *Elizabethan Popular Theatre: Plays in Performance*, London and Boston: Routledge & Kegan Paul, 1982

Hawkes, Terence, *Shakespeare in the Present*, London and New York: Routledge, 2002

Heal, Felicity, *Hospitality in Early Modern England*, Oxford: Oxford University Press, 1990

Heath, Peter, 'Urban piety in the later middle ages: the evidence of hull wills', in R. B. Dobson ed., *The Church, Politics and Patronage in the Fifteenth Century*, Gloucester: Alan Sutton, 1984

Helgerson, Richard, 'Soldiers and enigmatic girls: the politics of Dutch domestic realism, 1650–1672', *Representations*, 58, Spring 1997, 49–87

Helmholz, R. H., *Marriage Litigation in Medieval England*, Cambridge: Cambridge University Press, 1974

Helt, J. S. W., 'Women, memory and will-making in Elizabethan England', in Bruce Gordon and Peter Marshall eds, *The Place of the Dead: Death and Remembrance in Late Medieval and Early Modern Europe*, Cambridge: Cambridge University Press, 2000

Henderson, Diana E., 'Many mansions: reconstructing *A Woman Killed With Kindness*', *Studies in English Literature 1500–1900*, 26:2, 1986, 277–94

Hindle, Steve, *The State and Social Change in Early Modern England*, Basingstoke: Macmillan, 2000

Hinton, David A., *Gold and Gilt, Pots and Pins: Possessions and People in Medieval Britain*, New York: Oxford University Press, 2005

Hoffman, Dean A., ' "Both bodily deth and werldly shame": "Little Musgrave and Lady Barnard" as source for *A Woman Killed with Kindness*', *Comparative Drama*, 23:2, 1989, 166–78

Holmes, Jonathan and Adrian Streete eds, *Refiguring Mimesis: Representation in Early Modern Literature*, Hatfield: University of Hertfordshire Press, 2005

Hoskins, Janet, *Biographical Objects: How Things Tell the Stories of People's Lives*, New York and London: Routledge, 1998

Hoskins, W. G., *Provincial England*, London: Macmillan, 1963

Houlbrooke, Ralph, *Church Courts and the People During the English Reformation 1520–1570*, Oxford: Oxford University Press, 1979

Houlbrooke, Ralph ed., *Death, Ritual, and Bereavement*, London and New York: Routledge, 1989

Howell, Martha C., 'Fixing movables: gifts by testament in late medieval Douai', *Past and Present*, 150, 1996, 3–45

Hunt, A., *Governance of the Consuming Passions: A History of Sumptuary Law*, Basingstoke: Macmillan, 1996

Hutton, Ronald, *The Rise and Fall of Merry England*, Oxford: Oxford University Press, 1996

Hyde, Patricia, *Thomas Arden in Faversham: The Man Behind the Myth*, Faversham: Faversham Society, 1996

Ingram, Martin, *Church Courts, Sex and Marriage in England 1570–1640*, Cambridge: Cambridge University Press, 1987

Ingram, William, *The Business of Playing: The Beginnings of the Adult Professional Theatre in Elizabethan London*, Ithaca and London: Cornell University Press, 1992

Jackson, Bernard S., 'Narrative theories and legal discourse', in Christopher Nash ed., *Narrative in Culture: The Uses of Storytelling in the Sciences, Philosophy and Literature*, London and New York: Routledge, 1990

Jardine, Lisa, *Worldly Goods: A New History of the Renaissance*, London: Macmillan, 1996

Johnson, Matthew, 'Rethinking houses, rethinking transitions', in David Gaimster and Paul Stamper eds, *The Age of transition: The Archaeology of English Culture, 1400–1600*, Oxford: Oxbow Books, 1997

Johnson, Matthew, *Housing Culture*, London: University College London Press, 1993

Johnson, Matthew, *An Archaeology of Capitalism*, Oxford: Blackwell, 1996

Kastan, David Scott and Peter Stallybrass eds, *Staging the Renaissance: Reinterpretations of Elizabethan and Jacobean Drama*, London, New York: Routledge, 1991

Kastan, David Scott, *Shakespeare After Theory*, New York and London: Routledge, 1999

Keenan, Siobhan, *Travelling Players in Shakespeare's England*, Basingstoke: Palgrave, 2002

Keene, Derek and Vanessa Harding, *Historical Gazetteer of London Before the Great Fire. Pt 1, Cheapside; Parishes of All Hallows Honey Lane, St Martin Pomary, St Mary le Bow, St Mary Colechurch and St Pancras Soper Lane*, Cambridge: Chadwick-Healey, 1987

Keller, James R., 'Arden's land acquisitions and the dissolution of the monasteries', *English Language Notes*, 30:4, 1993, 20–4

Kendon, Adam ed., *Nonverbal Communication, Interaction, and Gesture: Selections from 'Semiotica'*, The Hague, New York: Mouton Publishers, 1981

Kermode, Jenny and Walker, Garthine eds, *Women, Crime and the Courts in Early Modern England*, London: University College London Press, 1994

Klein, Holger and Rowland Wymer eds, *Shakespeare and History*, Shakespeare Yearbook 6, Lewiston, Queenston, Lampeter: Edwin Mellen Press, 1996

Kopytoff, Igor, 'The cultural biography of things: commoditization as process', in Arjun Appadurai ed., *The Social Life of Things: Cultural Commodities in Perspective*, Cambridge: Cambridge University Press, 1986

Korda, Natasha, 'Household Kates: domesticating commodities in *The Taming of the Shrew*', *Shakespeare Quarterly*, 47:2, 1996, 109–31

Korda, Natasha, 'Household property/stage property: Henslowe as pawnbroker', *Theatre Journal*, 48:2, 1996, 185–97

Korda, Natasha, *Shakespeare's Domestic Economies: Gender and Property in Early Modern England*, Philadelphia: University of Pennsylvania Press, 2002

Laithwaite, Michael, 'A ship-master's house at Faversham, Kent', *Post-Medieval Archaeology*, 2, 1968, 150–62

Lake, Peter, *The Antichrist's Lewd Hat*, New Haven, London: Princeton University Press, 2002

Lamarque, Peter, 'Narrative and invention: the limits of fictionality', in Christopher Nash ed., *Narrative in Culture: The Uses of Storytelling in the Sciences, Philosophy and Literature*, London and New York: Routledge, 1990

Law, R. A., 'Yarington's *Two Lamentable Tragedies*', *Modern Language Review*, 5, 1910, 167–77

Lefebvre, Henri, *The Production of Space*, translated by Donald Nicholson Smith, Oxford: Blackwell, 1991

Leggatt, Alexander, '*Arden of Faversham*', *Shakespeare Survey*, 36, 1983, 121–33

Levine, Laura, *Men in Women's Clothing: Anti-theatrical Discourse and Effeminization 1579–1642*, Cambridge, New York: Cambridge University Press, 1994

Lieblein, Leanore, 'The context of murder in English domestic plays 1590–1610', *Studies in English Literature 1500–1900*, 23:2, 1983, 181–96

MacCaffrey, Wallace T., *Exeter 1540–1640: The Growth of an English County Town*, Cambridge, MA, London: Harvard University Press, 1975

McClintock, Michael, 'Grief, theater and society in Thomas Heywood's *A Woman Killed With Kindness*', in Margo Swiss and David A. Kent eds, *Speaking Grief in English Literary Culture: Shakespeare to Milton*, Pittsburgh: Duquesne University Press, 2002

Macfarlane, Alan, *Marriage and Love in England 1300–1840: Modes of Reproduction*, Oxford and New York: Basil Blackwell, 1986

McKendrick, Scot, 'Tapestries from the low countries in England during the fifteenth century', in Caroline Barron and Nigel Saul eds, *England and the Low Countries in the Late Middle Ages*, Gloucester: Sutton, 1995

McLuskie, Kate, '"Tis but a woman's jar": family and kinship in Elizabethan domestic drama', *Literature and History*, 9, 1983, 228–39

Martin, Randall, 'Arden winketh at his wife's lewdness, & why!': a patrilineal crisis in *Arden of Faversham*', *Early Theatre*, 4, 2001, 13–33

Maus, Katharine Eisaman, 'Horns of dilemma: jealousy, gender and spectatorship in English Renaissance Drama', *ELH*, 54:3, 1987, 561–83

Maus, Katharine Eisaman, *Inwardness and Theatre in the English Renaissance*, Chicago, London: University of Chicago Press, 1995

Meads, Chris, *Banquets Set Forth*, Manchester: Manchester University Press, 2001

Medick, Hans and David Warren Sabean eds, *Interest and Emotion: Essays on the Study of Family and Kinship*, Cambridge: Cambridge University Press, 1984

Mehl, Dieter, Angela Stock and Anne-Julia Zwierlein eds, *Plotting Early Modern London: New Essays on Jacobean City Comedy*, Aldershot: Ashgate, 2004

Melville, Jennifer, 'The Use and Organization of Domestic Space in Late Seventeenth-Century London', unpublished PhD thesis, University of Cambridge, 1999

Mendelson, S. and P. Crawford, *Women in Early Modern England, 1550–1720*, Oxford: Clarendon Press, 1998

Milward, Rosemary, *A Glossary of Household, Farming and Trade Terms from Probate Inventories*, Chesterfield: Derbyshire Record Society, 1977

Mitchell, W. J. T. ed., *On Narrative*, Chicago and London: University of Chicago Press, 1980

Mowat, Barbara A., '"The getting up of the spectacle": the role of the visual on the Elizabethan stage, 1576–1600', in G. R. Hibbard ed., *The Elizabethan Theatre IX*, Port Credit: published in collaboration with the University of Waterloo, 1981

Mukerji, Chandra, *From Graven Images: Patterns of Modern Materialism*, New York: Columbia University Press, 1983

Mullaney, Stephen, *The Place of the Stage: License, Play and Power in Renaissance England*, Chicago, London: University of Chicago Press, 1988

Murray, J. T., *English Dramatic Companies 1558–1642*, London: Constable, 1910

Nash, Cristopher ed., *Narrative in Culture: The Uses of Storytelling in the Sciences, Philosophy and Literature*, London and New York: Routledge, 1990

Neill, Michael, '"This gentle gentleman": social change and the language of status in *Arden of Faversham*', *Medieval and Renaissance Drama in England*, 10, 1998, 73–97

Newcomb, Lori Humphrey, *Reading Popular Romance in Early Modern England*, New York: Columbia University Press, 2002

O'Hara, Diana, '"Ruled by my friends": aspects of marriage in the diocese of Canterbury *c.* 1540–*c.* 1570', *Continuity and Change*, 6:1, 1991, 9–41

O'Hara, Diana, 'Sixteenth-Century Courtship in the Diocese of Canterbury', unpublished PhD thesis, University of Kent, 1995

O'Hara, Diana, 'The language of tokens and the making of marriage', *Rural History*, 3:1, 1992, 1–40

O'Hara, Diana, *Courtship and Constraint*, Manchester: Manchester University Press, 2000

Oakley, A. and S. Corpe eds, *Canterbury Freemen, Vol. 1*, Canterbury: Kent Records Collections, 1982

Orlin, Lena Cowen, 'Man's house as his castle in *Arden of Faversham*', *Medieval and Renaissance Drama in England*, 2, 1985, 57–89

Orlin, Lena Cowen, 'Familial transgressions: societal transition on the Elizabethan stage', in Carol Levin and Karen Robertson eds, *Sexuality and Politics in Renaissance Drama*, Lewiston, Lampeter: Edwin Mellen Press, 1991

Orlin, Lena Cowen, *Private Matters and Public Culture in Post-Reformation England*, Ithaca, London: Cornell University Press, 1994

Orlin, Lena Cowen, 'Boundary disputes in early modern London', in Orlin ed., *Material London*, Philadelphia: University of Pennsylvania Press, 2000

Orlin, Lena Cowen, '"The causes and reasons of all artificial things" in the Elizabethan domestic environment', *Medieval and Renaissance Drama in England*, 7, 1995, 19–75

Orlin, Lena Cowen, 'Fictions of the early modern English probate inventory', in Henry Turner ed., *The Culture of Capital: Property, Cities, and Knowledge in Early Modern England*, New York, London: Routledge, 2002

Orlin, Lena Cowen, 'Walls and their chinks in early modern England', paper given at the Putting Objects in their Places Colloquium, Shakespeare Institute, University of Birmingham, 18 June 2005

Ornstein, Robert, 'Bourgeois morality and dramatic convention in *A Woman Killed With Kindness*', in Standish Henning, Robert Kimbrough and Richard Knowles eds, *English Renaissance Drama: Essays in Honor of Madeleine Doran & Mark Eccles*, London: Southern Illinois University Press, 1976

Overton, Mark, 'English probate inventories and the measurement of agricultural change', in Ad Van der Woude, and Anton Schuurman eds, *Probate Inventories: A New Source for the Historical Study of Wealth, Material Culture and Agricultural Development*, Utrecht: HES Publishers, 1980

Overton, Mark, *Agricultural Revolution in England: The Transformation of the Agrarian Economy 1500–1850*, Cambridge: Cambridge University Press, 1996

Overton, Mark, Jane Whittle, Darron Dean and Andrew Hann, *Production and Consumption in English Households, 1600–1750*, London: Routledge, 2004

Panek, Jennifer, 'Punishing adultery in *A Woman Killed With Kindness*', *Studies in English Literature 1500–1900*, 34:2, 1994, 357–78

Parker, Vanessa, *The Making of Kings Lynn: Secular Buildings from the 11th to the 17th Century*, London and Chichester: Phillimore, 1971

Pearson, Sarah, *The Medieval Houses of Kent: An Historical Analysis*, London: HMSO, 1994

Platt, C., *The Great Rebuildings of Tudor and Stuart England: Revolutions in Architectural Taste*, London: UCL Press, 1994

Platt, C., *Medieval Southampton: The Port and Trading Community, A.D. 1000–1600*, London, Boston: Routledge and Kegan Paul, 1973

Priestley, Ursula and P. J. Corfield, 'Rooms and room use in Norwich housing, 1580–1730', *Post-Medieval Archaeology*, 16, 1982, 93–123

Prior, Mary, 'Wives and wills, 1558–1700', in John Chartres and David Hey eds, *English Rural Society 1500–1800*, Cambridge: Cambridge University Press, 1990

Rappaport, Steve, *Worlds Within Worlds: Structures of Life in Sixteenth-Century London*, Cambridge: Cambridge University Press, 1989

Raymond, Joad, *Pamphlets and Pamphleteering in Early Modern Britain*, Cambridge: Cambridge University Press, 2003

Relihan, Constance C., 'The narrative strategies of Robert Greene's cony-catching pamphlets', *Cahiers Elisabethains*, 37, 1990, 9–15

Reynolds, George Fullmer, *The Staging of Elizabethan Plays at the Red Bull Theatre 1605–1625*, New York: Modern Language Association of America, 1940

Richardson, Catherine, 'The Meanings of Space in Society and Drama', unpublished PhD thesis, University of Kent, 1999

Richardson, Catherine, 'Properties of domestic life: the table in Heywood's *A Woman Killed With Kindness*', in Jonathan Gil Harris and Natasha Korda eds, *Staged Properties*, Cambridge: Cambridge University Press, 2002

Richardson, Catherine, 'Domestic objects and the construction of family identity', in Cordelia Beattie, Anna Maslakovic, Sarah Rees Jones eds, *The Medieval Household in Christian Europe, c. 850–c. 1550 Managing Power, Wealth, and the Body*, Turnhout: Brepols, 2004

Richardson, Catherine ed., *Clothing Culture 1350–1650*, Aldershot: Ashgate, 2004

Richardson, Catherine, 'Early modern plays and domestic spaces', *Home Cultures*, 2:3, November 2005

Ricoeur, Paul, 'Narrative time', in W. J. T. Mitchell ed., *On Narrative*, Chicago and London: University of Chicago Press, 1980

Ringler, William, 'The first phase of the Elizabethan attack on the stage, 1558–79', *The Huntington Library Quarterly*, 4, July 1942, 391–418

Roberts, Peter ed., *Christopher Marlowe and English Renaissance Culture*, Aldershot: Scolar Press, 1996

Roberts, Judith, 'Tenterden Houses: A Study of the Domestic Buildings of a Kent Parish in their Social and Economic Environment', unpublished PhD thesis, University of Nottingham, 1990

Roberts, Sasha, ' "Let me the curtains draw": the dramatic and symbolic properties of the bed in Shakespearean tragedy', in Jonathan Gil and Natasha Korda, *Staged Properties*, Cambridge: Cambridge University Press, 2002

Roberts, Sasha, 'Lying amongst the classics: ritual and motif in elite Elizabethan and Jacobean beds', in Lucy Gent ed., *Albion's Classicism: The Visual Arts in Britain, 1550–1660*, New Haven, London: Yale University Press, 1995

Rutter, Carol, *Documents of the Rose Playhouse*, Manchester: Manchester University Press, 1984

Salgado, Gamini, *Eyewitnesses of Shakespeare*, London, Toronto: Sussex University Press, 1975

Sanderson, Margaret H. B., *A Kindly Place? Living in Sixteenth-Century Scotland*, East Linton: Tuckwell Press, 2002

Sarti, Raffaella, *Europe at Home: Family and Material Culture 1500–1800*, London: Yale University Press, 2002

Schama, Simon, 'Perishable commodities: Dutch still-life paintings and the "empire of things"', in John Brewer and Roy Porter eds, *Consumption and the World of Goods*, London: Routledge, 1993

Schofield, John, 'Urban housing in England 1400–1600', in David Gaimster and Paul Stamper eds, *The Age of Transition*, Oxford: Oxbow Books, 1997

Schofield, John, *Medieval London Houses*, New Haven and London: Yale University Press, 1994

Schutzman, Julie R., 'Alice Arden's freedom and the suspended moment of *Arden of Faversham*', *Studies in English Literature 1500–1900*, 36:2, 1996, 289–314

Sharpe, J. A., '"Such disagreement betwyx neighbours": litigation and human relations in early modern England', in John Bossy ed., *Disputes and Settlements: Law and Human Relations in the West*, Cambridge: Cambridge University Press, 1983

Sharpe, J. A., 'Defamation and sexual slander in early modern England: the church courts at York', *Borthwick Papers*, 58, York, 1980

Sharpe, J. A., *Early Modern England: A Social History 1550–1760*, London: Edward Arnold, 1987

Shepard, Alexandra, 'Honesty, worth and gender in early modern England, 1560–1640', in H. R. French and Jonathan Barry eds, *Identity and Agency in English Society, 1500–1800*, Basingstoke: Palgrave, 2004

Shepard, Alexandra, *Meanings of Manhood in Early Modern England*, Oxford: Oxford University Press, 2003

Simpson, Paula, 'Custom and Conflict: Tithe Disputes in the Diocese of Canterbury in the Sixteenth Century', unpublished PhD thesis, University of Kent, 1997

Skipp, V. H. T., 'Economic and social change in the forest of Arden, 1530–1649', in Joan Thirsk ed., *Land, Church and People*, Reading: Museum of English Rural Life, 1970

Skipp, Victor, *Crisis and Development: An Ecological Case Study of the Forest of Arden 1570–1674*, Cambridge: Cambridge University Press, 1978

Smith, Bruce, *Ancient Scripts and Modern Experience on the English Stage 1500–1700*, Princeton: Princeton University Press, 1988

Smith, Bruce, *The Acoustic World of Early Modern England*, Chicago: University of Chicago Press, 1999

Spufford, Margaret, 'Puritanism and social control?', in Anthony Fletcher and John Stevenson eds, *Order and Disorder in Early Modern England*, Cambridge: Cambridge University Press, 1985

Spufford, Margaret, 'The limitations of the probate inventory', in John Chartres and David Hey eds, *English Rural Society 1500–1800*, Cambridge, New York: Cambridge University Press, 1990

Spufford, Margaret, *Contrasting Communities*, Gloucester: Sutton, 2000 (originally published 1974)

Spufford, P., 'Mobility and Immobility', in M. Spufford ed., *The World of Rural Dissenters, 1520–1725*, Cambridge and New York: Cambridge University Press, 1995

Stallybrass, Peter and Ann Rosalind Jones, *Renaissance Clothing and the Materials of Memory*, Cambridge: Cambridge University Press, 2000

Stallybrass, Peter and Allon White, 'The fair, the pig, authorship', in Stallybrass and White eds, *The Politics and Poetics of Transgression*, London: Methuen, 1986

Stone, Lawrence, *The Family, Sex and Marriage in England, 1500–1800*, London: Weidenfeld and Nicolson, 1977

Sullivan, Garrett A., '"Arden lay murdered in that plot of ground": surveying, land, and *Arden of Faversham*', *English Literary History*, 61:2, 1994, 231–52

Sullivan, Garrett A., *The Drama of Landscape*, Stanford: Stanford University Press, 1998

Tennenhouse, Leonard, 'Playing and power', in David Scott Kastan and Peter Stallybrass eds, *Staging the Renaissance: Reinterpretations of Elizabethan and Jacobean Drama*, London, New York: Routledge, 1991

The British Atlas of Historic Towns, Vol. III, London, Oxford: Oxford University Press, 1989

Thirsk, Joan, *Economic Policy and Projects: The Development of a Consumer Society in Early Modern England*, Oxford: Clarendon Press, 1978

Thirsk, Joan, *Agricultural Regions and Agrarian History in England, 1500–1750*, Basingstoke, London: Macmillan, 1987

Thirsk, Joan ed., *The Agrarian History of England and Wales, Volume IV 1500–1640*, Cambridge: Cambridge University Press, 1967

Thomas, Keith, *Religion and the Decline of Magic: Studies in Popular Belief in Sixteenth- and Seventeenth-Century England*, London: Weidenfeld and Nicolson, 1971

Titler, Robert, *Architecture and Power: The Town Hall and the English Urban Community c. 1500–1640*, Oxford: Clarendon Press, 1991

Titler, Robert, *Townspeople and Nation: English Urban Experiences, 1540–1640*, Stanford: Stanford University Press, 2001

Travitsky, Betty S., 'Husband-murder and petty treason in English Renaissance tragedy', *Renaissance Drama*, ns, 21, 1990, 171–98

Turner, V., 'Social dramas and stories about them', in W. J. T. Mitchell, ed., *On Narrative*, Chicago and London: University of Chicago Press, 1980

Turner, V., *Dramas, Fields and Metaphors: Symbolic Action in Human Society*, Ithaca: Cornell University Press, 1974

Underdown, David, 'The taming of the scold: the enforcement of patriarchal authority in early modern England', in Anthony Fletcher and John Stevenson eds, *Order and Disorder in Early Modern England*, Cambridge: Cambridge University Press, 1985

Urry, William, *Christopher Marlowe and Canterbury*, edited with an introduction by Andrew Butcher, London: Faber, 1988

Van der Woude, Ad and Anton Schuurman eds, *Probate Inventories, A New Source for the Historical Study of Wealth, Material Culture and Agricultural Development: Papers presented at the Leeuwenborch Conference (Wageningen, 5–7 May 1980)*, Utrecht: HES Publishers, 1980

Vickery, Amanda, 'Golden age of separate spheres? A review of the categories and chronology of English women's history', *The Historical Journal*, 36, 1993, 383–414

Wall, Wendy, *Staging Domesticity: Household Work and English Identity in Early Modern Drama*, Cambridge: Cambridge University Press, 2002

Weatherill, Lorna, *Consumer Behaviour and Material Culture in Britain 1660–1760*, New York, London: Routledge, 1988

Weimann, Robert, *Shakespeare and the Popular Tradition in the Theatre: Studies in the Social Dimension of Dramatic Form and Function*, ed. Robert Schwartz, Baltimore, London: Johns Hopkins University Press, 1987 (originally published 1978)

West, William N., *Theatres and Encyclopedias in Early Modern Europe*, Cambridge: Cambridge University Press, 2002

White, Hayden, 'The value of narrativity in the representation of reality', in W. J. T. Mitchell, ed., *On Narrative*, Chicago and London: University of Chicago Press, 1980

White, Hayden, *The Content of the Form: Narrative Discourse and Historical Representation*, Baltimore, London: Johns Hopkins University Press, 1987

White, Paul Whitfield, *Theatre and Reformation: Protestantism, Patronage and Playing in Tudor England*, Cambridge: Cambridge University Press, 1993

Wiggins, Martin, *Journeymen in Murder*, Oxford: Clarendon Press, 1991

Wiggins, Martin, *Shakespeare and the Drama of His Time*, Oxford: Oxford University Press, 2000

Wiltenburg, Joy, *Disorderly Women and Female Power in the Street Literature of Early Modern England and Germany*, London: University Press of Virginia, 1992

Worthen, W. B., *Shakespeare and the Force of Modern Performance*, Cambridge: Cambridge University Press, 2003

Wrightson, Keith, 'Critique: household and kinship in sixteenth century England', *History Workshop Journal*, 12, Autumn 1981, 151–8

Wrightson, Keith, *English Society 1580–1680*, London: Hutchinson, 1982

Wrightson, Keith, 'The social order of early modern England', in Lloyd Bonfield, Richard M. Smith and Keith Wrightson eds, *The World We Have Gained: Histories of Population and Social Structure*, Oxford, New York: Blackwell, 1986

Wrightson, Keith, *Earthly Necessities: Economic Lives in Early Modern Britain 1470–1750*, London: Penguin, 2002

Wrightson, Keith and David Levine, *Poverty and Piety in an English Village*, Oxford: Clarendon Press, 1995

Zell, M., 'The social parameters of probate records in the sixteenth century', *Bulletin of the Institute of Historical Research*, 57, 1984, 107–13

Zell, M., *Industry in the Countryside: Wealden Society in the Sixteenth Century*, Cambridge: Cambridge University Press, 1994

Index